Stresses in Children

Dedicated by the Editor with affection and esteem to Dr Conrad Graham

Stresses in Children

Edited by Ved P Varma

University of London Press Ltd

ISBN 0 340 15789 5 Boards
ISBN 0 340 17171 5 Unibook
Copyright © 1973 University of London Press
Second impression 1974

University of London Press Ltd,
St Paul's House, Warwick Lane, London EC4P 4AH

Printed and bound in Great Britain by
Hazell Watson & Viney Ltd, Aylesbury, Bucks

CONTENTS

Introduction   *Page* vii

Handicapped children in the ordinary school   I
J. D. KERSHAW, *Consultant, World Health Organisation. Lately*
M.O.H. and School M.O. Colchester

Psychotic children   21
LORNA WING, *Member of the Scientific Staff, Medical*
Research Council, Social Psychiatry Unit

Slow-learning children   32
PHILLIP WILLIAMS, *Professor, Faculty of Educational Studies,*
The Open University

Delinquent and maladjusted children   41
JOHN MAYS, *Professor, Department of Sociology,*
University of Liverpool

Bereaved children   57
MARJORIE MITCHELL, *Lecturer, Rachel McMillan College of*
Education Annexe for Mature Students

The adopted child at school   72
M. E. HUMPHREY, *Senior Lecturer in Psychology, St George's*
Hospital Medical School

The immigrant (West Indian) child in school   82
WAVENEY BUSHELL, *Educational Psychologist, London*
Borough of Croydon

Injury-prone children   93
LINDY BURTON, *Research Psychologist, Nuffield Department*
of Child Health, The Queens' University of Belfast

Blind children   105
MYFANWY WILLIAMS, *formerly Lecturer, Birmingham*
University Course for teachers of blind and partially-sighted
children

Partially-sighted children   116
    J. KELL, *Adviser in Special Education, County of Buckinghamshire*

Deaf and partially-hearing children   127
    LAWRENCE IVES, *Lecturer in Educational Psychology, Department of Audiology and Education of the Deaf, University of Manchester*

Children with physical handicaps   139
    JOAN REYNELL, *Senior Lecturer in Educational Psychology, Wolfson Centre and Department of Developmental Paediatrics, Institute of Child Health, University of London*

Notes and References   152

The Editor: Ved P. Varma is Educational Psychologist with the London Borough of Brent Child Guidance Service

INTRODUCTION

All of us have experienced stress at one time or another, in our personal relationships, in our work, in our health or in all of these and in other areas as well. But adults are not the only people who experience stress. Indeed, it can be argued that stress is likely to be most evident during periods of most rapid change. And since childhood is the period during which we develop most rapidly, then a strong case can be made for stress being especially prevalent in children.

This book deals with stress in children. But the contributors are not concerned with discussing those periods of normal childhood stress to which research in education, psychology and the social sciences has alerted us. For some groups of children, stress in childhood is more permanent or more serious than is usually the case. The purpose of this book is to outline some of the problems which these particular groups of children face.

The content is interesting. Some of the chapters discuss children who are among those categorised by the special education regulations as 'handicapped': for example there are chapters on the blind child and on the maladjusted child. But other chapters discuss children who are not categorised in this way at all. For example there is a chapter on the adopted child and another on the bereaved child. This serves to emphasise that the concept of handicap, valuable though it has proved in helping to develop special education and other services, may perhaps be a little restrictive. Recent research has alerted us to the vulnerability of children other than the handicapped. The concept of stress – although a little complex as some of the writers point out – enables us to extend our understanding of which children need special care.

At the same time, in this broader view, the division between the handicapped and the non-handicapped begins to blur. The idea of stress, which everyone experiences, makes us realise how arbitrary this division is in many instances. Even arbitrary divisions and categories have their uses, but they also have their dangers. Thus categorising children as 'handicapped' sometimes makes it difficult for other members of the community to accept them fully. The use of the idea of stress helps to avoid this danger.

The importance of bringing even the severely handicapped child into the community both at home and at school is a matter of current concern. For this reason alone teachers, parents, social workers and others need to be aware of the special problems posed by handicapped children and imposed on them. This book meets this need in a non-technical and helpful way. But more than that, it alerts us to the existence of other groups of children, less well-recognised, whose special problems and particular stresses need to be more widely known than has hitherto been the case. These are the children of the middle chapters of the book, children who are to be found in every school and every community. The book performs another valuable function in bringing these children to our notice.

HANDICAPPED CHILDREN IN THE ORDINARY SCHOOL

J. D. Kershaw

Stress is a part of life; the art of living consists in the achieving of equilibrium within a balance of stresses. And because the nature and intensity of stresses are constantly changing, an important requirement is the ability to foresee those changes and adjust and adapt to meet them. It follows that learning to live must include experience of stress, experience which must be controlled so that in any situation the stress is enough to challenge but not so great as to overwhelm. Precise graduation is usually impossible and one must assume that the child will have sufficient resilience and tolerance to recover without harm if he should happen to be temporarily overstressed.

This process postulates the existence of an informed group of educators – prominent among whom are parents and teachers – who will strike a balance between too much protection and too much exposure and will guide and advise the child in dealing with stresses. The home and the school are ideally partners in providing a structured environment which progressively introduces the child to challenging stresses and leads him on to the point at which he can stand on his own.

When a handicapped child enters an ordinary school, a special situation arises. A large school cannot be infinitely flexible in organisation. Its buildings, its staffing and its administration are provided on the assumption that the pupils' requirements as individuals will vary within only a comparatively narrow range and that by a compromise between the adaptability of the pupils and the adaptability of the school system the needs of most will be met without either children or school suffering unacceptable strain.

By definition, a handicapped child is one who suffers from a disability which, because of its nature or degree, places him at a disadvantage as compared with normal children in the same circumstances. His disability must be accepted as a fact and therefore, initially at least, an ordinary school will have to accept the strain of having to adjust somewhat beyond its normal range to give him what he needs. The aim of the school, in the long run, must be not only to educate him in the ordinary sense of the term but to teach him to accept and adapt to the total circumstances of living.

He has several special points of vulnerability. His total powers of adaptation are restricted. His special disability may be a point of weakness in that too much stress may actually increase the disability. One of the important

All notes and references are given on pp 152 ff.

elements in the normal child's learning to bear stress is that in school most of his stresses are shared by others and a stress which is common is more easily tolerated. A stress which is special to oneself carries an element of 'unfairness' which makes it harder to bear and it is just this kind of stress which the handicapped child must face.

To understand this vulnerability it is useful to consider what it means to be handicapped. First and foremost there is a limitation of performance. There are some things which a handicapped child cannot do at all. There are others which he can do just as effectively as a normal child. In between there are many things which, though he can do them, he will do less well or more slowly than a normal child, or at the cost of pain or greater effort. Some activities are essential; others are not. Some, while not essential, are pleasant or socially desirable; others are less so.

Essential activities must have first priority. If the child cannot perform them himself then someone else must do them for him. If he performs them only imperfectly or with difficulty it becomes necessary to decide whether others must do them or whether he should deal with them himself and pay the price in time, fatigue or pain. Among the non-essentials it is necessary to help the child to a choice based upon priorities and upon his desires and his capacity to bear fatigue or pain, remembering always the possibility that the putting of too much of himself and his time into a non-essential, however pleasant, may reduce his ability to deal with essentials.

Many workers in this field, myself included, have urged in the past that we should concentrate on the achieving of maximum independence and that we should teach the child to see himself though 'different' as not necessarily 'inferior'. In view of the changing pattern of disabilities and the increased prevalence of multiple handicaps this approach can no longer be defended as realistic. In the sense that a handicapped child must have some essential things done for him by others – or be helped by others in the doing of them – he is dependent and must accept some measure of planned dependence. In the sense that he is unable to engage in some activities which normal children enjoy or are part of the accepted pattern of social life he is inferior to the normal child.

The necessity to accept dependence and inferiority is a producer of emotional stress in itself. To come to terms with a disability involves the acquiring of a special personal set of values which will differ from those of the group. To forego some highly regarded activities is to become isolated from the group in those parts of its life. But the development of satisfactory personal relationships is usually achieved through participation in group activities; it follows that the handicapped child is likely to be disadvantaged in this essential part of growing up.

Because his activities must be restricted and because the things which must be done must not involve excessive strain it is important that the handicapped child must so order his life, or have it so ordered for him, that as far as possible it shall be regular. It must be realised that any substantial unusual activity, when it has to be undertaken, should be foreseen and planned for and even some occasional special activities which the normal child can take in his stride may, for the handicapped, involve a good deal of quite detailed preliminary work. This considerably reduces the handicapped child's adaptability and his power to tolerate change; it is unfortunate for the individual and helps still further to limit his chances of fitting in with the normal majority.

Choice of school

The medical officer who is charged with advising the local education authority on the education of a handicapped child will approach his task with the feeling that it is desirable that every child should live in his own home and attend an ordinary school. Whether in fact he recommends special educational treatment will depend upon whether the child has some essential need which cannot be met while he lives at home and attends an ordinary school. The essential need or needs which are considered may be educational, social, emotional or therapeutic.

In making a choice it must be remembered that the ordinary school may carry certain important advantages, as compared with the special school. Its curriculum is probably wider and its ultimate standard of attainment is in some respects substantially higher. Socially it offers the child better prospects of learning how to adjust to life in a community of non-handicapped people, closer contacts with the community in which he will later have to live and probably more practice in activities of daily living. These certainly justify some degree of bias in favour of the ordinary school.

It follows, therefore, that handicapped children admitted to ordinary school will fall into two main groups. The first, and larger, is that of children whose disability is comparatively minor in character and degree and who can be confidently expected to benefit by normal education if they are understandingly managed and if a few small adjustments can be made to the curriculum and the general daily round. The second group consists of children regarding whom there is some element of doubt; it is considered that they will probably be able to succeed in an ordinary school but their initial placement is a quite deliberate trial procedure.

In addition, there are two smaller groups which must be borne in mind. The first consists of children whose disability is such that they will probably be able to profit by ordinary education in the easier atmosphere and at the moderate pace of an ordinary infant or even junior school but who are likely to need transfer to a special school when they reach the age at which stricter routine and educational pressures impose unacceptable stresses. For these the ordinary school offers opportunities for maturing, educationally and socially, without the disadvantages attendant upon early separation from their home and their normal peer group.

The second of these groups, fortunately very small, consists of children who unquestionably need special education from an early age but whose parents refuse to allow them to go to a special school. Compulsory powers exist to require their attendance at a special school but it is often a lesser evil

3

to permit them to go to an ordinary school than to enforce special school attendance with inevitable conflict between home and school. Often, though not always, the time may come when the parents accept that the child cannot benefit by ordinary school attendance and acquiesce in special education. Until that time arrives these children, with comparatively severe disability, may present serious problems.

In the first three groups – those most likely to be met with in ordinary schools, the following will be the commonest disabilities:

Moderate motor defect;
partial sight;
partial hearing (with or without hearing aids);
minimal cerebral dysfunction;
moderate intellectual disability;
minor or well-controlled epilepsy;
slight or moderate chronic illness (e.g. asthma and diabetes).

It is worth mentioning that there is a growing tendency to transfer some quite severely handicapped children from special schools to ordinary schools for the final years of their education. In some cases the principal reason for this is to enable the child to make the transition from a specialised environment to ordinary community life in two stages rather than to discharge him direct from the protection of a special school to the rough-and-tumble of working life. In other cases the intention is rather to give the child the opportunity to have fuller secondary education in special subjects which are not taught to an advanced level in the special school.

The stress periods

Some disabilities generate quite specific patterns of stress for the children affected and where this is so it is possible to predict the child's response and take anticipatory action. Indeed, this is part of the *raison d'être* of the special school. This is most likely to be the case where the child has a severe major disability but no other significant defect.

Handicapped children who are placed in an ordinary school are not likely to show this specificity. The picture is most often of a child whose disabilities make him generally vulnerable to stress and whose immediate trouble is that he has difficulty in coping with the stresses which are normal to school life. The importance of the nature of his disability lies mainly in the way in which it may affect the pattern of his stress symptoms and, also, in determining the lines on which care and therapy may be most profitably carried out.

All school life – one might indeed say all life – contains elements of stress, but the impact of the normal school stresses tends to be specially marked at particular periods; predictably periods when change is impending or taking place.

School entry

The effect on the child of his first entry to school has not received the detailed study it deserves. It is only within the past decade that workers in the school health field have realised that many perfectly normal children go through phases of what is coming to be described as 'school shock' and 'first year failure'. The former is a period of behaviour disorder or emotional disturbance occurring in a child who has hitherto appeared quite well adjusted. There is no standard pattern. The disturbance may show itself both at home and at school, but it is by no means uncommon for the child to be perfectly behaved in school and grossly disturbed at home, or *vice versa*. If this happens, it can set parent and teacher at odds, with the one imputing all the blame to the other, and the consequent antagonism between home and school adds to the child's problems.

It is probable that the main causes of school shock are to be found in the sudden change from family life to a group situation or from a home where the child's every wish has been met to a place where at any rate some rules have to be imposed impersonally by a stranger. The trouble does not usually last long and may well be over by the end of the first term or early in the second.

'First year failure' is probably to some extent a special form of school shock. A child who is, with reason, considered to be of average or high intelligence simply fails to manifest that intelligence in his school activities. He may have a spell of overt behaviour disorder, but the failure to progress may be the only outward sign. The trouble may persist throughout the first year but this is hardly surprising since in the permissive atmosphere of the reception class in a British school the challenge to the intellect builds up somewhat slowly. It has been suggested that one element in the picture is an inadequate relationship between child and teacher and that there is a more or less deliberate refusal to learn as a manifestation of hostility to the teacher. Needless to say, a refusal to learn hardly endears the child to the teacher and the relationship does not improve. It is perhaps significant that these children often suddenly leap ahead in the second year when promotion to a new class brings about a change of teacher.

Obviously, a child with a handicap is likely to start school at a disadvantage. In the first place it is probable that his disability will have restricted his social experience. He may have been impeded in joining with his peers in play, his parents may have taken him about in their normal activities less than they would have done if he had had no disability, he may have been helped in normal activities of daily living or he may have been overindulged at home. Any or all of these may have left him socially immature for his years and thus unready to fit into the group environment.

Social immaturity in itself is a substantial disability, but his handicap imposes other difficulties. School activities, inevitably in a systematised education, are based on the assumption that every school entrant will be capable of an average range of performance. The handicapped child is disadvantaged in some of the general activities in which he is expected to take part and probably for the first time in his life he has to face the fact that in some things he is inferior in performance. This is not a matter of failure in competition; the competitive element in education does not arise until appreciably later. Slowness in feeding, difficulty in coping with dressing and undressing, stumbling when one runs, clumsiness in handling simple class-room apparatus, all these may mark one as inferior. They certainly make a child feel 'different' from the others and if, in addition, his disability impedes him in communication or in joining in games or if it necessitates his receiving special attention from the teacher, the other children in the class will tend to see him as different from them and group integration will be retarded.

He may have a disability which specifically impedes his learning; if so the teachers will make appropriate allowances. What is not yet fully realised, however, is that *any* disability may make a child a slow learner. Education has moved out of the era in which children were bombarded ceaselessly with repetitive instruction in the hope that some of this would eventually adhere to them, and the keynote now is participation and activity, even to the point at which activity is recognised as a help to the acquisition of language. Any substantial disability impedes participation or activity with the inevitable consequences.

Change of school

In the British system the ordinary child will expect two changes of school – from infant to junior at 7+ and from junior to secondary at 11+. The first of these gives little cause for concern; in the larger schools in urban areas it usually involves no more than a transfer of a group of contemporaries from one department to another within the same school. In rural areas it may require that the child moves from a small village school to a somewhat larger centralised junior school, but he is still moving with his established peer group to a school which is not too large and in most cases the only extra stress is that of daily travel to and fro. It is consequently easy to underrate the stress this transfer may present to a handicapped child.

Since an important concomitant of disability is diffidence and difficulty in making personal relationships a handicapped child will become more dependent upon those relationships which he does form. Even in the infants department he will have to receive some special attention and consideration from his teacher, with the result that he tends to have a much more close – and even dependent – relationship with his teacher than do normal children. This relationship may often extend to other members of the school staff who have had to give him particular attention – the auxiliary who has helped him in the lavatory, the canteen assistant who has ensured that he is not crowded or impeded at mealtimes, the playground assistant who has kept a helpful eye on him.

For such a child, mere promotion to a higher class may have been a little traumatic because of the change of teacher; it is quite common for a handi-capped child to retain a relationship with his former teacher until he gets used to the new one and so long as he is in the same department or school this is practicable. Transfer to a different school at the age of seven or so requires that he must learn to live with a whole new set of adults, and however helpful and sympathetic they may be, they are still strangers for the first weeks and they have to learn his peculiarities just as he has to learn theirs.

Again, he may be vulnerable to the atmosphere of the junior school. It expects pupils to be more self-reliant and somewhat more responsible than they have been in the infant department. It also takes education more seriously; specific subjects begin to emerge, new skills have to be developed and inevitably there come the beginnings of educational competition as learning becomes less play and more work. During an acclimatisation period of one or two terms he may be reminded rather forcibly of difference and inferiority.

However, the most potentially traumatic change period is that from junior to secondary school. The comprehensive school system has much to commend it, but inevitably the comprehensive school must be large and draw its pupils from several primary schools. The pupil moves to it with his peer-group of classmates but this group may be only a small part of the new entry and the child has to learn to get on with a large number of contemporaries who are strangers to him. The age-gap between newcomers and seniors is greater than in his previous schools; he may well feel that he is under the shadow of young men and young women. Certainly even a normal child may be daunted by the change from being a big fish in a small pond to being a small fish in a big pond.

The handicapped child has new cause for feeling inferior. However much individual attention the teachers may give him, they do not yet know how to manage him, nor does he know anything of them. In any event, though he may have found an individual identity for himself in a community of perhaps two or three hundred he will have to start searching anew when he finds himself only one in a community of perhaps a thousand or more.

He has, one hopes, learned how to get around in his previous small school building with a minimum of physical difficulty. Now he must learn his way about something much larger and more complex which presents new practical problems. And, because he is among strangers, with a substantial age-gap between him and the majority of the others, he cannot expect the little, understanding concessions and acts of consideration which have made it possible to adjust to day-to-day school life. All in all, there is good reason to expect a period of emotional and social regression, quite probably associated with a spell of general or specific learning difficulty.

The last years at school

It is probably just as well that the first years of adolescence coincide with the last years at school; the child has at least the probability that he will be facing adolescent turmoil, physical, emotional and social, in an environment which offers him protection from the consequences of his most serious errors, some degree of understanding surveillance and even some perceptive guidance. On the other hand, it is unfortunate that he should be compelled to leave school in the middle of what is probably the most difficult stage of adolescence.

The normal child manages to survive this period of schooling successfully and, in the long run, makes the transition to adult life in the community without suffering too greatly. It cannot, however, be assumed that because the educational system does well by the normal pupils one can be complacent about the handicapped ones.

It must be remembered that the handicapped child who has reached stability is still only conditionally stable. He has learned how to live with his disability within his environment at the moment. To do this he has almost certainly had to restrict his environment, in the sense of limiting his activities to those within his range and, also, limiting both the extent and the nature of his social contacts with his peers. Essentially, his capacity for adjustment to deal with sudden changes and emergencies is below average and his physical and mental powers may be fully taxed in maintaining his equilibrium.

Physical and emotional instability are essential elements in the picture of adolescence. The handicapped child, on his tired or moody days, has no reserves left to meet the extra strain which comes from the sudden impact of the unexpected. To make matters worse, it is not uncommon for the changes of adolescence to exacerbate his actual disability – diabetes or epilepsy may temporarily slip out of control, asthmatic attacks become more frequent, irregular physical growth impose extra strain on a weak limb and so on. All in all, therefore, it is to be expected that an adolescent with a disability will be under multiple stress during these years and that, to make matters more difficult, the stresses will be variable rather than constant. Emotional and social problems, and also school performance, are almost certain to suffer.

Competition takes on a new form and a new significance. The adolescent naturally begins to experiment with his growing powers and matching himself against his peers is now to him a serious business. Group aggregation is also becoming a serious part of life.

This, in the early stages, probably bears more hardly on the handicapped boy than on the girl. The standards of the male adolescent herd at this point tend to be oriented towards physical sports. If a boy is to be highly esteemed among his peers it is necessary for him to be more competent than average at one of a small number of such sports. Conversely, if he is unable to join in any of them at a level of moderate competence he has no social standing in the major groups. The criteria of the majority are in fact such that a lad who shows interest and ability in his school work or in the less physical and more intellectual pursuits may be in some degree ridiculed and looked down upon; more urgently than ever before he finds that a physical disability, whether in vision, coordination or motor power, sets him among the inferior minority.

The girl is less likely to suffer in this way, because among girls physical sports are taken less seriously. Her problems come later but are no less painful. Competition enters the sexual field as the 'teens' come on. To achieve the highest esteem in his social group a boy must be good in sport *and* find himself a girl, but he will not suffer much if he concentrates on sport and makes girls his secondary hobby. A girl, however, has no such choice; she must find her boy or be branded as unsuccessful. To make matters worse, while the handicapped boy can often find a girl to take an interest in him – even though that interest be based on an element of sympathy or pity rather than on sexual attraction – the majority of boys at this age judge girls by superficial standards and the girl who is ungainly or unbeautiful, even if the thing which mars her appearance is nothing more serious than the wearing of a hearing aid or strong spectacles, is at a great disadvantage in the competition for personable boy friends. The results of this can be quite disastrous and may lead to long-lasting deformation of her ability to enter into normal relationships with the other sex.

Further disadvantages beset the handicapped in the final year at school. This is when the 'moment of truth' is approaching. It is normal and proper for the young to have optimistic daydreams about the future, with quite unrealistic ambitions for a career. The great majority settle quite comfortably for something short of these ambitions. The non-handicapped youngster has the assurance that he will find a job without great difficulty and that he can afford a period of trial and error when he goes into employment. The handicapped one begins to realise that the actual employments which some of his peers will find will be outside his powers, and even that finding work at all may be difficult for him. What he may not realise – but those in charge of him must be constantly aware of this – is that he cannot risk a period of trial and error. If he goes into a job and fails, not only is this a severe blow to his self-esteem and confidence, but the fact of his failure can too easily suggest to other prospective employers that he is a poor prospect because of his disability.

School has offered the handicapped child some measure of shelter and security within an ordered programme of living. If he is at all capable of forethought, he will realise that when he leaves school he will find life in general more difficult. The normal young person looks forward to leaving school with a considerable degree of eagerness. The day of leaving will bring 'grown-up' status, freedom from being treated as a child in that everything is arranged for him, and the prospect of having money of his own to spend. The handicapped youngster by contrast, knows that he will have new and undefined problems, that he will be going out into a community which will have comparatively little sympathy for his disabilities and shortcomings and that his earning power is somewhat dubious. It is hardly surprising if his fears take charge and he shows signs of social regression or attempts to compensate by becoming rebellious.

Care and management

Generalisations are dangerous in this even more than in other fields of child care, child health and education. However, it is reasonable to indicate a few

general principles which can serve as a useful guide, provided that in apply-
ing them one does not lose sight of the uniqueness of the individual.

Because of his disability a handicapped child tends to be below the
average in resilience. After any experience of stress he is likely to take longer
to recover his confidence and his equilibrium than would most normal children. If a new stress strikes him before he has recovered from the previous
one, his recovery will again be delayed and the cumulative effect of successive
stresses may effect lasting damage. The aim should be to see that as far as
possible he is not asked to face stresses beyond his capacity and that he
should not be faced with more than one source of stress at any one time.

The time of school entry is outstandingly the one at which a child has to
meet simultaneously a number of different stresses and the key to success lies
in prevention and anticipation. It is particularly important that he should not
be exposed at the same time to the sudden impact of group life, a formalised
environment and the need to start learning school subjects, even though the
teaching of these may be simple and not intensive. If he can be introduced by
degrees first to group life, second to formality and then to being taught, his
liability to school shock is greatly reduced.

Well before school age, therefore, he should begin this introductory
process. Probably the best sequence would be part-time attendance at a play
group, progressing to a nursery school and then entering an ordinary school.
The paucity of nursery schools makes this sequence impossible in many
places; an alternative is for him to go from nursery or play group to a nursery
class. In some cases the latter may be preferable; if the nursery class is
associated with the school to which he will go later he may become accustomed to the idea of school before he has to face schooling as such.

This process is more than acclimatisation. It offers a chance of assessing
him and discovering his strengths and his weaknesses and observing his progress toward maturity. His future teacher should be given full information
about him by those who have had charge of him and desirably she should,
before he enters school, meet them and him and get to know him personally.

It should go without saying that he ought not to enter school as such
until he is socially and emotionally mature enough to do so. Provided that he
is having adequate group life and social experience he will lose nothing by
starting school six months or a year after the standard age. If, however, there
are no facilities for group experience other than in school it may be better
for him to start part-time school attendance at the age of five.

Experience suggests that it is better for him not to enter school at the
beginning of term. For the first weeks of term the reception class is going
through a settling down process and to introduce a vulnerable child to a
group which has not yet reached some sort of stability is bad for the group as
well as for the child himself; not only will the staff be unable to give him
much individual attention but the normal children, not yet having learned to
accept each other, will be far from ready to accept him.

It not infrequently happens that a handicapped child, over quite a substantial period, is unable to tolerate school life for the whole day. If half-day
attendance is permitted for too long there is the risk that he may begin to fall

behind the other children educationally, and thus there exists the danger that he may have to face the extra stress of catching up with them or knowing that he is falling behind them. In these circumstances, an expedient worth trying is to combine half-day school attendance with part-time home teaching until the child is ready for whole-time schooling.

In the early days of schooling it is common for a handicapped child's disability to seem more handicapping than the history would suggest. This is partly because he is attempting some unfamiliar tasks and having to perform even the familiar ones in new surroundings. It may also be that part of the 'shock effect' of school entry is causing him to regress somewhat and to shelter behind his disability.

Whether this occurs or not, it is usually undesirable that he should be completely excused from any school activity which he is capable of attempting, even if it is obvious that he is not going to be able to do it as well as, or as fast as, the other children. He should be encouraged to try it and should be helped with it and his imperfections accepted. The reasons for this are fairly obvious – the longer he waits before trying, the more likely he is to assume that it is beyond him and observation of his attempts will help in the assessment of both child and disability.

However, he needs the confidence that only achievement can bring and it is most important that the school should discover as early as possible something which is part of the general pattern of class activities and which he can do competently, and let him have as much opportunity as possible to engage in it.

So far as giving him help is concerned, whether in classroom work or in daily living activities, full use should be made of any aids which will make tasks easier for him. Even so, he will probably need some assistance from one of the staff and initially it is desirable that all such help should come from one person. Not only is it going to be easier for him to learn to relate to one individual; it is important that the helper should be familiar with his powers and disabilities – and his idiosyncrasies – and know both how to help and when to help. Later, when he is beginning to settle down, the other members of staff may undertake the helping role.

At this age, normal children accept the presence of a handicapped child quite well, so long as he does not actively interfere with or impede their own activities, but the acceptance is passive rather than active. It is reasonable that they should be taught to show him some consideration, but the further, and important, stage of acceptance, the giving of positive help, must not be expected to arrive until the second or third school year.

Transfer from infant to junior department must be considered well in advance. It is desirable, from the point of view of his self-esteem, that he should not feel that he is being held back but it is equally desirable that he should not suddenly be faced with challenges which are likely to be too much for him. Where the two departments are in the same school, gradual transfer may be possible; he may, for a while, spend part of his time in the infant department and part in the junior. If, however, transfer is going to involve a move to a different school, with the need to find his way around a new building and to get used to different staff, there may be a good case for retaining him in the infants department as an 'over-age' child for one or more terms. In general, one year should be the maximum retention period; if he is not mature enough to move at the end of a year it is probable that placement in an ordinary school was not, after all, suitable and transfer to a special school should be considered.

By this time his assets and liabilities should be fairly well known to the staff and full information about these and any special needs should be passed to the junior school well in advance, so that appropriate provision may be ready from the day he starts life as a 'junior'. If this is done, it is probable that no substantial new problems will arise during the first three junior years. However, this is the period during which school work is becoming a more serious matter and a careful watch should be kept for the appearance of any specific learning difficulties so that these may be investigated and remedial teaching introduced if necessary. On this point it is worth mentioning that if there is any doubt the help should be given sooner rather than later; if one waits till failure is obvious the child will already have felt the stress of that failure.

The last year in junior school should be a time of special assessment and preparation, especially for the handicapped child. He is likely already to be somewhat apprehensive about his impending move to the secondary school and the staff should be looking ahead to the possible special difficulties he may meet there and considering how these may be minimised or circumvented. Consultation with the secondary school staff is highly desirable. Among the questions which need to be asked one must include whether the building will present any problems of getting about from classroom to classroom or from classroom to toilet block, whether the teachers whom he will first encounter have the right attitude and approach, whether the classes are unduly large and whether the pupils as a community are 'tough' or tolerant. It may be desirable for him to transfer to a secondary school other than the usual one which covers the catchment area in which he lives; if so, possible travel stress and the emotional difficulties which might arise from his being thrown into a community composed entirely of strangers must be balanced against the possible advantages.

A special point worth watching arises in the case of a handicapped girl. Not only does a girls only school tend to have less of a 'rough and tumble' atmosphere than a mixed secondary school, but the social and emotional problems already referred to, which arise out of competition over 'dating', may be less important. Even so, before specially assigning a handicapped girl to a school for girls only it is worthwhile remembering that girls have to learn to mix with boys at some time and that perhaps introduction to the opposite sex may be best effected in the controlled environment of a school.

Since any secondary school will contain a large proportion of children from junior schools other than the one the child has attended, the importance of a child's being transferred at the same time as the rest of his class is less than at the time of infant–junior transfer and it is consequently much easier to hold the immature junior back for a year, or even longer, to let him ripen for secondary education. This is specially useful if the secondary school to which he is to transfer is a large comprehensive school, as the flexibility of the good comprehensive school makes it fairly easy for it to accept a child whose attainment level is one or even two years behind the average for his age.

The good secondary school offers a fair range of choice in its curriculum and there should be little difficulty in finding for the handicapped child a choice of subjects which will fit the pattern of his abilities. The choice, however, must be forward-looking. It is well worth while, if his disability is substantial, to enlist the aid of the Youth Employment Service quite early – at the age of thirteen or possibly even twelve – for preliminary advice. It is not to be expected that any precise vocational assessment can be made at this age, but it is often possible to define certain broad areas of employment which would be either quite unsuitable or dangerously stressful for the child and others which might offer good prospects. If this can be done, then it is possible to orient the child's educational programme appropriately and achieve two useful ends – first to channel his interests and ambitions into the realm of the realistically possible, and second, to prepare him for that particular field of occupation and thus give him some advantage over the children who have had no purposeful preparation.

Given understanding care, guidance and management during the pre-teen years the moderately handicapped child will have learned his powers and limitations and will know how to live within the latter. The natural competitive instinct will tempt him now and again to venture beyond his powers and fail, but this need not be grossly traumatic. It is, in fact, part of the normal process of learning by experience and one can only discover one's limitations by a process of trial and error. The most difficult part of learning to live with a handicap is learning to accept it and, as already indicated, the worst dangers that face the handicapped teenager are those arising out of frustration and isolation.

To overcome or avert these it is essential that he should, by some means or other, attain an average or above average level of competence and achievement in some activity which has significance for him and is valued by at least some of his peers. There are very good reasons why this should be sought in the field of recreation. This field is a wide one and within it there is something which would be appropriate for virtually everyone. In every type of recreation there are group linkages which are particularly important socially and emotionally because they are based on common interests entered into of one's own free will and desire. They are among the very few parts of human activity where competition and cooperation go hand in hand, so that the expert is eager to welcome, help, encourage and train the beginner. They usually cut completely across most of the common social barriers. And, not least important from the point of view of the handicapped youngster, they have continuity. One of the most dangerous stress factors in adolescence is the complete and sudden break which comes on leaving school and leaves the handicapped young person groping for new contacts in a strange setting. If, before he leaves school, he has been initiated into the brotherhood of the swimmers, the model engineers, the stamp collectors, the bird watchers or any of a hundred others, he will have friends ready-made when the interruption of other relationships is imposed by leaving school.

The target of those who are working with and for him in the later school years should be to find some recreation which is congenial and for which he has the basic ability and aptitude. If it is possible to find more than one, so much the better. In the case of a boy it is desirable that one of his recreations should be in the physical field, because of the special value which young males attach to physical sports.

In the large, progressive comprehensive school there may well be a wide range of facilities provided, with staff available to give help, training and guidance. In the smaller secondary school, whether facilities are available for anything outside the few 'standard' competitive sports depends too often on whether the school is lucky enough to have individual staff members who are interested in some of the less orthodox and traditional school recreations. In the latter event – and even in the former – the school may have to enlist the help of local clubs outside the school. This, however, is good rather than bad because it gives the youngster a footing in the outside world before he reaches leaving age.

Special disabilities

The foregoing general discussion has covered most of the problems of stress which will have to be faced by any handicapped child in an ordinary school; it is worth reiterating that since his disability is minor or moderate his essential difficulties will arise from the fact that normal stresses have a greater than normal impact upon him. However, some kinds of disability may specially affect either his problems of adjustment or the task of the school in meeting his needs and these may be briefly indicated.

Partial sight

In the infant department the pace is comparatively slow, much work is oral or practical and the books in general use have large print. The majority of partially sighted children have little difficulty in coping with its activities whether in work or play, so that it is usual for these children to start their career in an ordinary school. At junior level, however, not only does the intensity of work increase but the actual techniques make greater demands on visual acuity. Not only does stress increase quite suddenly at this stage, but the work of the school includes basic processes which are fundamental to all the child's future education. That such a child has kept up with his peers in the infant department does not imply that he will be able to continue to keep up and transfer to a special junior school must be seriously considered. Many such children, given special school help during these critical years, may return to the normal school without undue stress in the secondary years.

Partial hearing

A partially hearing child, with an appropriate hearing aid if necessary, may have little trouble in keeping up with school work without stress. Much of it is visual and oral teaching, is usually given clearly and may be supplemented with visual demonstrations. However a level of hearing which is adequate for comparatively static class work may not be adequate for the general conversation of child with child outside the classroom. This means that the child may have difficulty in intercourse with his peers and may tend to become isolated from the group. This can lead to isolation and retarded social development. Moreover, ordinary conversation is one of the main agents in fostering language development and retardation in this can have repercussions on school work. There is no easy way of overcoming this difficulty. One solution which has been tried with varying degrees of success is the setting up of integrated partially hearing units within ordinary schools. Apart from the educational value of these, they offer the child the company of a special peer group – that of the other partially deaf children – where he will not be socially isolated to anything like the same extent.

Some children, especially those who have been fitted with a hearing aid rather late, are over-conscious of the aid as an outward sign of 'difference' and tend not to use it. In such cases the extra cost of providing an inconspicuous ear-level aid may be completely justified by the way in which it enables the child to mix successfully with the normal children in play as well as in work.

If, however, it becomes evident that a partially hearing child, though keeping up with the class in work, is substantially impeded in social contacts and integration one must accept the possiblity that the experiment in placing him in an ordinary school has failed and transfer to a special unit or school must be considered. It is not desirable to retain him in the ordinary school in the hope that he will overcome his difficulties spontaneously. If, after such transfer, he improves rapidly and becomes socially mature in the special environment, re-admission to an ordinary school may later be considered.

Physical handicap

An intelligent child with average vision and hearing, and with one normally functioning hand and another hand which can be used for steadying his work material, can be expected to cope with the general classroom activities of a normal school. There has been a general – and praiseworthy – tendency in recent years to place many such children in ordinary schools and this is, in fact, the only group of handicapped children of which a substantial number with really severe disabilities are likely to enter such schools. Given transport to and from the school and within the school they will have little trouble with their work. They will, however, be disadvantaged in extra-curricular activities.

Crippling disabilities are a matter of physically obvious fact. They are 'socially acceptable' by normal people, whether children or adults, and the handicapped child himself will perforce have become to some degree reconciled to them before he enters school. There are certain social-emotional risks which arise directly from these facts. The child himself may have become reconciled to inferior status before school age, and may already be convinced that competition is not for him. The kinds of help he needs are plain to see and not difficult to provide; too often the school as an entity and the other children, collectively and individually, rush to offer too much help too quickly.

If such a child is not to be emotionally and socially ruined for life the school must, from the start, face him with direct challenge. Initially, while he is facing the sudden impact of school, it is reasonable to indulge him somewhat and give him a little more help than is strictly necessary. Nevertheless, even at this stage the school must be assessing his abilities – of course in close collaboration with those who are providing medical or surgical treatment – and trying to determine what is the absolute minimum help or protection that he needs. As soon as he begins to settle down in school the help and protection must be gradually reduced toward that minimum.

The crippled boy will be likely to feel his position acutely as he comes to the age when physical sport is of special importance to boys in general. In the case of most severely crippling conditions it is probably best to have started the process of diverting the boy's interests toward non-physical recreations before he reaches the age of eleven or twelve. If, however, there is *any* physical sport at which he can hope to become competent, he should be helped to do so. The leg-cripple in particular may have potential for swimming. Many boys who are competent in other sports may make little progress in swimming and the crippled boy who is coached into competence in this sport can derive much moral support from the fact that he is succeeding where many normal youngsters fail.

Respiratory disabilities

'Chestiness' in children has many causes. Cystic fibrosis is a severe, mainly physical, disability which demands that the child shall have some special care and protection. Asthma has components in both the physical (infective and allergic) and emotional fields. Much respiratory illness diagnosed as 'chronic bronchitis' probably also has some emotional component.

Parents of children with respiratory disabilities lean toward overprotection and are often likely to keep a child away from school if he has only a slight cough or cold or if the weather is a little chilly or damp. This overprotection in itself may intensify any emotional instability in the child, while its repeated interruptions of education may delay his school progress and place him under strain in keeping up with his class. The only practical action which can be taken is to have the child's condition carefully assessed through the medical services – including, if necessary, the child guidance service – to determine whether and to what extent pressure should be brought to bear on the parents to ensure more regular school attendance. The earlier in school life that this can be done, the better for all parties; the child is initially likely to prefer coming to school to staying at home, but if the parents' over-protection continues too long he can easily become something of a hypochondriac.

Diabetes

Many diabetic children have their condition stabilised on a combination of insulin and special diet and attend a normal school quite successfully. If the diabetes is at all severe, however, the child may require a regular routine which can be somewhat irksome to him and restrict his participation in some activities. He may well try to depart from the routine in order to be 'normal'; the consequence is commonly excessive fatiguability, with the risk of physical stress leading to emotional stress. The only safeguard against this is to gain his understanding cooperation in the early years.

The physical changes of puberty may cause temporary instability in a diabetic who has been previously well stabilised. This may first show itself as an inability to keep up the pace, in work and play, with the children with whom he has previously mixed as an equal. The possibility of this should be borne in mind and his physical condition investigated before competition stress has become significant.

Epilepsy

Something like two-thirds of all epileptic children can now have their fits adequately controlled by drugs to the point at which they are able to attend ordinary schools. Occasional fits remain a possibility and the fear of them, together with the shock of their actual occurrence, often makes the child emotionally uncertain. One of the basic essentials is that such children must learn to live with their disability and the best and most important action to this end is that the manifestations of the disease should be accepted in school in the most matter-of-fact way. The other children quickly learn to do this; the difficulty may well lie in apprehensiveness in the teachers. Such apprehensiveness is understandable, for a child who may have fits imposes considerable responsibility on those in charge of him. When a child with epilepsy, however well controlled, enters an ordinary school, the staff should be fully advised and warned. To press for the admission of such a child to a school where the staff feel themselves already under such strain that they cannot accept the responsibility is unfair to both staff and child. If this is the case in the school which normally serves the neighbourhood in which he lives, admission should be sought in a school which is able to be more tolerant.

Puberty may bring a diminution of the epilepsy or may make a previously stabilised child unstable. In the latter event it is often better for the child to be temporarily transferred to a special school for a period of investigation and re-stabilisation than to try to re-stabilise him while he is attending an ordinary school. Not only are the special facilities more comprehensive but in a special school he is facing his crisis in the company of children who have the same kind of problem.

Minimal cerebral dysfunction

This not uncommon condition is still too little understood. Present opinion inclines to the view that it is in many cases due to a minor degree of brain damage, though sometimes it may be accounted for by a combination of minor intellectual defect with emotional disturbance.

Typically, the child with minimal cerebral dysfunction presents a combination of intellectual 'slowness', physical clumsiness, physical hyperactivity and emotional instability. In some cases it appears that the intellectual disability is irregular, in that the child may be at or above normal level in certain aptitudes but substantially below in others.

The most difficult aspect of the child's situation is that no single aspect of his disability may be severe enough to attract special attention in the early years of life. Any one of them – and often all of them, considered separately – may be within normal limits, or at least no more marked than might be expected in a child who had been somewhat deprived of social contacts and normal play activities or over-indulged by his parents. The consequence is that in many of these children no disability has been suspected before the age of school entry, so that they tend to be presented automatically to ordinary schools without any suggestion that there is anything special about them. The many-sided challenge of school life suddenly finds out all their weak spots simultaneously and they may consequently suffer from 'school shock' in a quite severe form. The school tends to hope and expect that they will settle down and they may not be brought forward for special investigation until late in the first year, when general retardation is becoming well established.

By this time the child is facing the situation of slight but definite all-round inferiority to his peers. Since all the disparities are slight he will be confused and even bewildered by the inferiority and may already have begun to 'contract out' of school life. The risks of incompatibility between child and school is specially marked when the intellectual deficit is patchy. It is both easy and natural for a teacher to assume that if a child has taken easily to reading, for example, but is failing with numbers he is an intelligent child with selective laziness who needs to be pressed in his weak subject or subjects.

Some of these children will inevitably need special education. Others, given special attention, appropriate remedial teaching and, possibly, drug therapy, can expect to succeed in an ordinary school. It is of paramount importance that schools should be aware of the existence of this bizarre disability, not only because those of its possessors who need special education should be identified early, before they disrupt the life of the class, but because those who are potentially educable in an ordinary school should not be allowed to add maladjustment to their problems by having suffered a year or more of frustration and misunderstanding.

There are no sovereign or universal techniques for helping children with minimal cerebral dysfunction through ordinary schools. Those who are in fact of normal school potential will, in general, be children who make slow all-round progress. Though somewhat below average in intelligence they can learn. Their clumsiness will grow less as they gain practice in motor activity and their emotional instability will be reduced as they settle into a stable social environment. Their predicament is perhaps best seen as one of slow maturing. If the disability is detected early after first entry it may be wise to transfer them to a nursery school or class for a year and, after they become established in the ordinary school setting, to re-assess their maturity every time promotion is due – even from class to class – and retain them for a year or so if necessary until they are considered really mature enough to move up.

There is always the possibility that they may have periodical episodes of regression, especially in behaviour, after any traumatic experience – a crisis in the home, an interruption of schooling by illness, a misunderstanding with a teacher. Again, no universal rule for dealing with this possibility can be suggested. The need for emotional experience for these children is certainly at least as important as that of any other children and excessive shielding is just as damaging. Certainly, if experience suggests that a given child is specially vulnerable to a particular type of experience it is worthwhile trying to anticipate the occurrence of such a situation and to minimise its impact. Often these critical situations have several elements and it may well be possible, as the situation builds up, to reduce at any rate some of the elements.

Perhaps more than in any other group of handicapped children the closest of understanding and collaboration between home and school is to be sought. A word of warning from parent to teacher or from teacher to parent that the child has had some disturbing experience which has put him on edge on one particular day, either in the home or at school, may make it possible to avoid adding any other stress which, though mild in itself, may light the fuse and precipitate the explosion.

In conclusion it is worthwhile to return to and emphasise something which has been implicit throughout this chapter; namely that the most important element for success in coping with any handicapped child in an ordinary school is the perceptiveness and understanding of the teacher. Too little is still being done to stimulate and develop those qualities. The training of teachers still assumes too easily that handicapped children go to special schools and many training colleges give little more than passing mention of the problems of handicapped children in their syllabus of general teacher training. This deficit needs to be remedied.

Even with such training, two dangers persist. One is that not every teacher has the special qualities of personality needed in the management of a child with a disability. The other is that even if she has that personality and training a teacher may be working under such general pressure or in such unpropitious circumstances that she cannot make use of her assets as she should. The placing of a handicapped child in an ordinary school should therefore be preceded by as thorough an assessment of the child and discussion with the school staff as one would enter into before special school placement.

The School Health Service is not merely a clinical assessment agency, though that is still one of its important functions. In partnership with the pre-school health services and in collaboration with the school and other agencies it will prepare the child for schooling, discuss the selection of the school, prepare the school for the child's admission and serve as the continuing provider of surveillance, advice and guidance. The care of any handicapped child, however minor his disability, is a task for a team working in the harmonious relationship which subsists when members of several disciplines forget 'demarcation lines' and professional possessiveness and join in the common pursuit of the total aim – ensuring that the child shall have the best possible chance of realising all his potentialities.

PSYCHOTIC CHILDREN
Lorna Wing

The word *psychosis* has no really satisfactory definition. The various schools of psycho-analysis apply the term to patients whom they consider have regressed to a very early stage of development.

In more conventional clinical psychiatry, when dealing with the illnesses of adults, the word psychosis is used as the general term covering a number of different conditions including, for example, mania, certain kinds of severe depression, schizophrenia, confusional states and dementias. These have in common the fact that they produce a profound effect (temporarily or permanently) upon the patient's behaviour and personality. In the field of child psychiatry it is even harder to find a precise meaning for the term *childhood psychosis*. Perhaps the best definition that can be given is that this diagnosis can be used when a child behaves in a way which is strange and unpredictable in the light of his age and level of intelligence. To take some examples, the average mongol child of ten does not behave like a normal ten year old, but he would not be called psychotic because his behaviour is predictable when one knows that he has the intelligence of a four year old child. On the other hand, some children with phenylketonuria behave in a way which is quite abnormal, whatever their intelligence level may be, and they could be called psychotic.

There are many different patterns of behaviour which can be grouped together under the general heading of childhood psychosis. Sometimes there is an obvious organic cause such as phenylketonuria as mentioned above, the after-effects of encephalitis (an inflammation of the brain due to infection), conditions causing destructive changes in brain tissue, or brain tumours. In most cases, however, the causes are uncertain or unknown, and the conditions have to be grouped in a rough and ready way according to the behaviour pattern shown.

One useful generalisation is to divide childhood psychoses into three groups according to whether they begin in early, middle or late childhood. Those starting in the first two or at the most three years of life mostly show the pattern known as early childhood autism. Those beginning in the middle years are a very mixed group, including a number with known organic causes, but the children affected do not show the typical autistic pattern. The psychoses of later childhood and adolescence include those which have the symptoms of adult psychoses such as schizophrenia, mania and very severe depression.

Although there are many different types of psychosis in childhood, probably the commonest single pattern found is that of early childhood autism. The rest of this chapter will concentrate upon this problem, since teachers are more likely to meet autistic children than those with other kinds of psychoses, and also because this is the group for whom most work has been done in the field of education.

Prevalence

A survey in the county of Middlesex, and a similar survey in Aarhus county in Denmark, showed that out of every 10,000 children of school age, four or five are likely to have early childhood autism. Of this number, about one half show the 'classic' pattern of behaviour, and the other half will have many but not all of the characteristic symptoms. Approximately one third of the children with this behaviour pattern have other abnormalities affecting the central nervous system, for example epilepsy, spasticity, or the after-effects of meningitis or encephalitis. The rest appear to be physically normal, except on careful observation as will be described later.

Nearly everyone who has written about autistic children agrees that boys are affected more often than girls, although estimates of the ratio vary, the highest being four boys to one girl.

The Middlesex survey was carried out in 1964 and 1965. At the time the children were seen, at the average age of nearly ten years, five were in ESN schools, two in special classes for maladjusted children, one was receiving home tuition and eight were in special residential schools, mostly Steiner. Nineteen were not under the education authorities and of these two were in a day unit, nine in junior training schools and eight were in a sub-normality hospital or other long term care. Although none was found in this survey, a few autistic children are placed in schools for normal children, especially small ones that are run privately, although sometimes in state schools also. In recent years a few schools and units which take only autistic children have been opened but the total number of such places is small, and it is still possible for a teacher in almost any kind of school to find that he or she has an autistic child in the class.

The behaviour of autistic children

Accounts of children with abnormal behaviour very like that of autism can be found in books and papers written well before this century, but the first person to describe them as a special group was Professor Leo Kanner. His original papers on the subject appeared in the early 1940s. His observations were excellent, and give a clear picture of many of the outstanding features. However, as virtually the first, and at that time almost the only, worker in the field, he concentrated upon the points that were most obvious. These were the apparent aloofness and social withdrawal, plus the childrens' insistence on sameness, refusal to tolerate any change and their intense attachment to objects. He considered these to be symptoms of a profound abnormality of social response, and went on to say that the parents of these children tended to be cold, distant and over-intellectual in their personalities and especially in their approach to their children. Later on Kanner and his co-worker Eisenberg wrote that this type of personality was found especially in the fathers.

Since that time there has been a steadily growing interest in these children, and people have had the opportunity to observe and to test them and their parents in much more detail, and to notice things that Kanner never described at all. From this work new ideas are emerging. There are now a small number of controlled studies which have found that parents of autistic children do not have any specially abnormal attitudes to their children, except those induced by having a handicapped child, nor any special personality features, apart from higher than average intelligence. Work with the children themselves suggests that their difficulties are cognitive rather than emotional in origin and that they have severe problems in comprehending and using any kind of language (speech, gesture, facial expression, miming, sign languages, etc.). They also seem unable to organise the information coming in from the outside world, to link it with past experience, or to use it as a basis for future action. These two problems are probably closely related to one another. This leads to the hypothesis that the cause lies in a delay in development of the parts of the brain responsible for organising information and for all aspects of language function, although this must remain a theory until more is known about brain structure, function and pathology. The behaviour pattern is most obvious between the ages of two and five years, after which there is a tendency to improvement, but the elements can still be seen during the school years.

The children respond to sound in an unusual way, ignoring some sounds completely, being fascinated and completely absorbed by others, and reacting to some noises as if they were painful and distressing.

At first they tend to ignore speech as if it had no more interest and importance than the sound of passing traffic or the patter of rain upon the windows. By school age most of them can understand at least a few simple instructions ('come and have dinner', 'put on your coat'), but they may be easily muddled by too many items in one sentence ('go upstairs and put on your hat, coat and gloves') and have no understanding at all of anything abstract or complicated.

Speech is almost always delayed and many never begin to speak at all. In those who do talk, repeating words spoken by other people, or repeating phrases heard some time ago is very common and the mimicry may be phenomenally accurate. In contrast the childrens' spontaneous speech tends to be laboured and badly pronounced, sometimes loud or too soft and sometimes spoken in a toneless voice or one that rises and falls in the wrong places. They are very confused about pronouns, usually saying 'you' instead of 'I' ('you want biscuit' meaning 'I want biscuit'). They have trouble with little words like in, at, to, from and so on, and often drop them altogether.

They muddle the sequence of letters in words and of words in sentences. Even those who learn to speak quite well tend to be pedantic, and very literal and concrete in their use and understanding of words ('what will you be when you grow up?' – 'a man!').

The majority of autistic children appear to be graceful and agile, although there are some who are rather clumsy in their movements. However, close observation of both kinds of children shows that their movement patterns are immature for their age, as for example in the way they hold their arms when running, and that they have marked difficulty in copying movements made by other people. They seem to confuse up and down, right and left and back and front, and this may also show in their attempts to read and write.

The children have many problems with interpreting the information coming to them through their eyes. They seem to dart rapid glances rather than to fix their eyes on people or things, which leads to the impression that they avoid looking at people's faces. They pay attention to small trivial things in the environment and ignore those that seem important to a normal child. They may walk downstairs or even ride a tricycle without appearing to look where they are going, but without mishap. They are sometimes, wrongly, thought to be blind. Like blind or nearly blind children they explore the world through touch, taste and smell although they sometimes appear oblivious of pain or cold. Again like blind children, they have many odd movements such as grimacing, jumping, tip-toe walking, spinning round and round, or rapidly twisting their hands, or shiny objects, near their eyes. They also have problems in understanding and using gestures, facial expression and miming. In their early years when they can neither talk nor gesture, they show what they want by grabbing someone by the hand and leading them to a desired object.

Given all these difficulties in understanding, it is not surprising that the children find the world unpredictable, confusing, frightening and extremely stressful. They have numerous emotional problems which are secondary to their handicaps.

The most striking of these is the appearance of aloofness, or rather unawareness of other people, which Kanner thought was so important. People who meet a young autistic child for the first time feel that he is living in a world of his own, quite oblivious to everyone else. This feeling is caused by the behaviour I have just described (lack of response to speech, tendency not to look at faces and so on) and also because the young child is so muddled and confused that he is at first unaware that human beings are any more important than the inanimate objects that he can pick up and handle.

As they mature the children tend to become much more aware of people and to become friendly and affectionate, although this is usually shown in immature ways. An autistic child of twelve or more may want to be cuddled like a toddler.

Living in a confusing world, the children try to cling on to what they know, so they become rigid about routines, and react with fear and anger to any change, or to the loss of any object to which they are attached.

Another direct result of lack of language and lack of comprehension of the world is the inability to play. Autistic children handle toys to obtain a series of simple sensations, and do not see them as trains or buses or dolls or whatever. They cannot play with other children except perhaps at very simple games of chasing, hide and seek, or throwing a ball.

Lack of language leads to lack of social sense, and this in turn leads to socially embarrassing behaviour such as screaming in the street, grabbing things in shops, biting and kicking. Temper tantrums or extreme fear may also result from exposure to too much noise and movement and confusion in the environment.

Despite their handicaps some of the children do well at tasks not requiring language. Most of them love music and a few sing or learn to play an instrument. Some can do arithmetical calculations and others are good with mechanical things. Their intelligence quotients on non-verbal tests range from above average to severely subnormal, with the majority scoring well below average.

Differentiation from other conditions

Each of the elements of the behaviour shown by autistic children can be seen for short periods in young normal children. The difference is that an autistic child shows all or most of the features at the same time, the pattern changes very slowly indeed, and it represents almost the whole range of his behaviour. By the time of school age the differences between autistic and normal children are clear. A child who is very withdrawn because of extreme shyness or anxiety does not show the other odd behaviour characteristic of autism, nor does a child who, for example, may speak at home but never at school ('elective mutism').

Children with deafness, aphasia, or visual perceptual difficulties often have parts of the autistic pattern when they are very young, for obvious reasons, and diagnosis depends upon a complete assessment of all the handicaps. Some children born both partially deaf and partially blind, especially if this is caused by the mother having had German measles in pregnancy, behave almost exactly like autistic children. Here the history and physical examination give the diagnosis.

Other forms of childhood psychosis can also be distinguished from autism from a detailed history and the pattern of behaviour.

Early childhood autism causes learning problems and is often associated with mental retardation. There are many different kinds of mental retardation and most retarded children do not have this special pattern of behaviour because they do not have the special difficulties of perception. The mongol child for instance is usually equally backward in speech and motor skills. In contrast an autistic child's language and social development is far below that of a mongol child of the same intelligence level, although his skill with music, arithmetic and mechanical things may be far superior.

Problems of teaching

Although all autistic children have the behaviour pattern in common, they vary a great deal in the severity of their handicaps, number of secondary behaviour problems, and whether or not they have other conditions as well. A teacher in a normal school may have an autistic child in the class who, apart from being very quiet and lacking in skill with subjects needing good language ability, does not stand out from the rest. At the other extreme, a teacher in a junior training school may have to cope with an autistic child who is ten times more disturbed and hard to teach than all the other children put together. All variations can be seen between these two ends of the scale. It is therefore impossible to discuss problems of teaching which will apply to all autistic children, so I shall mention various kinds of difficulties that may be met, with the proviso that only some of them will be relevant to any individual child.

They can be discussed under four general headings, namely, managing disturbed behaviour, teaching basic skills, teaching more academic skills, and helping the child with his emotional problems.

Managing disturbed behaviour

Difficult behaviour arises primarily because the child does not understand the ordinary rules of social conduct. However, it is often made worse because the bewildered parents rarely receive any advice on how to help their child, and in despair they tend to give him the things he wants in order to restore some semblance of peace and quiet. The child, lacking guidance and any framework to help him organise his world, becomes even more confused and distressed. The way to deal with this situation is gradually to introduce some simple rules of conduct and to insist very firmly upon the child's cooperation. He cannot be expected to obey verbal instructions in the early stages, so he must be shown in more direct ways. He can learn that he must sit quietly while his teacher is with him, if she holds him firmly in his chair and shows quite confidently that she will not allow him to run around during the allotted time. Screaming, spitting, kicking, biting and so on must never be rewarded for the sake of a quiet life. They must be discouraged at once. It may be necessary to remove the child from the classroom if he screams and it is important to have an assistant to stay with him in another room. All this takes a long time, but at least some improvement will certainly occur, providing the staff are consistent, and they begin with very simple rules so that the child can grasp what he has to do, even if he does not know why.

Sometimes teachers, like parents, worry that a child will dislike them if they stand firm against his tantrums, but experience soon shows that the children are much happier and more loving towards people who set limits and make them feel safe and secure.

A few people hold the theory that it helps autistic children to behave better if they are allowed to regress to the baby stage, to bottle feed, and, so to speak, 'start again'. There is no evidence that this is helpful, and in my view it could do harm by teaching the child even more immature and undesirable habits than he has already.

Once the stage of screaming and tantrums has passed new social problems may appear, because the children lack any sensitivity to social nuances. Those who can talk may make embarrassing remarks in a loud voice in public about other peoples' physical peculiarities, or concerning subjects that are not usually discussed in company. They may appear in public half clothed, or without any clothes at all, and are very surprised that this excites comment. The teacher and the parents have to be aware of these possibilities and lay down reasonable rules. The children usually obey when they know these rules, but do not understand them and tend to apply them quite inflexibly to all situations.

Teaching basic skills

Many autistic children, even by school age, lack basic skills such as dressing, washing, using a knife and fork and also cannot ride a tricycle, throw a ball, or use outdoor play equipment. If they watch other people do these things and try to copy them they become muddled and miserable, or frankly uncooperative.

The best way to teach these skills is to move the child's fingers or limbs through the necessary movements until he gets the 'feel' of what is required. This takes time and patience, and usually needs two adults to one child. At first the child may resist furiously and then become limp and passive. Eventually, however, you begin to feel his muscle movements following your own, until he can do the whole action for himself. He may need a guiding finger, perhaps just touching his arm, for weeks after he can perform perfectly well, but in the end this can be removed (by stages) and he manages on his own. Many simple skills can be taught in this way and each new success gives the child more control over his environment, more self-confidence and helps to make his life less stressful and more enjoyable.

Teaching academic skills

Teaching 'academic' skills is considerably more complicated than improving behaviour. The eventual level of attainment depends upon the severity of each child's handicaps. All I shall do here is to mention some of the difficulties that may be encountered.

The children at first react with fear and anger to attempts to teach them new things, probably because any change is seen as adding to their confusion and therefore as a threat. Some teachers have found that they can make use of the fact that the children have certain routines, bodily movements that they repeat endlessly, or objects to which they cling. The teachers use these 'obsessions' as starting points for making contact with the child and from there move on to more constructive activities. Once they have learnt something they often resist moving on to anything new, and want to do the same things over and over again. The teacher must be understanding but firm, making each new step very small, but insisting that the child tries if she feels he is ready.

The children have severe learning problems, which underlie their reluctance to try. Even the brightest of them cannot understand or use complicated ideas and most of the children have very limited comprehension. Added to this they may have the same difficulties as children with dyslexia. In order to plan lessons the teacher must be very familiar with each child's pattern of handicaps and she must be aware of the difference between an emotional refusal to learn and a genuine difficulty of comprehension. It is very rare in these children to find the first without the second as well. Teachers should beware of thinking that the child can understand and talk perfectly well simply because he puts his coat on when told. This is the same as assuming that a child in the first year of grammar school can speak French fluently because he can answer the question 'où est la plume de ma tante?'

Emotional problems

Autistic children have the best chance of making the most of their potentialities if they have families who give them love and security, and if they are taught by an experienced and understanding teacher. Under these conditions the emotional problems arising directly from their handicaps gradually improve and may in some cases almost disappear. However, if a child's understanding of the world increases sufficiently he may develop new kinds of emotional problems that do not trouble the more handicapped child. Children of this kind begin to be aware that they are different from other people, especially if they are in a class with pupils who use language normally. They may become very miserable, even depressed. If they are good at some subjects they may place too much value on this and become upset, and even badly behaved, if they make any mistakes in their work.

Occasionally a bright autistic child will make pathetic attempts to be as normal as anyone else, and will try to do things like writing essays for a competition at which he is doomed to failure. He sees that other people fall in love, get married and have children, and he will think about these matters and perhaps worry about his lack of social success in this direction. The more handicapped autistic children enjoy physical contact and have an open, childish, simple curiosity about their own and other people's bodies which may lead to socially awkward behaviour.

There is no simple answer to the problems of an autistic child who develops insight. Nothing anyone can do can hide at least some part of the truth from him. In this situation the teacher can show sympathy and understanding, try to be a sure source of comfort and friendship and listen if the child is able to put some of his feelings, however haltingly, into words. This kind of child does, however, have some compensating abilities and it helps to direct his attention to the things he can do, rather than those which he cannot.

In all these problems of management and teaching it is most important that teachers and parents should see each other as equal partners. Both should consciously strive to avoid feelings of possessiveness about the child and jealousy of each other. Both have a role to play and the child benefits if they work in harmony, and suffers if there is antipathy and distrust. The latter is particularly liable to arise if the teacher automatically assumes that the parent is responsible for the child's handicaps, or if, on the other hand, the parent resents the fact that the teacher tries to lay down some rules to control the child's behaviour.

Autistic children in different kinds of schools

There has been much discussion as to whether autistic children do best in schools which specialise in their problems, or in schools where they are mixed with other handicapped children or with normal children. In my view the specialist school or class has, in practice, the most to offer, but I shall not go into the arguments here. This section will deal with the various problems that are found in different educational settings.

One disadvantage of schools accepting only autistic children is that staff and children alike are isolated from contact with children whose behaviour is normal. This matters less for the autistic children themselves, since they seem to learn little from other children unless they reach a fairly high level of development. The staff, however, lack the stimulus of discussion with teachers in other fields. They also tend to forget the levels of social and academic achievement of normal children, and perhaps see the progress of the autistic children too optimistically. One way round this may be to arrange contacts with a nearby school for normal children, or children with other handicaps, and to combine for various social and recreational activities.

Schools which mix autistic and other handicapped children have to reconcile the conflicting demands of many different learning and behaviour problems. This is particularly true in a junior training school from which disturbed overactive autistic children are often excluded simply because the staff cannot cope with them and teach the other children as well, all of whom need some individual attention. The fact that autistic children have to have much of their teaching in non-verbal ways makes it hard to organise lessons with children who learn through spoken language.

Autistic children are rarely able to defend themselves against attacks from other children. They do not have the almost automatic movements of defence and attack which so readily appear in most schoolboys. They are bewildered and helpless if hit and they usually cannot complain to adults, so they suffer in silent misery. They do not learn to look after themselves through experience, and they may be most unhappy if mixed with mal-adjusted or other aggressive children. Teachers must be aware of this problem and close supervision may be necessary to prevent physical attacks on a child who is so vulnerable. His distress may show itself in screaming, self injury or further social withdrawal, if he cannot tell his teacher what is happening.

Very few autistic children are accepted into normal schools, since their handicaps are usually too severe and their behaviour too difficult. A few with mild handicaps, however, are educated with normal children. Quite often the child starts in the infant's school and settles down quite well. He manages in the first classes of the junior school, but as the 11+ exam approaches and the pressures begin to build up, he begins to fall behind. This is mainly because, at this level, work involves the use of language and the manipulation of ideas, and the child's weaknesses begin to be exposed. He may have to leave at this stage and move to a special school, either because his work is not good enough, or, unfortunately, because his behaviour has deteriorated as well. When he is placed in a school where he can cope and where his handicaps are understood, such behaviour problems usually settle down rapidly. His pace of development tends to be slower than that of normal children and this can be catered for in the right kind of special school.

A small number of autistic children are able to stay in normal school up to school leaving age, or even, in very rare instances, go on to higher education in music or mathematics. Here one of the biggest problems is to ensure that the child is accepted by the normal children and has some social life. Unless this is tactfully supervised by the teacher he may lead a very solitary life indeed. At first sight it may seem that he prefers to be alone, but the usual experience is that the children love social events and outings even though they are passive participants. They are often not asked because they appear so little involved, but this makes them very hurt and unhappy, although they may not talk about it. Normal children can be thoughtless, but they also respond to explanation and guidance from adults as to how to behave towards someone who is handicapped.

As in schools with aggressive or maladjusted children, bullying may also occur in normal schools. This may take the form of teasing rather than physical assault but can be just as harmful to the apparently slow-witted autistic child who is as little able to defend himself with verbal wit as he is to win a fight.

Wherever he is placed, an autistic child will need a great deal of individual attention from his teacher, at least until he has settled down, become used to the routine and has begun to learn. Supervision is often a particular problem in residential schools. Whereas the time in class is organised, evening and weekend activities are usually freer and these are the times when the autistic child may be left on his own, and when he may revert to his unconstructive repetitive activities, through boredom and lack of stimulation. Without special attention, a child may become too disturbed to remain in the school, or he may be so quiet and withdrawn that he escapes notice, and gains nothing from his school experience.

Aims of education and prognosis

Whether one is dealing with autistic children who are mildly, moderately, or severely handicapped, there are certain basic aims which are the same for all. The first of these is to try to improve each child's social behaviour so that he can live in the community (even if he always needs a protected environment) and does not have to be admitted to an institution. The second aim is to help the child to compensate for his handicaps, and to learn as much as he can so that he understands something about the world around him. Thirdly, education should aim to teach skills so that he has an occupation as an adult, whether he is employed on the open market or, as is more likely, in a sheltered workshop. The last aim, which involves all the others, is to help autistic children to find some interest and pleasure in life, instead of leaving them in frightening chaos.

A few years ago a research worker followed up a group of autistic children into early adult life. He found that about fourteen per cent made very considerable progress towards normality, twenty five per cent showed a fair improvement and the rest had not changed very much. None of these children had received any specialised education, although a number had attended various kinds of schools for other handicaps. It is to be hoped that the recent developments in education specifically designed for these children will improve the prognosis.

Teachers who work with these children have stresses of their own to face. They need to be able to accept painfully slow progress, and the possibility of only limited gains. Their pleasure and reward come from each child's gradually developing awareness of things around him, and the long worked for, triumphant moments when the penny drops and the child acquires a new piece of knowledge.

SLOW-LEARNING CHILDREN
Phillip Williams

Summary

This chapter presents snapshots of a slow-learner in a primary school from the teacher's point of view and the mother's point of view. It then introduces in a non-technical way a few key findings from recent educational enquiry into the factors which relate to learning difficulties in children. Later, it touches on some of the additional problems which the slow-learner may face in the school and in the family. Finally, it examines three ways through which teachers can identify the existence and possible causes of stresses in slow-learners.

John Smith

This section introduces John, a child with learning problems. The descriptions given are not of course intended to constitute a case-study, but simply to provide background material to which later sections of the chapter can refer.

John Smith, aged 9 years 7 months – date of birth: 3rd December 19...
Attending Acacia Primary School

John is a slow-learner. On the recommendation of the educational psychologist, he will be transferred, with the consent of his mother, to the special class for slow-learners which has been established at Boxford Primary School.

THE TEACHER'S STORY   'I have had John since September. The first thing that struck me when he came into my class was the very poor quality of his work. I run the class very much on activity lines with children arranging themselves in two's and three's for small-group work. They follow the instructions on a series of cards which I have prepared and often work from then on from books which are available to them from the library or which I lend to them. John just couldn't cope with this approach. To begin with he had no reading attainment at all. He literally could not read the first sentence of our new maths book. I gave him a quick test on a graded word reading test and he was unable to read more than three or four words. He had been following the new maths scheme which we have been running in the school but when he came to me he was still unable to distinguish simple number concepts and when I gave him a quick check on some of the Piaget-type exercises which I have available, he obviously had not passed through the stage of conservation of number.

'His learning problems were matched by his personality difficulties. He did not really belong with the other children. No one wanted to work in the same group as John. Had I carried out a study of social relationships in the class through sociometry or a similar technique, I am almost certain that John would be an "isolate" or at least a "neglectee". He has no friends at all in the class.

'My concern about John is how he is going to develop as he grows older. It is fairly obvious that he doesn't fit in the class with which he has been placed until now. In the playground he occasionally plays with some of the children from the first year juniors or the top infants but his physical size, which is about average for his age – he is quite sturdily built and fairly robust – means that he is really out of place in mixing with these younger children. I foresee considerably greater difficulties for him as the rest of the class gain more independence in their work and progress to more difficult exercises. It is for these reasons that I feel he is a lad who needs some form of help other than that which we can provide for him in this school.

'Naturally I have discussed his problems with the Head and I have also had a talk with his previous teachers. The Head felt we should look into things in more detail and we called in the school psychological service. As a result of the conferences which have been held John has been recommended for a place at the special class for slow-learners, and we think that this may well be the best decision which we have yet taken about John's education.'

THE MOTHER'S STORY   'John is the middle one of my five children. He has always been a bit slower than the others and has never come on quite as well as they have. They are not great scholars, but they do manage to hold their own at school. He didn't have a good start, of course – his birth wasn't easy and the doctor told me that I was lucky to keep him at all. I suppose on looking back that he reached his milestones later than the other children did and he was perhaps very slow in talking. He didn't really begin to talk in reasonable sentences until he was three or four, whereas the others were well away by the time they were two or three. His speech has never been really clear, I suppose.

'He has not been a very awkward child but he did find school difficult. He didn't seem to settle well when he had to start at the infants' school and we had a lot of tears when the time came for him to go to school in the mornings. But he did get used to it in time and he goes fairly happily now, though I have noticed recently – I suppose this last six months or so – that he isn't as keen to go as he used to be. He is very ready to suggest that he has a cold or isn't very well if he has the chance. I suppose it may be that the work is getting harder for him and he is not quite as able to cope as he was when it was easier.

'I don't find that he has many friends. At home he plays fairly happily with Tommy – that's my youngest – although Tommy is almost four years younger than John and has in fact only just started school. I haven't really been able to go along to school and see exactly how John is getting on. I would like to have done this and I suppose I feel really a bit guilty that I haven't. But since my husband left me four years ago and we had to move to this very small flat, I have been far too busy trying to keep the home together to be able to come along and sort out the kiddies' problems at school.

'So when Mr Tomlinson – the headmaster, that is – suggested that it might be a good plan if John went to this special class and when he told me that the bus would take John to the class and bring him home again without him having to worry about crossing roads and so on, I was really quite pleased. I am hoping that this will be a very good thing for John. I must admit I am a little worried that it will make him different from the other children round about. But everyone tells me that it will be good for John so I think that we must try it and see how it goes.'

It might be appropriate to head our next paragraph 'John's Story'. This we will not do because it is very hard for John to describe eloquently to us the way in which he views his own situation at the moment. It is not easy for young slow-learners to communicate their feelings in an adult way, a point which is discussed later, since it has implications for the identification of stress. If it is not possible for us fully to enter his world, nevertheless we must try to understand the reasons for John's learning difficulties. These will help us to evaluate the stresses which led to his slow-learning and help in our handling of him. Stresses which lead to the slow-learning condition can be called determinant stresses, as opposed to stresses which flow from the slow-learning condition. These latter we can call resultant stresses. Let us now consider these two kinds of stresses.

Determinant stresses

Basically the stresses which have led to the slow-learning condition are similar to the stresses which nearly all children have to meet during their development. But the slow-learner has usually met those stresses in a more severe form than the educationally normal child. In John's case relationships between the parents had deteriorated so far that his father had left home, a much more acute situation than the mild parental bickering that many children meet.

In addition the slow-learner has often encountered several stresses, not just one. John had not only to meet the problem of poor parental relations: he also had a difficult birth, which may well have led to other learning problems. Handicaps caused by combinations of stresses like this, are sometimes said to show 'multiple causation' or 'multifactorial causation'.

One of the major concerns of present research is to find the relative importance of different stresses in causing the slow-learning condition. There are stresses within the environment which lead to learning difficulties. For example, John came from a family of five which father had left. Inevitably the mother's problems are more concerned with the economics of keeping the household going than with the needs of the individual children; the limited time that she has at her disposal for the children will in any case be still further reduced when it is shared between each of the five. So there is bound to be a degree, not so much of neglect, as of lack of attention.

This leads us to consider the attitude which the home has towards school. Here the mother's statement that she has been feeling guilty about her lack of contact with school may suggest an attitude which is basically good. But if we were to assess her attitude by her behaviour, this very lack of contact may lead us to a different conclusion.

In addition, the physical condition of John's home, the overcrowding that his mother mentioned, brings in train a number of complications. A quiet room for looking at comics or for putting out the stamp-collection is obviously out of the question. What effect have restrictions like these had on John's development and learning?

The most careful recent analysis of the stresses which relate to learning performance in primary schools has been carried out in the Plowden Report (Department of Education and Science, 1967). In the enquiry for this report, Peaker (1967) analysed the relationships between the characteristics of children's environments and their attainments. He grouped his information about the children's environments into three areas:

1   parental attitudes to education (e.g. how educationally ambitious the parents were);
2   home circumstances (e.g. the material conditions of the home); and
3   schooling (e.g. the amenities the school possessed).

He then examined his results to see which of these areas of the environment was most closely related to attainment in school. Peaker writes:

'Qualitatively the results are in no way surprising. Common sense and common observation lead us to expect that a child's school achievement will be determined, to some extent, by the attitudes of his parents and that these attitudes in turn will partly depend upon their material circumstances. It was indeed this common sense expectation that guided the planning of the enquiry. What could not be foreseen, until the enquiry was complete, was the quantitative aspect. We could foresee that parental attitudes, parental circumstances and schooling would each make a contribution. What we could not foresee and what the enquiry has shown, is the relative size of these contributions . . .

'Before the enquiry, it was plain, as a matter of common sense and common observation, that parental encouragement and support could take the child some way. What the enquiry has shown is that "some way" can reasonably be interpreted as "a long way" and that the variation in parental encouragement and support has much greater effect than either the situation in home circumstances or the situation in schools.'

The over-riding importance of parental attitudes and interest in affecting attainment has been confirmed by other investigations. Thus Wiseman (1967) writes that '. . . economic level and social class are much less important than aspects of parental attitude, attitude to education and attitude to books and reading. A high wage packet and a middle-class home does not guarantee a favourable background for educational progress, and literate homes with good parental attitude to school may be found in the slums as well as in the suburbs.'

Attempts have been made to elucidate these attitudes and interests more specifically in relation to children with very poor attainments – the slow-learners. Wiseman (1967) has contrasted the stresses which relate to attainment in backward children with those which relate to attainment in bright children. He concludes that 'the factors affecting backwardness tend to be those denoting maternal attitude to the child, while for brightness the parent's attitude to education seems the more important.'

What is of fundamental importance here is not so much the finding, as the principle. Slow-learners are a group with special problems. Research findings which apply to 'every day' children in the ordinary classes may not apply to that small group of children we call the slow learners.

Let us look again at John. If his mother's attitude to her children is poor, we must ask why John alone seems to be the slow-learner? We have no evidence from our brief case-description that she has a particularly poor attitude to John in comparison to his brothers and sisters. But we do know that his early development – of speech for example – was relatively slow and we also know that he had a difficult birth. We cannot help wondering, therefore, if John's case is an example of the effect of a combination of stresses, a damaged environment combining with a damaged child to produce a slow-learner.

In order to examine this hypothesis we would rely, in the real-life situation, on a medical evaluation of John's physical condition and history, a psychological assessment of the important attitudes and interest and a social assessment of the environment in which he is growing up. The important point, however, is that schools admit children whose slow-learning condition is the result of many different determinant stresses, but most notably stresses associated with poor parental attitudes, poor environmental circumstances and physiological handicap.

Resultant stresses

There is, however, another set of stresses which are a consequence of the slow-learning situation. Let us look at these under the headings of school and of family.

The school situation

The main character in the school situation is, of course, the teacher. As far as the slow-learning child is concerned the teacher can too readily be the powerful adult whose standard he (the child) so rarely reaches. He spends most of his school time in the charge of an adult whom he may well try hard to please but whom he rarely succeeds in pleasing. He may, of course, have an understanding and capable teacher who is able to treat each one of his thirty to forty children as individuals, and meet each one at his own level, but this is rare. The teacher inevitably distributes praise and blame among the class and on the whole a slow-learner is a child who is less likely to receive praise than is a 'quick' learner.

In the school situation a slow-learner mixes with his peer group, that is the children of his own age or class. These are the children with whom in many schools he is in competition. Even if the school is organised on co-operative lines, as seems to be so in John's case, he soon realises, particularly when he enters the junior school, that others manage to solve problems and answer questions which he himself cannot do. This raises the question in his own mind of his own adequacy – 'how capable am I – why is it I find school work hard when others don't?' These are some of the questions which pose themselves, perhaps not in so clear a form, perhaps not even in the form of words, but more as a vague unease. He may not appreciate why the unease is there but he senses it nevertheless. The attitude of the teacher and the comparison with his peers may well lead to a damaged self-concept, a feeling of inferiority and lack of worth.

The family situation

In the family, the slow-learner tries to please his parents, but in many families the parents themselves have anxieties about his progress. 'Why is it that John cannot read whereas Tommy, who is four years younger, is already making a start with simple words? Will he ever learn? What will happen when he is sixteen? Will he ever manage to hold down a job?' Sometimes lying at a lower level there is the unspoken question of whether John is somebody who will depend on his mother for the rest of his days.

Many of these anxieties can be eased, if not removed, by skilled discussions and by meeting with understanding specialists. Often the questions are not answered and the doubts not alleviated until they have been in existence for some years. And they are easily communicable to the slow-learner, again with serious implications for the way he thinks of himself.

In the family, too, the slow-learner cannot help but be aware that his brothers and sisters in many cases manage to succeed in situations which he himself cannot meet. 'Why is it that my younger sister or younger brother can manage to read and to be praised by mother whereas I cannot?' Again, questions of adequacy and competence exist and have meaning for slow-learners, although adequacy and competence exist not as words within the slow-learners's vocabulary, but as feelings which he senses.

How do resultant stresses such as these affect the child? One very obvious effect is, of course, in the behaviour that he shows. Thus we see that Chazan (1964) found a high proportion of maladjustment in slow-learning children. Here, of course, we have to be very careful, because it is just possible that the maladjustment is not an effect of the slow-learning but that slow-learning may be an effect of the maladjustment. However, the evidence of research suggests that the former is more probably the case; see, for example, Yule (1970). The relationships between maladjustment and learning problems are discussed in Cashdan and Williams (1972).

Identifying stresses

Teachers have little difficulty in recognising stresses which show themselves in behaviour problems and are very sensitive to a much wider range of behaviour problems than was the case years ago. When Wickman (1928) reported a study of the seriousness of behaviour problems in children as viewed by American teachers it was the aggressive, difficult behaviour which teachers viewed as serious. More recently, studies have shown that today's teachers are as sensitive to the problems of a quiet, withdrawn child as they are to those of an aggressive, difficult child.

But nevertheless teachers seek confirmation of their identification of stresses in their slow-learners. Extra information can be gained through a variety of ways.

In essence there are three additional sources of information:

1   adults who know the child – especially his parents;
2   the peer group – especially his class-mates;
3   the child himself.

Information from adults

John's teacher, for example, would find it profitable to hear the mother's story – and no doubt he did in the conferences which he tells us were held at the instigation of the school psychological service. Indeed, he would have been a poor teacher if he had not been aware of some of the home story beforehand, certainly some of the basic data – size of family, for instance, should be available in the school records.

Often teachers will have met parents at school. Where parents do not respond to invitations to come to discuss their children's difficulties with the school staff, the school can ask for a link to be made via the education welfare officer. Some schools have the services of a school social worker available, who can call at the house and obtain the picture of the child in his home setting. Interviews of this sort are usually informal, in which the parents talk freely in response to those questions which the interviewer feels are important. Sometimes the interviews are formalised, with a group of set questions to be completed. The questions are designed so as to fill a particular need, as in the home-background schedule of the Schools Council Project in Compensatory Education (Schools Council, 1969), aimed at acquiring home-background information in order to measure the likelihood of entrants to infant schools needing extra help. But whichever way the information about home background is acquired, it is essential for the teacher to learn how the child behaves, or is seen to behave, outside school, and especially at home.

Information from the peer-group

The teacher had also considered gaining information from John's classmates. This is the sociometric enquiry which the teacher said he had considered using. This type of enquiry provides information above the social structure of the classroom. Often information of this sort corroborates the teacher's own observations. Occasionally, it provides surprising data, which change dramatically the way in which teachers perceive children.

The sociometric techniques which can be used to identify the child whose relationships with his peers are poor are described in Evans (1962). These approaches are very easy for the teacher to use, although the analysis of the relationships by a sociogram or sociomatrix can be time consuming. For this reason a 'guess who' technique is probably better. Children can be asked to 'guess who' fits a specified role, e.g. 'an unhappy child, who is never chosen to play with the other children'. An estimate of the way a class sees a particular child is obtained by counting the number of times a child is chosen by his classmates as fitting the negative descriptions given. Bower (1969) uses a set of class pictures to help sharpen the roles described and has devised his own method of scoring.

The material is presented to one child at a time, so that the process is not speedy. But it does mean that children who have reading and writing problems are not excluded, since reading and writing skills are not required.

Quite apart from any score, the overall picture of how a slow-learner is viewed by the rest of the class is helpful and valuable information for the teacher.

Information from the child

The easiest way for the teacher to obtain information from the child himself is, of course, by talking to him. All teachers talk to their children, but not all have the skill and experience to help a child express the stresses he feels. There is a story of an interview conducted at an outpatient clinic, in which a young houseman was dealing with an adult patient referred for hearing problems. The houseman's attempt to explore whether the patient had any psychological problems associated with the hearing difficulties consisted of a staccato 'Any worries?' inserted between a number of rapid routine questions on the nature of the problem. There are skills needed to discuss issues of this nature with adults. For children, the skills are different and at least as difficult to acquire. For young slow-learners, as we saw before, the information may be very difficult to obtain. For this reason, a careful observation of behaviour is probably the best way of gaining information from the child himself. A check list, such as the Bristol Social Adjustment Guide (Stott, 1963) or the Rutter Scale (Rutter, 1967) will help the teacher who would like some guidelines as to which sorts of behaviour indicate stress.

It is not easy for young slow-learners to communicate feelings easily and teachers may have to infer feelings from behaviour, rather than from discussion. For the same reason questionnaires which require children to check problems which bother them, valuable though they are in many circumstances, usually require reading skills which many slow-learners have not gained.

When the teacher has this three-dimensional picture of the slow-learner he has a much clearer idea of the sorts of problems with which he is trying to deal. But the vital question, which cannot be overemphasised, is 'What will the teacher do with the information he has obtained?'. The information has not been gained in order to place on a file, or to write on a report; it has been obtained in order that the teacher shall take some action in the interest of the slow-learner.

In John's case we know that the teacher felt that John needed specialist teaching. He discussed the situation with the headmaster, who called in the school psychological service to investigate the situation more carefully. John was placed in a special class.

The way in which John's case was dealt with is outside the scope of this chapter. But the investigation disclosed that John's intellectual development was generally limited. His language skills were particularly weak and although his non-verbal abilities were better, they were still well below average. On the assessments made it was estimated that overall, he fell in the bottom three per cent of his age group.

The investigation also disclosed the existence of anxieties connected mainly with John's school difficulties but also, to a lesser extent, with the absence of a father in the family. As a result of the ensuing discussions between the school, the mother, and the school psychological service, the decision to try John in a special class was taken.

This is only one of a number of actions which might have been taken to deal with the stresses in this pupil. There is no set list of prescriptions which can be issued for dealing with the hundreds of thousands of Johns in our schools. Each one is an individual, in his own unique situation. Each needs a teacher who is sufficiently concerned to attempt to see his pupil from different viewpoints, sufficiently sensitive to interpret his observations accurately and sufficiently energetic to take suitable action to improve his pupil's lot.

DELINQUENT AND MALADJUSTED CHILDREN

John Mays

Pressures on school children

Many people, if they are quite honest with themselves, will look back upon their own childhood with very mixed feelings. They will, of course, remember the happy experiences and the good times, although these by now are probably tinged with an unreally golden after-glow and nostalgia of *temps perdu*. But there were also many unhappy experiences which stand out. Childhood, even now, is far from being a happy phase. There is still much to frighten, to frustrate and to intimidate the growing child. How many, if we had our time over again, would want to begin it much before mid-adolescent years, I wonder? More particularly, how many would want to relive their schooldays and go through once again the boredom of most lessons, endure the petty restrictions and humiliations of the regime and experience again the endemic feelings of uncertainty and lack of confidence which were often so hard to cope with or to communicate to an adult, be it teacher or parent?

There is as little sense in enthusing over formal education as there is in becoming idolatrous about childhood. There have, of course, been changes and nowadays child-centredness is certainly a vogue concept, especially in primary educational circles. But children are still and always will be immensely vulnerable and at the mercy of adverse social influences and personal pressures. This is why school life can so easily be soured by noxious contacts and disturbing situations, and why, even in these latter days, when so much has been written and so much is known about the causes of social and personal maladjustment, school often proves, for some unlucky youngsters, to be a painful and sometimes a permanently damaging experience.

It is important to realise that school life, like any other form of human experience, must necessarily generate a certain degree of stress and strain. Tension is not, of itself, undesirable. It is merely that too much tension over a period of time becomes psychologically damaging. We must also remember that individuals are very different and that an experience which for one child is bearable and even stimulating may, for another child, prove crippling. Such considerations have a direct bearing upon educational practice and what takes place in the classroom. Furthermore, there are transitional stages during a child's school life when changes of status and orientation occur (usually on a purely chronological basis) which expose every child to a certain amount of apprehensive anticipation and which induce in some a state of positive anxiety. Starting school in the first place is an obvious example of a transitional stage which is so fundamental in its implications that it has often been compared to a weaning process – in this case the child is being weaned from complete dependence upon his family and home and obliged to have formal and informal relationships with parent-figures and with other children in an entirely new setting.

So, too, passing from the infants' to the primary school involves a change of status and outlook; and, more noticeably, of course, the move from primary to secondary education which may mean that children have to leave their known physical and educational environment and become initiated into a strange and perhaps, at times, an alien-seeming institution.

That children do in fact experience the onset of a new life stage as disturbing to varying extents is evidenced in the well-known connection between the statutory school leaving age and the peak age for delinquency. The latter falls near the fourteenth birthday. But when the school leaving age was fourteen, the peak age for delinquency was thirteen. There is probably a causal connection between the two which could be tested critically when the leaving age goes up another year from 1972 onwards. It does seem a reasonable hypothesis that the approach of school leaving, with its associated increase in responsibility and entry into the more demanding work situation of adult society, is seen by some children as somewhat frightening and that they give release to this rising psychological tension by sudden outbursts of vandalism, uncontrolled aggression and even crime. Certainly the delinquency rate falls after schooldays are over, which suggests something of a settling down process, only to rise again to a fresh subsidiary peak at seventeen when, one is entitled to hypothesise, a new challenge (this time associated with the assumption of adult autonomy) may be seen to be approaching.

In addition to having to adjust to new schools and new environments, pupils are also obliged during their school lives to adjust to a great many different teachers and to vastly different teaching methods and disciplines. It is widely recognised that children do better at the same subject with one teacher than they do with another, and that in an incalculable yet very real way the scholastic progress that a pupil makes, or fails to make, is not so much a reflection of his own ability as of an interaction process between his personality and the personality of the teacher – except, of course, in cases of gross psychological disturbance or of critically low intelligence.

A great many factors in the everyday life of school and classroom are stress producing. In schools with a 'high academic' tradition which teach traditional subjects in standardised ways, which stream and restream the cream with the cream, where the mark book is always out and being entered up, where examinations are accepted as the proper and only yardstick of progress and measure of achievement, where competitiveness is built up between pupil and pupil (each one urged on to outdo his immediate challengers for primacy in test scores) the net results are often emotionally disastrous. In such schools, as Philip Taylor has pointed out, 'the achievement of the children is bought out of their diminished self-regard.'[1] This is a case in which we can see that social class or, at least, upward social aspiration, does not necessarily buttress a child's self-image against pedagogical damage. As Himmelweit [2] has shown, many teachers are prejudiced against children from working class backgrounds even when they are trying to conform to grammar school norms and expectations. The same teachers can help to demean pupils' self-esteem further by dividing them into more or less ability groups, by streaming and highlighting differential performances in unending tests and examinations.

The pressures of mark-obsessed teachers (backed up by over-keen parents) can frequently be seen to produce irritability, jealousy between classmates, psychosomatic disorders, and sheer fatigue. The academic puritanism of such not uncommon secondary schools produces unbalanced personalities or obliges those who are strong enough to avoid the drudgeries to take refuge in lies and daydreams and deceptions, while others, permanently discouraged by their inability to catch up with brilliant classmates, lapse into frustration and despair.

That an education employing such methods is not an education at all and should be suppressed is obvious enough to those who see education as a self-enriching experience. Nevertheless, such schools do exist in quite substantial numbers in spite of the alleged abolition of the 11+ and the growth of more relaxed teaching methods in much primary education. Middle class parents and lower middle class parents who are ambitious for their children realise that, while the educational system is dependent upon examination performance and while access to higher education is immediately tied up with A level marks, they cannot afford to relax and encourage their children to develop at their own pace. It is only children from non-aspiring homes who can be allowed to regard learning as fun.

For the majority of children, however, stress in school due to academic pressure is rare. Lower class children probably receive too little scholastic pressure and encouragement and the adverse influence of the school is more likely to be seen in a failure to provide adequate out of school activities, and in an attitude of social rejection on the part of the teachers who seem consciously to be preparing their pupils for second class citizenship.

So far, it will be apparent, I have been dealing with children in general and not specifically with delinquent or maladjusted children as the title of this chapter requires. This is a deliberate choice on my part because I want to emphasise that most delinquent and even a great many maladjusted children are not very different from other children and it is what they all have in common, not their alleged difference, that we need to bear in mind when we are considering them in sociological terms. The normal shades off into the abnormal, the non-delinquent into the delinquent, the adjusted into the maladjusted, and the dividing lines are both hazy and arbitrary and should not be allowed to mislead us into thinking that there are different kinds of children rather than children with differing needs and different environments.

Neither delinquency nor maladjustment are solely products of school life, yet we can see how strain and tension induced by formal education could produce such results in children who are particularly stress-prone or who are already emotionally disturbed, either because of a confused family background or because of hereditary predisposition. Since no generally agreed definition of maladjustment exists, it is not possible to gauge its incidence within the school population at any one point of time. D. H. Stott estimated that between eleven and fifteen per cent of the boys and eight per cent of the girls are maladjusted in Britain judged by the criterion of twenty or more indications of behaviour disturbance as tested by his own Bristol Adjustment Guides.[3] The authors of the Plowden Report, *Children and their Primary Schools*, showed that the proportion of children who were either receiving or awaiting special school education in 1966 and who were categorised as 'maladjusted' was 10·9 per 10,000 of the school population of England and Wales.[4] The 1961 figure was only 7·9. Both figures seem remarkably low. M. Chazan, on the other hand, who carried out a study of 169 ESN pupils, making use of the Bristol Social Adjustment Guides, found that the incidence of maladjustment for this group was as high as thirty six per cent.[5]

While conservative estimates put the maladjustment rate at no more than one per cent and others suggest a much higher figure, we must wait for further research to decide which is the more accurate assessment. Perhaps as much depends upon how we define the word itself as upon accuracy of measurement. But like delinquency, we may conclude that maladjustment may, in some shape or form, be regarded as a not unusual hazard even for 'normal' children. Thus, the apparently adequately adjusted individual can easily, as a result of some new stressful experience, exhibit signs of maladjustment, just as, in a similar manner, an 'honest' person can be led into crime under the influence of some peculiarly strong temptation or novel set of circumstances. Both maladjustment and delinquency can be thought of as existing along more general continua, between whose extremes there lie a vast number of intermediate positions. To be somewhat delinquent or to be a little maladjusted may hence be thought of as a part of the normal human condition.

At the same time it would be a mistake to equate maladjustment with delinquency although they quite frequently overlap. Maladjustment is essentially a psycho-social concept while the concept of delinquency, although incorporating important sociological and psychological components, is also strictly legal. For the purpose of the law a delinquent can be defined with some precision, as someone who has committed an offence. A maladjusted child, on the other hand, seems to be one who is judged by the adult world of teachers, parents and social workers to be seriously out of step with his peers and generally at odds with his environment; in terms of the 1945 regulations for the guidance of authorities sending children away to special residential schools, one of those who 'show evidence of emotional instability or psychological disturbance and require special educational treatment to effect their personal, social and educational readjustment.'

Two further points may perhaps be made. First, not all children who break the law are apprehended and second, not all psychologically disturbed children are ascertained and treated. A great many delinquents seem to slip through the net and similarly no doubt do maladjusted children. Perhaps it may also be just as well that they do. Just as a great many delinquents fairly soon grow out of their delinquent phase, so mildly maladjusted children may successfully pass through temporary periods of maladjustment without deterioration. In other words, both certain kinds of delinquency and certain kinds of maladjustment may be regarded not only as phasic in character but also as not abnormal aspects of personal and social maturation.

The school as a possible cause of maladjustment

So far we have been considering the personal problems that arise from the failure of a child to adapt adequately to the ordinary demands and programme of average schools. We have suggested that the fact of having such adjustment problems is not necessarily a sign that a child is to be categorised as 'maladjusted'. We have suggested further that most normal children at some time or another experience difficulties in learning and that they also occasionally will have conflicts with the teachers and with the authority of the school. When Professor Valentine called a well-known book of his *The Normal Child and Some of His Abnormalities* [6] he clearly had a similar idea in mind. It is only when these not unexpected difficulties either of work or of discipline persist and fail to submit to any of the usual methods of handling which the average school has at its disposal that we need to think of an individual child as becoming truly maladjusted. In such cases the teacher and the parent need to call in skilled outside help in the form of educational psychologist or child psychiatrist. But it is probably dangerous for teachers to run too quickly for expert help from outside school and home. A flight into maladjustment is conceivable as an astute method whereby a child who wishes to evade issues, perhaps to avoid fresh challenges in the shape of demands for harder work and a reduction in time available for recreation, may properly and with full adult acceptance do so. Teachers and parents do a child no service by encouraging a flight into pseudo-maladjustment and they should at least be aware that such a danger exists. Almost all children can in fact behave in extremely odd ways, manifesting many of the textbook symptoms of psychological disturbance without being truly ill enough for outside help to be necessary.

Much more, however, remains to be said about the kinds of problems that can and do arise in formal education and about the personal and social difficulties that the school itself can create. All too frequently difficulties that a school child experiences are attributed either to his own shortcomings or to some failure on the part of the parents to perform some necessary task at the appropriate time and in the appropriate manner. But it should also be clear that the school itself is sometimes to blame for pupils' maladaptation. This can arise from two possible sources. First, from the incompetence or malignity of a member of staff who either wittingly or unwittingly mishandles a pupil. There are many documentations of this kind of pedagogic injustice and inhumanity. Most readers will be able to recall some instances from their own childhood of individual teachers who seemed to 'pick on' some unfortunate classmate for excessive punishment or, worse still perhaps, to use as a butt for sarcasm and verbal assault against which, of course, children are almost entirely unprotected. Dr Leslie Weatherhead, former Minister of the City Temple, London, has described how he 'hated and dreaded school because the teachers resorted to the cane on the slightest pretext' and how being 'a shy and delicate child, often away with illness when new lessons were learnt, I came in for innumerable beatings.'[7] Such experience of injustice at so early an age may be uncommon; it may not happen in schools today as it most certainly did in schools a generation or so ago but we cannot deny that the danger of oppression is always there. The Illingworths have a very distressing chapter in their book *Lessons From Childhood*[8] in which amongst other things they show how in so many cases famous and creative men endured bullying and excessive punishment in their early days at the hands of teachers or parents or sometimes even both. Luther, Samuel Johnson, Coleridge and Lamb, to name only a few of earlier geniuses were so abused, and, to come nearer our own day, so were H. G. Wells, Paul Nash and Conan Doyle. Though we live in less violent days and the cane is much less resorted to, it is by no means done away with and the obstinacy with which the teaching profession clings to its so-called right to administer corporal punishment while in theory acting *in loco parentis* demands a thoroughgoing explanation at both conscious and subconscious levels.

It may well be, however, that of the two evils physical assault does less permanent damage than mental cruelty, and that scapegoating and derision, if carried on for a fairly long time, can undermine a child's self-confidence to the point of despair and even suicide. Certainly teachers need to be most carefully vetted and trained to carry out their vital social task and even when they have graduated need to be scrutinised and supervised in a way that we have never been able to do in this country on an adequate scale. How much harm bad teaching does and how much misery is still inflicted upon children in school (as in their own homes, too, for that matter) it is quite impossible to estimate. No sensitive parent can be unaware of the hazards involved in schooling, and no sensitive parent by the same token can be too grateful for the contribution to mental health and simple human happiness that a sympathetic, experienced and dedicated teacher can make in the upbringing of his children.

No doubt some of the harm that inflexible or punitive teachers do arises from their own psychiatric ill-health or from chronic frustration of ambition. But this does not seem to account for all the unhappiness and lack of sympathy which, even in so-called 'good' schools, often becomes apparent in the form of resentment from juniors and rebelliousness from older pupils. Nor can one account for this kind of manifestation solely in terms of youth's inevitable reaction against paternal authority and its benign need to seek autonomy by repudiating the values and standards of the older generation. There is much more to it than the sum of the psychological disorders and personal shortcomings of the individuals, young and older, pupils and teachers, who make up the educational institution and compose the school community. Emile Durkheim, one of the great pioneers in the application of sociological methods of education, touched on this raw spot in his lectures on Moral Education.[9] He was very much against the use of physical punishment in schools, and attributed its existence to some extent to the growth of the great teaching guilds in the middle ages. Durkheim considered that there must be 'something in the character of the school itself, something that inclines it in this direction', and later, in the same essay, wrote, 'it seems one is justified in seeing here a special case of a law, which might be stated this way: whenever two populations, two groups of people having unequal cultures, come into continuous contact with one another, certain feelings develop that prompt the more cultivated group – or that which deems itself such – to do violence to the other.' The situation in traditional schools, hence, may be regarded as a species of domestic colonialism. In schools, as Durkheim points out, there is no intervening countercheck to put a brake on the chronic impatience of the older people in their relations with the youngsters (or of the colonisers with the natives). So much is this the case that Durkheim is led to ask: 'Is there not at the core of pedantry – that trait so characteristic of our professional make-up – a kind of megalomania? When one is continually in relationship with subjects to whom one is morally and intellectually superior, how can he (the teacher) avoid developing an exaggerated self-conception, expressed in gesture, attitude, and language? Such a feeling readily gives rise to violent expression; for any behaviour which offends it easily takes on the character of sacrilege.'

So far, indeed, did Durkheim carry his analysis of the legacy of authoritarianism handed down from the mediaeval teaching guilds that he advanced what in his time must have been a quite shocking idea, that 'the make-up of the school is the source of the evil', and that, furthermore, this arose because school is so cut off from the rest of the social world, so insulated from the ordinary checks and balancing factors of everyday society.

Durkheim was, let it be said at once, not against teachers or anti-schools as such. On the contrary he gave formal education a vital function to perform in his sociological theory, seeing the teacher's role as similar in many respects to that of the priest, as 'the interpreter of the great moral ideas of his time and of his country.' So important indeed was the role of educator in society, so great was the teacher's contribution to the stability and moral integrity of the nation, that only the best would do. Nevertheless, that so subtly analytical and so morally committed an educationist as Durkheim saw the inherent dangers in the traditional institutionalisation of authority within educational structures is far from being without significance in our evaluation of the impact of schools on the lives of pupils in our own society and in our own day and generation. Quite recently, Professors F. Musgrove and P. Taylor[10] have launched a critical attack on the teaching profession and accused it of exerting a despotic influence upon the qualities of the rising generation, and, as far as the majority of the population is concerned, without very much reference to the wishes of parents. By their choices of what is deemed worth learning, by deciding whether or not to stream, by insisting on the wearing of school uniform, and by imposing various other regulations regarding conduct and organisation they have a great influence in deciding the characters and attitudes of their pupils. Musgrove and Taylor seem to be arraigning the teaching profession for doing precisely what Durkhein considered they ought to be doing – shaping the future of the nation. But they are concerned that teachers may not be up to so stupendous a task. It may well be asked 'who is?' And it may also be asked who else there is to undertake this vital task or, at least, to take a major part in it, if teachers opt out?

Fortunately or unfortunately, the teaching profession is by nature and almost by definition conservative in outlook, which means that, by and large, the social influences perpetuated and promoted by formal educational institutions embody much of the past and pioneer only in exceptional cases and unusual circumstances. All of which means that Professors Musgrove and Taylor are guilty of exaggerating the domination of the culture by the scholastic fraternity and need fear their impudence very much less than they apparently think or, at least, imply that they do.

But the charges against teachers and against educational institutions are by no means cleared merely by showing that their influence is mainly exerted in the direction of maintaining the *status quo* and is seldom even innovatory, let alone revolutionary. The indictment is not merely that there are some bad schools and some bad teachers, although it must be accepted that many substandard schools and many incompetent teachers do exist. It goes very much further and penetrates very much deeper than a simple criticism of ineffectiveness. It involves a critical analysis of the way in which the educational system operates and the way in which schools as individual institutions are organised. In fact the indictment is that *in certain respects* the apparently less effective schools are only too effective in performing their socially divisive task of separating the cultured sheep from the uncultured goats.

A small but growing body of sociological research concentrated on the study of schools as functioning institutions has shown that schools are active agents rather than passive witnesses in the process of selection and allocation of pupils for their future social and economic roles. In so far as both primary and secondary education are complementary parts of a gigantic social conditioning process, they are almost equally culpable in the acceptance of a competitive system and of an individualistic ethos. It would, indeed, be very hard to imagine average schools doing other than produce the results that society in general wills from them and sets them up to do. But there is no doubt that families' status frustration and pupils' depressed job prospects, together with lowly socio-economic ranking of whole neighbourhoods, contribute to many of the most severe social problems which in terms of mental illness, nervous instability, retreatism, crime, drug taking, alcoholism, work-avoidance and general social incompetence become manifest at the level of personal behaviour.

If we look at the findings of a fairly recent research project such as that reported by Havighurst and his colleagues for the mid-western community of 45,000 in the U.S.A. which they named *River City*,[11] we can see how serious may be the consequences of school failure for the rising generation in a culture which rewards the abler and more enterprising and as a consequence depresses the life chances of the less able and more inert of its citizens more acutely. This longitudinal study of boys and girls passing through *River City* schools and on to their later working or non-working lives up to the age of twenty vividly describes a process set on foot by early failure in school 'that leads them into delinquency and other forms of maladjustment' and from which, as time goes by, they find it increasingly difficult to release themselves. The outcome is, for a substantial number of these school drop-outs and failures, alienation from the mainstream of normal social life to an extent and to a degree that is disturbing to contemplate from this side of the Atlantic. The *River City* authors conclude that 'About thirty per cent of the age group are unmotivated for school work' and furthermore that 'at least half of this group are alienated from the values of the community and of the school'. From such careful documentation of evidence it is clear that what we are dealing with here is a major social problem far outstripping in its ultimate consequences the personal deviations and psychological maladjustments of individual children with poor biological endowment or emotionally disturbed home backgrounds. We can catch a glimpse here of society itself at work manufacturing, as it were, its own eventual misfits and cast-offs in a routinised and unrecognised way that is very frightening.

British society is, of course, very different from American. But the two have so much in common and so clearly belong to the same great cultural stream and general philosophy of life that we would be foolish to imagine that such a degree of alienation between young and older people could never happen here. The out-croppings of violence at street level, sparked off by racial conflicts and even by football matches, and some of the simmerings of unrest from the student population are straws in a wind that blows from dangerous quarters and indicate that all is far from being well. Experience in some of the less attractive schools in downtown areas, and especially in districts which are blighted and impoverished to a point of being clearly designated as slums, indicates more precisely how school systems and teacher attitudes serve to reinforce the rejection that society in general has already in store for a large number of its non-conforming and its less gifted pupils.

A perceptive article contributed to *New Society* by a schoolmaster in which he describes his experience as a member of the staff of a not-untypical boys' comprehensive school in the East End of London most vividly illustrates this rejection at work.[12] The author reveals a number of significant points about the policy of the school as directed by the headmaster. Contact between staff and parents was officially discouraged. Ninety three per cent of the intake were graded as academically below average although there was evidence from other sources that they were not so much basically below the national standard as very backward in reading achievement. A rigid streaming system modelled on the orthodox grammar school system and geared up to G.C.E. split the pupils into a ten per cent academic minority and a ninety per cent non-academic majority: the former receiving all the attention and limelight, the latter being treated as inferiors and gradually made aware of their lowly status. 'By the time they are third year', the author comments, 'they become dimly aware of their true position; educationally and socially they have been sold down the river.' As a result discipline becomes a serious problem and, at the remedial class end of the pupil hierarchy 'the bottom stream, the dregs of the dregs' are located 'and the secret is not kept from them'.

To some extent the system can be blamed for such a state of affairs. Rigid streaming and specialised subject teaching, a general lack of personal interest from a cheerfully cynical staff, a hierarchy of authority in which graded posts are awarded to those who accept the *status quo* and back up the head all combine to produce a school that is academically inefficient and, more seriously, reveals how an opportunity of helping a great many socially disadvantaged children has been lost for ever. But the individual teachers who accept the system, above all the rigid headmaster, whom we hear in an aside is a lay-preacher on Sundays, who perpetuates such an inflexible system, cannot be exonerated on the moral level. It is difficult not to believe that, on the evidence of the article, most of the staff either acquiesced in the regime for the sake of a quiet life or even supported it for ideological and political reasons.

John Partridge's study of a secondary modern boys' school in the Midlands shows that such a state of affairs is not confined to the East End of London.[13] Once again it is a tale of a rigidly repressive system backed up by streaming, reliance upon physical punishment rather than on responsibility built up by sound personal relationships, quick staff turnover and timetable and curriculum of a stodgy, repetitive and pseudo-academic kind. 'The general mood of apathy, disinterest, indifference, and even contempt, which typifies the attitudes of our boys to their classroom work and in some cases to all school activity' makes a mockery at secondary level of the proud claims for educational advance under the banner of child-centred education which, we are often told, has transformed infants' schools and primary education. Moreover, it casts a new and highly critical light on the sometimes maidenly smugness which creeps into such well-known reports as Newsom and Plowden. All too often, it seems clear, the writers of official publications fail to see that it is the schools themselves that are frequently failing their pupils and the public that pays for them.

So the evidence continues to mount up to suggest that schools – especially those serving poor districts – are themselves criminogenic. David Hargreaves' impressive study as a participant-observer of the life of a secondary school, this time one serving the Manchester area, is particularly acute and penetrating in the way in which we are shown how the school actually operates over time to divide the pupils from one another and to instil hostile attitudes between in-group and out-group members.[14] Here again rigid streaming systems, pseudo-academic objectives and an inflexible and often authoritarian structure are shown to be the villains of the piece. According to Hargreaves streaming divides the pupils into two subcultural groups: one aligned to authority, accepting the formal goals of the school and receiving all the honours and favours that the staff can offer them, the other rejected as low ability nonconformists and given the dirty end of the stick wherever possible. The outcome of such a process traced over four years of school life is to separate friend from friend and to dichotomise the school into 'good' A stream boys who are successes, and 'bad' D stream boys who inhabit a delinquescent subculture. The lower the group in the school status system the greater the extent of both known and admitted delinquency, revealing a range between forms 4A and 4D of three to fifty five per cent for actual court appearances and of seven to sixty four per cent of those admitting to current undetected thieving. Not surprisingly the D streamers in their delinquent group evidence strongly negative attitudes towards school, find lessons boring and do not wish to pursue formal education any further.

Hargreaves has argued, and attempted by his data to show, that this dichotomy between the two main pupil groups extends and deepens over the years because of the operation of the school as a value-laden system upon its participants. At the end of the second year in school there was little or no evidence of the normative and subcultural differences between the two extreme streams later identified, and it is hence not unreasonable to suppose that the school itself was the major cause of the ultimate differentiation in behaviour and attitudes. The hypothesis is, of course, not proved but it is presented as one of high plausibility. This plausibility is also receiving considerable support from the evidence that is accruing from the work of the Social Medicine Research Unit of the Medical Research Council which has been studying the incidence of juvenile delinquency in the area served by the London Hospital.[15]

Observing that some schools in the area have comparatively high delinquency rates while other schools not very far away have comparatively low ones, the research workers have suggested that some schools have effectively protected their pupils against local subcultural influences, and more particularly against delinquent associations, while other schools have failed to do so. This is perhaps another way of viewing Hargreaves' findings, this time from a positive and therapeutic angle. It may be that schools in bad areas actively promote delinquency and other forms of protest behaviour as Hargreaves has suggested. It may equally be true that, given a different kind of school regime, schools can prevent their pupils from developing delinquent self-images and from the impulse to break the law. Indeed, Sir Alec Clegg's presentation of certain evidence from West Riding Schools in high delinquency districts suggests that this is the case, and that, more particularly, this is due to the leadership, skill and sympathy of specific headmasters.[16] Further research is, of course, necessary to know whether this is so or not but, once again, there is strong *prima facie* evidence to suggest that the damage that 'bad' schools and indifferent or rejecting teachers can do to their pupils, 'good' schools and concerned and sympathetic teachers can undo.

In other words, schools are institutions on which remedial and preventive efforts can be hopefully centred. The remainder of this chapter will be devoted to a discussion of how schools may be developed in this way to reduce the incidence of stress and avoid strain in all kinds of children, some of whom may be reacting to stress by delinquent acting-out behaviour and others by excessive passivity, withdrawn-ness and even timidity.

The teacher's role

In the light of what we have said above, attention needs to be directed both to the relations between individuals in the school setting and to the way in which the school is formally organised. Enough was probably said about the latter in the preceding section of this chapter, and at this point it is perhaps only necessary to add that we need to organise schools in such a way that many if not all the problems discussed earlier are greatly reduced if not entirely done away with. It should be pointed out, however, that education alone, however radically reformed, cannot solve all our child-training problems for us, that schools are particularly handicapped by a lack of suitable employment for school leavers, and that the level of attainment aimed at and the motivations encouraged must to some extent be related to the existing opportunity structure. This may be regrettable but it is a fact, since both educational systems and opportunity structures are subject to more fundamental social structures and political systems which, in the last analysis, exert a decisive influence on the educational process as a whole.

This need not mean that teachers are entirely ineffective or helpless in initiating and guiding social change. It does mean, however, that there are limits to their effectiveness and that, like social workers, they frequently find themselves prevented from doing for their pupils all they would wish to do by forces which lie outside their control as teachers.

Clearly teachers and, above all, head teachers, have a vital role to play both in preventing juvenile delinquency and social maladjustment, and also in helping with its treatment. There is little point in arguing whether or not the job of preventing and dealing with delinquency is more properly the province of the social worker rather than the teacher. Indeed, I believe it is a mistake to conceive of these two roles as being widely different. They are in fact convergent. Education of its very nature involves favouring one kind of behaviour rather than another, and social work, too, can hardly begin unless its exponents have a set of values they are striving to promote and maintain, however obliquely. The roles overlap and interweave and quite clearly the two distinct professions must not only be prepared to tolerate each other's presence in the field but also to collaborate actively and openly.

Since all children go to school, schools seem to be the obvious place where early detection of troubles of various kinds can begin. It may be that the teacher's role is, as Alfred Khan for example has argued, more appropriate for the detection than for the treatment of delinquency or maladjustment as such.[17] Others, conversely, might seek to involve teachers more actively both in preventive programmes and in social treatments of various kinds.* Prob-

---

* Such as, for example, in the new so-called 'intermediate' methods which have been proposed in the White Paper *Children in Trouble*, Cmnd. 3601, 1968.

ably at the present moment what really matters is that teachers should become diagnostically alert (but not, of course, to a morbid degree!). They need to become sensitised during their training period to signs and manifestations of maladaptation and also, in a general way, to become more sympathetic to the special needs and problems of stress-prone youngsters.

What sort of problems should a teacher be on the look-out for and what signs ought he or she to take very seriously? Moreover, how can these be distinguished from 'normal' behaviour?

As I have already said, the categories of normal and abnormal cannot be readily distinguished and even experts can make mistakes. Teachers must accept their fallibility but not be depressed by it. Provided they do not take too sudden and too drastic steps probably little harm will accrue from a failure to distinguish behaviour which is symptomatic of distress and hence a kind of cry for help from behaviour which is just the result of a passing cloud or even a healthy reaction to some frustrating circumstance, or a normal result of physical illness or emotional stress occasioned by grief or bereavement. Signs which may be symptoms of maladjustment need to be watched to see whether they pass away or grow. Truancy, petty thieving, rule-breaking, insolence in class, unpopularity with other children, bullying tendencies, extreme withdrawal and passivity, listlessness, regression, and many other symptoms will be noted in the many text books and they are all forms of potentially disturbed behaviour which the teacher should unobtrusively study. As we have said, where these behaviours persist or grow more noticeable, there are grounds for inferring that some deeper cause lies behind the child's aberrant conduct and, at this stage, it would be wise to call in the help of child guidance specialists and child care officers.

The question of how more precisely a teacher can spot a delinquency-prone child has been tackled over a number of years by D. H. Stott. Stott believes that signs of behavioural disturbance usually show themselves before delinquency actually occurs and, if this is so, it would seem logical to try to detect and help potential delinquents before they actually break the law.[18] Stott also ties up his concept of delinquency with psychological maladjustment and seems to imply that, although these are distinct categories, they greatly overlap and that, in the main, delinquency rarely occurs without maladjustment also being present. Hence he believes that the Bristol Social Adjustment Guides which he himself developed could be adapted in a simplified form for use in schools and so assist teachers to spot children who look like being high risks. For convenience of administration he reduced the number of factors employed in his Bristol Guides to six simple questions covering the forms of maladjustment which, in his view, are most often associated with delinquency. The application of these six questions to whole classes, and indeed the entire school population, would be a comparatively speedy and quick operation and could be used as a preliminary combing out operation to pick out those children who require further study and those who could be left alone. Stott's idea is attractive in many ways but to the best of my knowledge has not been adopted, although he himself and several other research workers have employed it, apparently with results satisfactory enough to justify further experiments.

Some people have expressed repugnance at the very idea of testing for delinquent potentialities in the same way that we may make blood tests, or apply intelligence or other psychological or even medical examinations. There is little doubt that these adverse feelings are largely responsible for the fact that simple predictive devices such as the Bristol Social Adjustment Guides provide have not been utilised, but the time may come when public opinion will change and their viability will be more open to empirical validation and evaluation.

Behavioural problems which become evident in school may well have been operating even before the child entered the school and may derive in the main from deep-seated emotional disorders in the family life. Problems which manifest themselves in the form of quiescence, withdrawal, regression and low educational attainment are probably just as serious in potentiality as those that issue in unruliness, aggression and overt delinquency. The pupil who constantly disrupts the class or who is obviously attention-seeking is in all probability emotionally disturbed and lacking in security and perhaps in affection. It is by no means true that the school should avoid intervening even in cases where the root cause of trouble lies in the home and in family relationships. Children rejected by the parents or in doubt about parental affection can receive support from caring, sympathetic and kindly teachers which – for all anyone knows to the contrary – could prove to be crucial in preventing serious breakdown. Moreover, in the case of broken families, a teacher can sometimes become a true parent-substitute. This could be especially useful in the case, say, of an adolescent boy who has no father or father figure in his own immediate home circle if he can identify in the psychological sense with a male teacher. Even if such identification leads to idolisation it is almost certainly in the long term a beneficial and health promoting relationship. As a general principle there is everything to be gained and nothing to be lost if a child's environment in school, home and neighbourhood provides a great many adults of either sex with whom children can associate frequently and who take an active and benevolent part in their lives. Youth workers, again, are obvious examples of most valuable parental and avuncular deputies, and in schools which are fortunate enough to have their own youth wings and fulltime staff this kind of natural relationship can develop all the more easily.

The same considerations apply to the new counsellors who are being appointed in some areas to deal with a variety of problems.[19] Such counselling is many sided and involves, in different instances, *educational guidance*, e.g. with regard to courses, qualifications, etc., *vocational guidance*, which aims to relate aptitude with future employment and *personal counselling*, which is related to both the foregoing but which also involves fairly close contact with parents, welfare workers and child care specialists. It is this latter function which is of primary concern for the topic of this chapter. Clearly the counsellor who sees his job mainly in terms of helping children with their personal difficulties will have an adjustive role to perform in relation to everything that happens to a child in all aspects of his life, not excluding his relations with other pupils and other members of the school staff, and most certainly he will be concerned with the child's relationships within the family and with the peer group in the neighbourhood.

When I describe the counsellor's role as adjustive I do not wish to imply that this always means helping the child to adjust to his circumstances and learn how to put up with things which are troublesome. I would also wish to imply that a very real aspect of the personal counsellor's role will at times involve speaking up for the child and, if possible, getting parents and teachers to modify their treatment and attitude towards him if these are seen by the counsellor as direct sources of unnecessary anxiety and misunderstanding.

We have already raised the vexed question of the relationship between home and school, teachers and parents, and there can be very little doubt that this is one of the storm centres of educational discussion in Britain. A fair number of teachers do not see that their claim to be in *loco parentis* also demands, as its corollary, close collaboration between school and home. Moreover, the findings of several nation-wide surveys and research reports in recent years have shown beyond any reasonable doubt that scholastic performance as well as conduct depend to a very considerable extent on the degree of rapport achieved between parents and teachers. The Plowden Report, which comes at the end of a long and imposing line of such studies, suggests that the problem that now faces us is how links between home and school can be more effectively formed and how liaison between teachers and parents can be successfully brought about and institutionalised. We need to know a good deal more about how particular schools faced and overcame their difficulties in this field. We want to find out what forms of parent teacher association are most likely to work in relation to precisely what kinds of school and what kinds of neighbourhood.

Evidence is slowly accumulating and the Department of Education and Science, amongst others, has collected some of it and offered useful examples of what has in fact already been done in this direction.[20] Technical aspects apart, what chiefly matters is that the idea of strong home-school links and collaboration should be adopted and the underlying reasons for its adoption should be more widely understood by both parents and teachers.

If a pupil is showing disturbance in his behaviour, the school, either through its counsellor or perhaps through some member of staff given the special job of liaising with the neighbourhood, in a teacher-social worker ole for example, should be able to get in touch with the parents very quickly to see what is happening and to discuss what might be done to help. But the success of this kind of operation depends absolutely upon planning and organisation. If there is no established means of communication between school and home valuable time may well be lost. If there is no general rapport already existing between parents and the school in some cases it may prove impossible to give any positive help at all to a child in difficulty or to a child detected in a delinquency. Rapport and communication take time to build up and cannot await a crisis to develop. The school that is outward looking, the school with a staff and especially, of course, with a head so minded, which is looking for ways in which to express its concern for its pupils in every aspect of their lives (without arbitrarily butting into its families' private affairs) will obviously have an immense contribution to make to the social health of an entire neighbourhood. In time it will come to be the natural focus for every creative social, educational, cultural, recreational and welfare activity going on or starting up in the area. Such schools do exist and are a model for the majority which have not yet accepted such an extension of their role and function. There are still too many teachers who, in Charity James' terminology, are 'thugs' and 'hired assassins', busy discouraging talent and depressing achievement, teachers who too blandly accept that aspect of their job which is in reality an 'entrepreneurial role for the economy' rather than embracing joyfully 'an interpretive one for the community.' [21]

If it is true, as Dr Wall said some little time ago, that one child in every five or six is in need of special help and if, as a community, we are really serious about mounting effective anti-delinquency programmes, there is a really vital social task ahead of the teaching profession which will stretch to the uttermost limits their humanity and competence. The educator as a kind of social priest and cultural missionary is a concept which is undoubtedly daunting, but I am convinced that unless we make substantial strides towards its realisation in everyday educational practice and service, the great social problems of maladjustment, youthful boredom, alienation, aggressiveness and delinquency which currently afflict a disturbing number of young people in our society will be neither solved nor even contained.

But the odds against a substantial number of teachers agreeing to such an extension of their role are very long indeed. For many years we have tended to concentrate upon a minority of the more academically able children; we have stressed and probably exaggerated an ability to pass routinised examinations and seriously undervalued moral and aesthetic development. One outcome of this process has been to divide society into potentially hostile camps of the more and the least successful people, facing each other with mutual incomprehension and aversion. Such social cultures provide seed beds and forcing ground for delinquency and maladjustment, for social isolation and individual despair. Schools obviously have a vital part to play in purifying the life of their communities and in promoting personal happiness. Moreover, recent interest in counselling as a new facet of the scholastic institution suggests that there is at least a realisation of the nature of the challenge being presented and a growing desire to take it up.

BEREAVED CHILDREN

Marjorie Mitchell

Pattern of bereavement in the U.K. today

Today, in this country, the bereaved child is a rarity, and the chances of his losing a member of his nuclear family while he is still at school, and becoming stressed as a consequence, are more remote than those of his being subjected to some of the other adverse circumstances described by contributors to this book. With the expectation of life at one year of age in the United Kingdom being 75·4 years for women and 69·5 years for men in 1967 (Registrar General's Returns for 1967) the child is also less likely to experience death of a grandparent than were his own forebears when they were children. An examination of the Annual Abstract of Statistics for 1968 (H.M.S.O.) will throw further light on the pattern of deaths by age and sex in this country, showing conclusively that the death rates of parents and siblings are so low that it is rare for a teacher to be confronted with a bereaved child.

If the child suffers bereavement of a brother or sister it is more likely to be that of an infant in the first year of life. The act of dying, like the death rate, has also changed during the last century and few children now are confronted with protracted death bed scenes following long periods of sickness and decline. Death in hospital may be more frequent than death at home and children do not share the last moments of dying relatives. Indeed they may be refused admittance to the ward during the terminal illness. In any case, death is frequently sudden today, from accidents or from coronaries rather than from infectious disease or mysterious disorders and, with the exception of some forms of cancer, the child is unlikely to witness prolonged pain and suffering. Drugs help the dying, and tranquilisers may ease bereaved parents through the first sad days, so even signs of adult grief may be muted.

Bereavement as a traumatic experience

Nevertheless, though the patterns of dying and death have changed both qualitatively and quantitatively over the past century the traumatic experience of the bereaved has not altered basically and it may have been intensified. This basic experience is 'a cry of absence, absence in the heart'. The small nuclear family grown in upon itself intensifies all the contained relationships –

parents and children, brothers and sisters. It does not expect to lose half its members before the parents are middle-aged or the children grown up. If death comes it does not arrive as a frequent and almost accepted visitor as it did in the nineteenth century, even personified as an angel by some of the religious, but rather as the 'new obscenity' which one covers up quickly and is embarassed to acknowledge or discuss, especially in front of the children. The bereaved schoolchild is unlikely to be singled out by a label, not even a black armband, certainly not full mourning, and he is also probably unique in his situation. There are not many others in the same boat and one of his reactions may well be 'Why have I been picked on?'.

Quite recently, particularly since Gorer's seminal work *Death, Grief and Mourning* (1965) and *Man's Concern with Death* (1968) by Toynbee and others a great deal of re-thinking about problems of death and bereavement is going on amongst the general public. For although there may be few bereaved children in this country it is the *individual* child with whom, as teachers, parents and social workers, we are concerned. One such child in a home or class has not only the right to be helped for his own sake and for those whom he may disturb, but those in charge of him need to know as much as has been discovered about childrens' reactions to death.

The child can never be wholly saved from the devastating experience of the death of a loved person but we may hope to save him from prolonged disturbance and permanent damage. We need, of course, to remind ourselves that young children are deeply disturbed by any form of separation. As soon as they become aware of themselves as entities distinguishable from familiar people and things, the removal of these will be experienced as a kind of bereavement, and as Bowlby (1960, 1961) has shown there will be reactions of mourning. Later, prolonged absence of a parent, particularly the mother (Bowlby, 1968), may be experienced as a death. Nursery teachers receiving a child at three, or sometimes earlier, will be familiar with this kind of experience, but of death itself the child under five has only very hazy concepts. The finality of it is not yet grasped and the mother's death or disappearance abroad may bring forth the same reactions.

Researchers such as Piaget, Gesel, Ilg and Bates include references to childhood bereavement in their studies of reactions to environmental factors during phases of development and these are readily available in most libraries. Sylvia Anthony's *The Child's Discovery of Death* (1940), based on first-hand observations of children, gives a useful account of how and when children form concepts of death.

First-hand observations on reactions of fifty three nursery school children to bereavement supplied by Miss Babb, Inspector of Nursery Schools, to Dr Brown (Gould, 1968) reveal both how nursery school children react and how these schools can help the children concerned.

Older children who realise the difference between going away and dying and whose parents and siblings may be in robust health, may nevertheless worry about bereavement in the future. The child who can be brought to terms with such fears before such an event happens, if it does, is more likely to weather a future traumatic experience. The boy who verbalised his terror while his parents were flying to New York – 'They'll get killed. I *know* there'll be a plane crash' – and was given statistics showing the relative safety of flying as a means of transport but was not told such an accident simply would *not* happen, was in a sounder position when bereavement came subsequently than one who was told that 'the angels would look after mummy's and daddy's plane' and they would not be killed. Teachers and parents can do a great deal to help children to accept the rare possibility of bereavement before it happens – by stories, poetry, drama, scientific discussions, observations of death in nature and by creative activities. They also can reassure them that children are helped, that they will be looked after if death of a parent occurs. I do not mean that this should be done directly but there is plenty of opportunity to build up security during day-to-day talk with children now that they are not expected to be seen and not heard. 'What would happen to kids like me' said a ten year old boy 'if they fought in England like in Vietnam?' We have to remember that the mass media have presented death to children by instant communication and they are well aware that events in this country might involve them in death and bereavement before they are grown up. The precariousness of the human situation is dealt with by some teachers and parents by religious faith but we have little evidence that this necessarily helps the child.

There is no space in this short section to deal with aspects of personal loss except as bereavement through a specific death. We shall consider some of the changes which have been observed in bereaved children, and how these may be recognised by those who are their guardians, and what they can do to help the children back to 'normality'. If the child's development is arrested or regresses over a prolonged period of time, expert psychological help is needed, and if the child concerned is disturbed to begin with this help is needed at the outset.

Recent researches on bereaved children referred for psychiatric treatment, and retrospective studies of disturbed adults, are well described by Dr Felix Brown in *The Prevention of Damaging Stress in Children* (Gould, 1968), including his own work on depressively ill patients, and point to the necessity for considering the child at the time of bereavement as at high risk.

Role of the teacher in dealing with bereavement

Teachers in primary schools usually have access to records of their children or, if not, can obtain information from the head if a child shows signs of stress; the position is more haphazardous in some secondary schools but those with tutorial and house systems, even in a school of two thousand pupils, are usually able to provide the adolescent with a teacher-guardian who can help. But there are still too many complaints from class teachers that they are not informed, or only half informed about their children. This is especially true when a teacher is new to the class. In spite of growing teacher-parent cooperation true neighbourhood schools are few and far between, and all the local repercussions of a death in the child's family, and the variables combining to determine his degree of stress may be only partially known to the teacher. Likewise, the repercussions in school, the attitudes of other children and staff, may not be drawn to the attention of the parent until it is too late. Derek Miller, in his recent book *The Age Between* (1969), stresses the dangers of faulty cooperation between home and school in the case of adolescent stress.

So the first point to make is that in dealing with the bereaved child, or for that matter with any deprived child, parent-teacher cooperation is essential, but it may well be that the teacher who is outside the intense confines of the family, and who by training and experience understands the development patterns of the 'normal' child is the one to play a major part in suggesting and carrying out the remedies.

Multiplicity of variables acting on the bereaved child

In determining the reactions of the bereaved child, many variables will be operating. Some of these are almost too obvious to mention, e.g. the age of the child, the degree of intimacy with the dead person, the presence or absence of immediate substitutes, previous experience, the attitude to death of family and neighbourhood, the degree of stability of the child. What we all sometimes fail to recognise in this age of child probing, is that children are always a new generation in a rapidly changing environment. We can never be quite sure what they are up to in terms of our own adult theorisings. We know they go through sequences of physical, mental, emotional and social development but the details for each child are unique, and while we are trying to record our findings in terms of standardised tests the child himself may have slipped away, hidden from our researches in his private world of the imagination. So much depends upon the individual child and, as Felix Brown (Gould, 1968) points out some children may react to parental loss by developing outsanding talents. A friend of mine who lost his father at fifteen remembers his feeling of 'raised status' and subsequent desire to 'outshine' his contemporaries. However, most children react to bereavement by behaviour patterns indicating deprivation and, as Bowlby has shown, young children may pass through three distinct phases when a parent, particularly the mother, dies. Protest and denial may be followed by a phase of despair manifested by withdrawal and other forms of disorganisation as the child comes to accept the reality of the death. The recovery, which comes sooner or later, will depend on the age of the child and the help given. A very young child may become completely detached from a mother who has died or even gone away for a period. An older one may discover that he can, in fact, survive the loss and hope again. When questioning grown-ups who remembered their childhood reactions to bereavement I found that most of them did pass through recognisable phases but as one, a social worker I will call Helen, expressed it when referring to her reactions to her father's being killed in the war when she was seven, 'I haven't read the Bowlby things for ages but, as I remember, I think I went through the three stages he discusses except that they weren't finished with at one go, and I had to go over them again and again over a long period and this had social implications.'

A biology teacher in a comprehensive school in London recently took a lesson on the endocrine glands and was interested in a fifteen year old girl who suggested that secretions from the andrenals may have helped her to cope with the stress caused by the death of her father a year ago. The teacher talked this out with her a little later and gave me the following verbal report.

Child's attitude to bereavement

Age at time of bereavement 14 years. Two younger brothers.

1 *Denial*   At first could not accept her father's death, thought death happened only to other people's families. Even now one year later sometimes feels it has been all a dreadful nightmare and that her father is not really dead.

2 No feeling that someone else near to her would die or that

3 she herself might die.

4 *Withdrawal symptoms*   Had feelings of withdrawal to people outside the family and especially feared the return to school afterwards, feeling that she, herself, was different from the others.

5 No over-excitement or bad behaviour.

6 For a time found difficulty in concentrating on work and had to force herself to do it, realising that life must go on in spite of what happened. She knew that her father was most interested in her progress in school and wished her to do well.

7 No real guilt feelings felt but wished she had paid more attention to her father and tried to do what he wanted her to do and listened to his advice.

8 No anger or resentment experienced but felt overwhelmed and bewildered that this should have happened to them.

9 *Idealisation of the dead*   She had realised that her father was a pillar of strength on which they all depended and his death had made them less secure.

10 *Overconscientiousness with regard to helping mother and replacing father* Felt closer to her mother than before and much more responsible, particularly to her two younger brothers. Her mother had taken over her father's business and they discussed with her details of business, whether good sales, etc. Obviously greatly involved with it (her father rarely discussed such things at home).

11 *Physical symptoms, etc.*   Losing her father was 'Like the end of the world' to her but she felt she had somehow been given strength to carry on. (It was in a biology lesson discussing adrenal glands that she suggested that secretions from these glands might have helped her.) Some loss of appetite and feelings of exhaustion at the time of his death. She feels more mature as a result of her suffering than other girls in her form, says her brothers have matured too.

In a book which should be most useful to those dealing with bereaved children *Explaining Death to Children* edited by Earl A. Grollman (1967), there is a chapter on 'Handling the subject and affected students in schools' by Helen Moller quoting case histories of children who reacted to bereavement by symptoms easy to recognise, such as regression in school work. Other contributors to this symposium and to Toynbee's *Man's Concern with Death* (1968) cite a great number of common behaviour patterns in both children and adults which, for the sake of brevity, I shall attempt to summarise, and in doing so shall also refer to case histories which I myself have investigated. For the sake of clarity I shall group these under three headings: 1 the death of the mother; 2 the death of the father; 3 the death of a sibling.

Death of the mother

Without exception this is regarded by research workers as the most traumatic experience of bereavement which a child can experience. It was more frequent a hundred years ago and often complicated by the mother dying in childbirth, thus affecting the attitudes of father and siblings to the baby if it survived. The maternal death rate in the U.K. is now 0·21 per 1,000 live births, and if mothers die while all or any of their offspring are still children it is more likely to be due to an accident or to one of the still recalcitrant diseases such as cancer. The age of the child and the kind of support and substitutes present will influence subsequent behaviour patterns more strongly than in the death of other relatives. Those concerned with the child bereft of its mother may expect some or all of the following symptoms.

1   *Shock of unbelief and denial followed by panic*   A major wound has occurred, the child being as it were amputated from its mother and unable to survive without help and rebuilding of another relationship. This reaction may include feelings of anger towards the mother for abandoning the child and towards doctors, God, father, and siblings and the child itself for not preventing the death. Some guilt feelings are almost inevitable. The child may become apathetic, appear dazed and completely uninterested in school, playmates or toys, unnaturally good and, in the worst cases, completely withdrawn. Another child may react by expressing his panic in violently aggressive behaviour, verbally and even physically attacking relatives, teachers and companions. Or he may indulge in undue showing off with fits of crying and laughter, amounting to hysteria in the most disturbed cases. The degree of these manifestations will vary from child to child but at some time or other during the bereavement uncontrolled behaviour and/or depression and withdrawal is likely to occur.

These symptoms are usually more intense if the child has suffered from evasion or lies about the death, from being excluded from family grief and mourning and particularly if he has not been aware of the final removal of the body of the deceased. A child of four denied the reality of his mother's death until the father allowed him to see the body being carried away from the bed to the coffin and finally out of the house. 'Now I know mummy is dead and won't never come back' he said, almost with relief. Four girls aged between two and five lost their mother in a car accident as she was driving away from the school where she had just left the oldest daughter. Not only did they never see the body but were immediately whisked away to the country until the father's grief had died down. When they returned home the house had been rearranged and their mother was said to be ill. All four became 'wild and uncontrollable' according to the neighbourhood and the five year old was sent to a boarding school soon after. To be sent away at such an early age was, of course, another sort of death and this girl, now grown up, still shows personality disorder.

Even when the bereaved children remain at home with a loving father and mother substitute and have been allowed to know the truth and to participate in the mourning, there will be disturbed behaviour patterns for a time and these may recur in adolescence, as was found to be the case with three boys and a girl between the ages of six and twelve who lost their mother from leukaemia. After an initial period of disturbance all four seemed to settle well at school, work normally, make friends, until one by one, as they reached the later years of adolescence from sixteen onwards, they showed signs of disturbance, expressing itself in wild rebellion and off-beat behaviour not wholly accounted for by the teenage subculture norms of today.

A child of eight expressed his terror of abandonment to a sister of twelve – 'Who will look after me now mummy is dead? Will you?' The sister said 'yes' and suffered in consequence. A friend of mine, who lost her mother, also at the age of eight, had participated in the terminal illness, the death and mourning which were typical in those days in working class families in small provincial towns. On the surface it would appear that this child was being allowed to take a full part in the expression of grief but in actual fact the wearing of black, the drawn blinds, the heavily scented lilies, the white clad corpse, the crying relatives and the funeral meats were merely outward trappings and techniques. She had been brought up in a Midlands milieu that scorned to show its feelings and she remembers being utterly terrified of giving way to her sense of panic. She made a vow – 'I must endure to the end, whatever the end may be' – and when further stresses occurred reacted by long moods of silence and withdrawal, accompanied by bodily distress. Mere mourning for mourning's sake, the ritualisation of death without the overt cry of absence is unlikely to help the bereaved child. We have no real evidence that the American way of death with its funeral parlours and gardens of rest, or the Victorian paraphanalia either helped or hindered the deprived child. True mourning and a time for sorrow is a different matter but it must be part of the true culture in which the child is growing up and I am not in full agreement with Gorer that we can recreate social mourning by establishing secular rituals.

2   The child may *regress* to a more infantile stage, including what the Americans call 'lowering his grades at school'. He may experience fears and anxieties which the adults in charge of him thought he had grown

out of, such as fear of the dark, of animals, of becoming ill and dying himself, of being punished by illness for some misdemeanor. An infant teacher told me of a child of six in her class who screamed violently every time she had the slightest accident and when asked why she was making such an undue fuss said 'So's I won't die like mummy'. He may become fixed in a fantasy relationship to the dead person, and cases have been known where this can persist into adulthood when a boy loses his mother, so that he is unable to make mature relationships with any woman. Adolescents, in particular, may idealise the mother to the extent of adopting her beliefs and thus never progress to their new adult identities. 'I could never find a lady to hold a candle up to my dear, dead mother', said an unmarried clergyman to me. 'She died when I was eleven and I've been faithful to her ever since.' One obvious comment here is that there had been a faulty mother-son relationship in childhood. Sometimes a child will deliberately remain babyish because he is frightened that maturity may bring death.

3   The child may drown his sorrow in *compensating activities*, school work, sport, hobbies, almost to the point of obsession. As this has been observed more frequently in father loss, I shall deal with it in that section.

4   A common symptom is *clinging to a mother substitute* who may be a teacher, father, sibling, aunt or anyone else available. Another infant teacher told me of a child who 'nearly drove her up the wall' by following her about perpetually and Bruno Bettleheim in his book *Love is Not Enough* (1965) on disturbed children describes Mary rushing into the schoolroom before breakfast to make sure that the teacher is really there, and in *Truants from Life* he describes other childrens' reactions to separation by death. Reluctance to leave familiar people and surroundings may become so intensified that the child growing into adulthood may be afraid of all forms of change.

If some of the symptoms described above are prolonged or obsessional it is imperative that teacher or parent should seek expert help.

Death of the father

All the symptoms noted in the death of the mother may be present in the child suffering father loss, some of them tending to be accentuated, others diminished. There would also appear to be sex differences perhaps more obvious than occurs in mother loss. For instance, boys experiencing death of a father with whom they were beginning to identify may continue to romanticise and idealise him, while the girl may be more concerned with identifying through her mother's relationship to the dead husband. A boy may also try to take on the father's role towards his mother and siblings; a girl may try to please her father's memory by working hard or by making a match which she thinks would be favoured by him. These may be fairly positive and helpful reactions, but are easily distorted.

Rutter and others (quoted by Brown [Bowlby, 1968]) have found that children tend to be more disturbed by the death of a parent of the same sex though there is by no means agreement on this. There is some evidence that the child can be helped most by teachers, psychologists, social workers and psychiatrists of the same sex though much more research is needed to establish this firmly. Studies of children referred for child guidance, maladjustment and delinquency point to a higher ratio of bereaved children compared with their peer groups considered to be normal, and also to a difference in reactions of boys and girls in relation to their own age at the time of bereavement and to the sex of the deceased. Sylvia Anthony (1940) finds that the ages eight to twelve are the most traumatic with regard to the loss of parents but Brown says that loss of the mother is significant at all ages.

The social worker, Helen, whom I have mentioned previously described a whole gamut of reactions to her father's death. Her first reaction was 'to swear at God and tell Him that he was useless because I had been taught each night to pray for my father's safety'. She expected God to retaliate and was terrified of going to sleep in case he killed her, too, in the night. Bodily distress persisted around bedtime – difficulty in breathing, feeling that her heart had stopped. She never told anyone of these symptoms, merely complained about not getting to sleep. Several children known to me have had these sleep disturbances, including nightmares following a bereavement. One child was terrified of 'dad coming alive again'. Another expressed it as 'He might come through the window as a ghost'. A highly intelligent girl said 'Fancy being afraid of your father for the first time when he's dead'. There seems to be less fear of mother ghosts.

Helen went on to describe what 'I think was a psychosomatic illness' four years after her father was killed and coinciding with the death of a close adult friend. It took the form of vomiting and such severe headaches that a specialist was consulted and E.E.C. readings taken. She explains this as due to the fact that she had never mourned her father because she had never really accepted the fact of his death. She had always expected him to turn up, this being reinforced by the doubts of adults around her who would suggest that in war mistakes were made and he might be amongst the missing. She thinks that when the second adult died, and subsequently others she went through delayed mourning and gradually accepted that her father was dead. To the child of seven 'there was no body, nothing'. But when she was eleven she saw the body of her mother's friend and was afraid to touch it in case it came alive again. She compensated by plunging into academic work at school and finally went to Oxford but all through her childhood and adolescence she experienced symptoms common to bereaved children – anger that she, her brother and mother had been abandoned by the father, idealising him and yet deeply resenting it when people expected her to behave like her father's child, proud when they said she looked like him and jealous when they said her brother resembled him even more closely. She was terrified every time she got home from school and her mother was not there or, in earlier years, when she was late getting to school to collect her. She always thought she had been killed. When she was fourteen her mother took another partner and Helen found this particularly distressing and actually insisted that they should sleep apart. This, too, seems to be a strong reaction in the case of girls who are not present at their father's death and are excluded from displays of grief and mourning at the time of the death. Another girl, Janet, the youngest of three sisters, was the only one not present when her father died suddenly while cleaning his motor cycle. She neither saw his body nor was involved in the grief of the family. She was eight at the time. Like Helen, when her mother re-married when she was seventeen, she was 'beside herself' with anger and distress, regarding her mother as a traitor to her father. Her sisters accepted it quite naturally. Helen, too, with her brother had been excluded from family grief at the time of her father's death on the grounds that the mother could 'have some peace'. Helen also reported that her case was further complicated by 'social implications' meaning mainly a working class background. Deprived of the main breadwinner, father loss may entail financial hardship to the mother and children, and put an excessive work burden on the mother. Helen said she resented free dinners and not having the same pleasures as her class mates.

Jim's father, who was a teacher, died when he was nine and his only sibling was a sister of seven. He, too, underwent the usual reactions but the major stress in his case was that his mother, hitherto a kindly, rather submissive woman became over-strict and dominant, obviously trying to take over the paternal role. Almost at once as it seemed to him later, he was sent to what he described as an orphanage and this, too, was extremely authoritarian. His reports described him as uncontrolled, undisciplined and at one time even violent. When he was fourteen he tried to get into bed with one of the domestic staff – a much older woman – and was regarded, therefore, as deeply disturbed. But, as in the case of Helen and others, there was no actual treatment and he compensated by working 'madly' academically. When he grew up work obsession scarcely declined on marriage.

A recent case brought to my notice concerns two brothers, one who has the added stress of being an adopted child. Another variable in the case was that the father was ten years older than the mother and died of a second stroke following on the first. The mother would not allow either of her sons to see the father during his last illness on account of his degenerated appearance and semi-consciousness. The younger son, aged ten, mourned deeply, unashamed of tears but constantly complaining of 'bad luck'. This boy idealised the father and stabilised by taking up his father's hobby of boat building and boating. The father ideal was thus expressed concretely and was far removed from the prolonged and exaggerated fantasy idealisation which may happen in the case of less balanced children. But the older brother, the twelve year old adopted son, expressed no overt grief at all. He became extremely hostile to his mother in particular, erratic in work, petulant and aggressive, reverting to a more childish type of behaviour such as asking for treats and then refusing to participate, letting the air out of the tyres of his mother's car and sulking in company.

A girl, Joan, who lost her father by suicide, thus adding another major variable to the multiplicity of factors which hit her at the time, was said to have overcome the stresses she experienced after actually discovering her father's body with his throat cut in the bathroom, by her iron will. Her mother would not accept the suicide and pretended that Daddy had just died and constantly talked of him – how he would do this and that. Joan was fourteen with a younger sister of ten who was unaware of the suicide for some time, and an older sister who was engaged to be married. Joan, like so many bereaved children, found difficulty in sleeping and suffered from nightmares, more frequent and intense in her case because of the horror of the suicide. She, too, compensated by hard work at school but found relationships with boys and men impossible. She became lesbian, 'finding great consolation in falling in love with women'.

A very penetrating account of a mature woman student's reaction to the death of her husband from lung cancer and brain tumours, written in 1969, includes a paragraph on how she helped her four young children to cope with the bereavement, after stating 'unfortunately, as the mortality rate decreases, death has become the "forbidden subject". Even among doctors and nurses there is a reluctance to discuss that the illness is terminal. I had to be quite forcible in showing them I knew he was dying and wanted to face the fact from the beginning. I had the same difficulty with people I met in the street. Remarks of "miracles happen" or "I knew someone with the same symptoms who got better" did not help, however kindly meant.'

'On our eldest daughter's sixth birthday my husband died. When I came home from the hospital I knew that how I acted would make a tremendous difference to the way this tragedy would affect our children's lives. It would be wrong to dwell upon sorrow, equally wrong to hide all grief. The children for several months played at dying, played at being wife, mother, child bereaved. Through play they learned to live again.'

The death of siblings

Reactions to the death of a brother or sister are so dependent on the ages of all the children concerned, the roles hitherto played by the deceased and the behaviour of the bereaved parents that it is not possible to generalise. But some of the same factors that have been observed to change behaviour patterns in children bereaved of parents also operate in the case of sibling loss and similar symptoms of deprivation may occur. Guilt feelings may be complicated and intensified by ambivalent emotional attitudes to the deceased. The rivalry and jealousy the bereaved child may have experienced in his relationship to the dead sibling may give rise to a sense of relief as well as of loss, and the child may be horrified by this and so feel guiltier than ever. 'Did Brenda die because I kept on teasing her?' 'I wish I had lent Jonathan my bike when he was alive.' 'I didn't really mind that Tim was better than me at school.' These are some of the remarks that teachers and parents may hear and be thankful for, because they may be talking points which will help to delve deeper into the bereaved child's problems. Another reaction, rarely found in the case of parent loss, has been reported to me by several grown-ups, remembering their reactions to loss of a brother or sister. One colleague referred to it as a sense of 'one upmanship'. When her infant sister died and she went back to her private little girls' school everyone was nice to her and she felt important. Although sympathy of peers may also be overtly shown at parent loss, this is usually too devastating for a compensatory sense of importance to develop. The most damaging experience in sibling loss is undoubtedly the reaction of parents and the following case history emphasises this so well that it will speak for many other examples. Deirdre and Diana were twins of nine when their oldest sister aged nineteen was taken to hospital, suddenly, with acute appendicitis. Next morning, very early, they heard the telephone, followed by a hasty rushing away of the car carrying their parents to the hospital. In the late afternoon, as they watched at the gate, the car came back. Deirdre saw her sister's suitcase in it and 'I knew she was dead'. Nothing was said to the two little girls. They were sent off to stay with an aunt in the country almost at once but not before Deirdre had been 'horrified by my mother's eyes all red with crying'. She became timid, withdrawn and afraid of change.

Another factor in sibling loss may be an attempt on the part of one or both parents to identify the surviving child with the dead one, sometimes going so far as to use the dead child's name as a replacement. Undue stress may be caused by the bereaved child forcing itself into a role which it adopts only to please the parents.

I have only been able to give some of the symptoms recognisable in children bereaved of mother, father or siblings. Other relatives and particularly grandparents who are particularly loved will cause similar stresses but these will leave the nuclear family intact and the child will normally survive them more easily. Losses of friends and beloved animals will also cause temporary disturbances and teachers have sometimes been puzzled by bad behaviour in hitherto amenable children until they have discovered that a favourite dog or cat had been run over the day before. In the last section of this article I shall try to suggest how adults can help children stressed by bereavement.

How adults can help

The most difficult to help quite obviously are children who are disturbed to begin with – before the bereavement – or those who are suffering from a second dose. Felix Brown (Gould, 1968), working with disturbed patients matched with control groups, found amongst the former a high percentage who had suffered from bereavement while under the age of fifteen. This, he thought, had left them with mental illness.

The parent, teacher, social worker or any other guardian of the bereaved child who is not an expert psychologist should first of all know what symptoms to expect and above all watch out for any distortion or undue prolongation. For a time the child may appear unwell both in body and mind. All the experts are agreed that mourning or expression of grief is important and should not be delayed. Nor should the child, even the young one, be told anything but the plain truth and he should be helped to accept the finality of death. Mother will never return. But what is the teacher to do if a child at home has been denied this truth? I am not referring to religious beliefs in the after life which no teacher would be likely to disturb and might feel impelled to affirm but it must be made clear to the child that the beloved person is physically dead and cannot ever again be present in the family as mother, father or brother. Some children are more curious about the fate of the body than the possible immortality of the soul and questions about burial and cremation should also be answered truthfully. The scientific explanation of death as something which happens to all organisms, and the cycle of integration and disintegration, can help to channel the child's interest into something less personal. With older children the possibility that one day scientists may be able to counteract senility and postpone or even 'abolish' death is not beyond their powers of discussion in this age of tissue transplants and new discoveries in biotechnics. There is no real comfort to be offered for the absence of the loved one. There is no real substitute; nor should there be if love is to mean anything. The parent and teacher can offer the greatest sympathy while admitting to the child that his loss is something which he has every right to express in intense and overt grief until time heals.

The play *Rosencrantz and Guildenstern are Dead* brings this out very clearly – 'death is not the act, it is the disappearance'. And the child who yells out his agony is more likely to recover quickly than the one who never cries. Teachers report that children enter a phase of general sadness after the first shock is over and frequently lament that the dead can no longer share the ordinary, day to day pleasures of life. 'My Mum would have loved these daffodils.' 'My Dad used to love steak and kidney pudding.' Talking this out, without undue emphasis, and sharing the child's regret may bring to light other problems such as guilt feelings. Is the child worried that he did not participate sufficiently in the dead parent's pleasures? Does he feel that in some way he was a hindrance? 'If my Dad hadn't bought me that bike he would have been able to go for a holiday', one guilt-ridden child said.

Another important discovery that the parent or teacher may make in talking with the child is what he really knows of the causes of death. Might he be worried that he, himself, is suffering from the same unknown obscure complaint, or might it have been prevented or cured if the deceased had gone to a cleverer doctor or better hospital? Must he now be on the watch all the time that another parent or sibling does not disappear? This burden can be removed by cheerful, wise discussions about death in general, and the child re-assured that death today except amongst the old is rare in this country and that in no way is the child responsible for the death of his relative.

Bruno Bettleheim in *Love is not Enough* (1965) describes a deeply disturbed child, Carol, aged eight, whose brother 'the preferred child' whom she hated had died a year ago. She believed that she herself should have died as she was so wicked, and that actually this would happen to her as a punishment. Although in Carol's case her behaviour was distorted something like this may be an ingredient of the complex reactions of more normal children. A child may ask himself if the parents would have preferred him to die rather than his little sister. Bettleheim also refers later on to the playing out of death by a disturbed child and most nursery and infant teachers would certainly recognise the value of play as therapy in the normal classroom.

The tendency to idealise the dead may be augmented by parents who may refer only to the attractive side of the deceased's personality. 'He was always such a sweet, kind boy.' 'My wife was an angel.' 'My husband was the best man on earth.' A child hearing this may believe it and try to behave like the paragon so described or he may feel so inferior that he gives up and decides it is impossible ever to catch up with his dead brother or become a man like his father. It is far better for his guardians to be strictly honest about the deceased and show that they loved him for himself alone with all his strengths and weaknesses.

There are two major environmental factors necessary if a child is to mature properly. One is security and the other is adventure, and these operate on all levels, physical, mental, emotional and social. The child stressed by bereavement must be cared for in each of these four aspects. Bodily stress must be treated by appropriate diet, rest, exercise and even clothing. The teenager may be helped by trendy clothes, the younger child by a new bright sweater, the child with loss of appetite by more attractive and/or more easily digested foods, the one who is compensating by over-eating by a careful check on weight and a supply of less fattening foods, and the withdrawn one skulking in the house or classroom by tempting new kinds of exercise outside. Buying a child flippers and goggles may tempt him to swim, or a course in horse riding may help. Middle class children will have this sort of help more frequently than those whose parents are in lower occupational grades. Financial help should be given in needy cases, interpreting the word needy to include more than a balanced diet. Some necessary luxuries may be the answer. A holiday away, not at the time of bereavement, but later, so that the child does not feel he is being excluded, may also help and school journeys where a teacher pays special attention to the hurt child may work wonders. Mental security can be re-established by discussions, by helping with school work, sometimes by buying a particularly desired new book or record. Or, alternatively, the child may be reassured that a period of mental fallowness will not be permanent. He may be encouraged to relax, to learn when he wants to do so, and to follow his own interests, even to drop out for a time from the examination racket. It would be interesting to study the effects of bereavement on children in the more progressive type of school with those in the more formal type. Emotionally, if he is deprived of a parent another attachment is the best answer, though not too soon after the bereavement and, of course, depending on the age of the child. It is essential that both peer group friendships and adult contacts should be encouraged. The worst thing is for the child to find all his consolation in the broken nuclear family. Bruno Bettleheim in *Children of the Dream* (1969) says that Kibbutz youngsters are fully supported by the group in cases of bereavement and, though he does not believe that this sort of extended family is necessarily a good milieu for child rearing, he certainly stresses the stability of those so brought up. Socially, the community should do more to help bereaved children regain their security. No bereaved child should have to suffer poverty or early school leaving, leading to denial of further education.

The second factor – the need for adventure, should be given more attention in cases of bereavement. Parents, teachers and others in the adult community can help the child back to the abundant life which is his birthright. More play groups, nursery schools, adventure playgrounds, sports facilities, travel, hobbies and exciting, creative work can help. We might learn from some of the communist countries here and provide palaces of recreation and culture. In my own study, *The Child's Attitude to Death* (1966) I have suggested in more detail how creative activities may help to neutralise the destructive aspects of death.

Bereavement plays its part in establishing many kinds of deviant behaviour, including violence and drug addiction in adolescence. A higher ratio of bereaved has been found in prison, approved school and Borstal populations as well as in psychiatric wards. Prophylactic treatment during the time of bereavement could have prevented some of these reactions.

Finally, we cannot ignore either genetic factors or the very first relationships which the child establishes soon after birth.

In *The Human Zoo* Desmond Morris (1969) says 'Good early imprinting opens a large emotional bank account for the child. If expenses are heavy later on, it will have plenty to draw upon. If things go wrong with its parental care as it grows up (such as parental separation, divorce or death) its resilience will depend on the attachment quality of the first vital year.'

Parents in the nuclear family may need information and help, classes in child rearing during the infant years of *each* of their children, as all children are different, as well as advice in times of stress, and this goes for teachers, psychologists, doctors and social workers, too, who may need to be acquainted with up to date researches on child rearing in their own and other cultures, especially as our community may become multi-racial.

Sula Wolff (1969) says that 'we cannot know what the psychological hazards of parental death are for children unless a special study of bereaved children in the community is undertaken.' Such studies are being pursued now but we have to realise that the variables are many and complex and, as culture patterns change, so will the reactions to death.

THE ADOPTED CHILD AT SCHOOL

M. E. Humphrey

Children do not like to differ conspicuously from others in any important respect, and their contemporaries – and sometimes even adults – can be quick to exploit a sensitive area. We may take it as self-evident that adoption is a significant event in any child's life, but the extent to which it remains a conspicuous event will vary with individual circumstances. The aim of this chapter is to consider how far – if at all – adoptive families merit special treatment.

Much has been written about adoption in recent years, and several major research studies have been carried out. However, with one exception (Kirk, 1964), the emphasis throughout has centred on the family. Relatively little attention has been given to community attitudes, and the teacher's viewpoint seems to have been largely ignored. And although the quality of family relationships is probably the most decisive factor in a child's development, he is also a member of society and must learn to function outside the home. Other far-reaching influences will affect his capacity to do so, and the nature of his school life is predominant among them.

As few teachers will be familiar with adoption statistics it may be as well to begin by presenting some of the relevant facts. Legal adoption was not practised on a wide scale in Britain until after the second world war, when a post-war peak of 21,000 adoption orders was reached in 1946. This was doubtless a reflection of war-time separations, in that many reunited couples will have wanted to confer legitimate status on the child born out of wedlock while the husband was serving overseas. Adoption by the natural mother has indeed always accounted for between a quarter and a third of all adoption orders, but this is not how most people think of adoption. After declining to a steady annual average of between 13–14,000 orders in the 1950s, the rate has again risen steeply in the current decade until a total of nearly 25,000 was reached in 1968. Despite this increasing popularity of adoption, however, the adoptive family belongs to a very small minority group. Thus not more than between one to two per cent of all children are legally adopted.

Hazards of adoption

The question of whether adoption is the best solution for children deprived of their natural parents must be viewed against the available alternatives, namely long-term fostering and institutional care. In both these situations the natural parents will normally retain their rights and obligations, but this may be at the cost of divided loyalties in the one case and inadequate emotional relationships in the other. Now that most child care experts have come to believe in adoption as providing the richest opportunities for vicarious family life, the real challenge is how to recognise good adoptive parents in advance. Since the great majority of today's adoptions are arranged by either registered societies or local authority childrens' departments, one might suppose that the child's interests were usually guaranteed. It is therefore somewhat disconcerting to find that the psychiatrist has been seeing more than his fair share of adopted children (Humphrey & Ounsted, 1963). Does this mean that, no matter what legal and social precautions are taken, adoptive families must remain vulnerable? Or in other words, are extra hazards inherent in adoptive parenthood?

Commenting on the recent eruption of American studies of adopted children brought for psychiatric help, Kadushin (1966) has pointed out that adoptive families have certain distinguishing features. The parents are generally well educated and tend to espouse middle-class standards. They begin their family rather late, and seldom have more than two children. Indeed, only children are likely to be more numerous among couples who come to parenthood late, and in one large sample of adoptions they accounted for no less than forty per cent (Kornitzer, 1968). (We have no reliable estimate of the frequency of one-child families in the general population, but it is certainly much lower than this). In view of the obvious pressures on the only child of middle-class parents, this factor alone – or possibly combined with the greater readiness of well educated couples to seek professional help – may explain why the psychiatrist has been faced with this surfeit of adoptive families. On the other hand this provides a less convincing explanation of why adopted children are grossly over-represented in schools for the maladjusted – eight per cent according to one survey (Pringle, 1961). In the present state of our knowledge we are probably justified in assuming that adoption poses special problems for both parents and children; but although some of these problems are easily identified, few of them have been fully explored. Here we shall consider only the least controversial issues.

Almost half of the children seen by Dr Ounsted and his colleagues in the Oxford area had been placed for adoption after the age of six months. Details of the pre-adoptive history were meagre, but there were several instances of gross parental deprivation in the first two years of life. In such cases one cannot necessarily blame the adoption for what has gone wrong. The couple who adopt a two-year-old can, of course, expect trouble whatever the previous history, merely because this happens to be an awkward stage of normal development. The suggestion that adoption becomes problematical even beyond the first six months of life may be harder for some readers to accept, yet it is typically between six and nine months of age that the child is forming its first specific social attachments. Thus even if he has spent the whole of the pre-adoptive period with a loving mother or foster mother, he will take longer to settle in his adoptive home if he has to part from someone he has learnt to recognise as an individual separate from himself. There is also the fact that most women prefer to adopt as early as possible in a child's life, and those who accept an older child may be either less realistic or less eligible by the standards of adoption societies. This combination of circumstances not uncommonly results in an already disturbed child being received into a far from ideal home.

There is an association between delayed placement for adoption and liability to character disorders. The latter are apt to come to a head in adolescence, when the boy may offend against the law and the girl may become promiscuous or beyond parental control. Stealing and destructiveness are the commonest complaints, and the parents may be tempted to blame the unknown heredity. Developments of this kind are by no means inevitable, and it has yet to be shown conclusively that damage sustained in the early years is irreversible. Warm and sensitive parents may well be capable of averting this danger. Moreover, today's disturbed adolescent was adopted in a less enlightened era, and today's adopting couple may hope to reap the benefits of improved social services and a better social climate. Evidence from biased samples must in any case be interpreted with caution, and wider surveys have yielded a more encouraging picture. For example, when a series of nearly five hundred adoptions arranged privately in Florida were followed up nine to fifteen years later it was found that the children were only marginally behind their classmates in social adjustment, and age at placement was immaterial where family relationships were good (Witmer *et al.*, 1963). The main findings of a British national survey of adoptive families who were placed under long-term surveyance (Seglow *et al.*, 1972), were equally reassuring.

Other possible complications of adoptive parenthood will include the age factor already mentioned, but the duration of childless marriage is likely to be more crucial than age itself. Some couples adopt within a few years of marrying late, but more often those who adopt in their late 30s or early 40s have had many years in which to become sufficient unto each other. That they should be alarmed by the prospect of a childless middle-age is understandable, but this is not a sound basis for adoption. The causes of infertility are various, and in some cases psychological factors may be wholly responsible. The couple whose childlessness stems from marital disharmony or sexual inadequacy may be ill-fitted for parenthood, as may those who have become unduly depressed by their reproductive failure. In a long teaching career one is likely to encounter children adopted by elderly, depressed or inhibited couples, but the true situation may be masked and its implications for family life are uncertain.

Of much clearer significance is the problem of uneasy or insufficient communication within adoptive families. A study of adults adopted in early life has revealed that a child may sense the parents' reluctance to discuss his origins and he therefore refrains from asking them embarrassing questions, which leads them all too readily to conclude that he is not really interested (McWhinnie, 1967). So whereas complete suppression of the truth is rare, a stalemate of this sort may be fairly common. The only child, or the only adopted child in a family, is particularly vulnerable in this respect. A child who shares his special status with another member of the family may find it easier to grasp, and those who adopt more than one child may be more relaxed about it anyway. The communication factor is therefore best discussed in the context of family structure.

Patterns of adoptive family

The majority of first adoptions outside the family circle are undertaken by childless couples, but the proportion of adopting couples who already have one or more children of their marriage is not accurately known. About twenty five per cent of a series of applications to The City of Oxford Children's Department fall into this category, and whether or not this figure is representative we can be sure that this kind of mixed family is no rarity. The motive of providing a companion for an only child is suspect, since the latter has usually reached school age before this solution is contemplated. Quite apart from the difference in status, the age gap between the two children will prevent this from ever becoming a normal family unit. Sometimes the older child will come to think of his position as inferior, since his younger 'sibling' was chosen whereas his own arrival could be interpreted as an unwelcome accident. This will almost certainly arise where the parents have adopted to ensure that their second or subsequent child is of the approved sex (I know of two cases where a girl was adopted to obviate the risk of a fourth boy, and in each case the third son became extremely disturbed in adolescence). When a child's self-esteem is threatened in this way the normal sibling rivalry will be intensified, and he may lose no opportunity of informing the adoptee that she is 'not Mummy's proper child'. Another motive for adding to a family is the philanthropic one. An increasing number of fertile couples are prepared to offer a home to a coloured or physically handicapped child rather than bring more children of their own into an overcrowded world. This is clearly an excellent idea in principle although the long-term outcome has yet to be assessed (for an interim account see Raynor, 1970).

Different problems may arise when a couple produce their first child after adopting. This situation has been invested with magical significance, but is less common than we have been led to suppose (Humphrey, 1969). Rapid conception by a previously infertile adoptive mother has been reported only occasionally in the medical literature, but where it does occur the adopted child may find it harder to understand how he came into the family. This is because a second adoption provides a convenient starting point for explaining the situation to the first child, who will learn a lot merely from taking part in the ceremony. Where the adoptive mother gives birth instead she not only loses this opening but has to define the adoptee's position in terms of differences rather than similarities between members of the family. So although the first child may have been wholeheartedly accepted – and there is seldom any reason why he should be rejected merely because fertility has been achieved – he is nonetheless handicapped in his biological research.

Adoptive families as a minority group

Even where the adopters have risen nobly to the challenge of timely disclosure, the fact remains that infertile couples belong to a minority group. Census returns have shown that twenty per cent of married couples are childless at any one time, and in the early years of marriage absence of children creates no problems. In time most of the couple's friends will have had children, until eventually they join the hard core of the involuntarily childless. This accounts for ten to twelve per cent of the married population, but is no mere statistical minority since society is inclined to disparage the childless couple. Yet although the social pressures towards adoption may prove considerable, they are frequently outweighed by such inhibiting factors as distrust of parental capacity or lack of agreement between partners. Consequently more couples remain childless than embark on adoption, while fertile couples who adopt are an even more eccentric group. In creating a family by this artificial means the new adoptive parents may have achieved social conformity, but they are actually joining a still more select club. Henceforth they may tend either to acknowledge or to deny the special features of their situation. Denial will involve them in self-deception, but too open acknowledgement might play on the children's sensitivities. These subtleties of adoptive family relationships are not to be underestimated even if they do not make or mar the outcome.

Community attitudes

While the nuclear family has come under severe scrutiny in the 1960s, much less attention has been given to its interaction with the community at large. Members of the adopted child's extended family can exert a considerable influence from the start, and adoption workers will commonly ask questions about the attitudes of potential grandparents and other relatives during their preliminary interviews. Although a grandparent's resistance to the idea of adoption will almost invariably melt when it becomes a *fait accompli*, prejudice dies hard. 'You don't know what you're taking on' implies a profound belief in heredity, and misgivings of this kind are commonly expressed by the older generation. It is true that the adopters' own convictions will carry more weight in the long run, yet the child is exposed in varying degrees to many other adults besides the parents. It would be unrealistic to expect a consensus of outlook, and the impact of significant figures in the child's life must therefore be taken into account. These will inevitably include his teachers, some of whom may harbour strange ideas about adoption. Even if we may hope that the stigma of illegitimacy has died out, there are plenty of professionals who hold that nature knows best and that infertility should be accepted as an act of God. The teacher who starts from such a premise will be looking for trouble in any adopted child, and where he or she goes home to an uneasily childless marriage this tendency may be reinforced.

Whereas the teacher's attitudes to adoption are usually unspoken, children are notorious for speaking their minds. Tactless remarks such as 'Peter isn't your *real* brother, 'cos you're only adopted' are inflicted on some children by their classmates, and the victim may feel devalued as a result. Even where no slur is intended the seeds of confusion may be sown. An intelligent eight year old surprised her adoptive mother by inquiring innocently on her return from school, 'Mummy, you *are* my stepmother aren't you?' This suggestion came from a friend to whom the child had confided that she once had another mother, which was construed by the friend as meaning that she must now have a stepmother. When the difference between an adoptive mother and a stepmother was explained to the child, she enlisted her mother's help in composing a simple statement for her friend's benefit. This supervised account was lost and replaced by her own unaided version which stated: 'Mummy is my real mother, my first mother was my stepmother!'

Where children are comfortable about their adoptive status it will not matter if they become muddled from time to time, but where the channels of communication within the adoptive family are blocked then casual interchanges at school may have lasting repercussions. And the parents whose child does not feel free to confide in them because the subject of adoption has become imbued with mystery, or because he is anxious to save their embarrassment, will never know about these episodes. Some adopters will for this reason advise their children not to discuss the subject outside the home, yet there are also disadvantages in treating it as a closely guarded family secret.

Teachers' attitudes

Presumably most adopters follow their own inclinations in the matter of whether or not to confide in others, but a recurring question which seems to produce conflict is whether to tell the school. Neither the parents' nor the teacher's viewpoint has been put on record, and in the hope of strengthening this chapter I undertook a small enquiry among head teachers of various state schools in Surrey. This was not designed as a statistical survey since time did not permit this, but I considered that a few informal soundings of opinion would be a useful first step. Visits were made to two secondary modern, three primary, two junior and two infant schools, representing a fairly wide range of catchment areas yet all within twenty miles of London. Only two requests for interview were declined, in one case owing to pressure of administrative reorganisation and in the other on unspecified grounds. The interviews (with five women and four men) lasted between half an hour and an hour and covered the following topics: number of adopted children on the school register; source of information and whether it should be volunteered by parents; attitudes of staff; kinds of problems experienced and methods of dealing with them (including psychiatric referral). These aspects will be examined in turn.

Estimates of the incidence of adopted children varied in reliability. One primary school head speaking off the cuff thought that he had about half a dozen in a population of 250. Another had checked the register before my visit and could muster only a pair of twins from a total of 280. Other estimates were close to the national figure of one to two per cent. All my informants emphasised that they could talk only of cases known to them, and there might well be others which had not come to light. However, apart from the plausibility of the quoted figures, it is worth noting that the fact of adoption could often be extracted from the school medical officer's records. Some heads did not appear to have access to these but others had learnt of more than one adoption in this way. Understandably most of my informants preferred to hear direct from the parents as this would make the subject easier to raise if it became necessary on any future occasion. Some parents were visibly embarrassed at introducing the topic but the majority referred to it quite naturally. Most teachers expressed some awareness of the possible relevance of this information – as one junior school head put it, 'one is in much the same position as a G.P., you need to know about the social situation in order to deal with the individual'. Only one head, a man with a grown up family of his own, thought that he would rather not know that a child was adopted in case it might bias his assessment. There was general agreement that class teachers should not be informed routinely.

Class teachers' attitudes could not be explored directly except in one case where the headmaster of a secondary school had assembled a third of his staff for my visit. Here there was a refreshing absence of negative feelings about adoption, and when names were quoted most teachers were surprised to learn that these children were adopted. This is all the more significant in that the school operates on a family group tutorial system, with the pupils remaining in their original group throughout their whole secondary school career. The fact of adoption might be expected to emerge more readily in these circumstances, but this had not happened. It was only the biology teacher who had learnt that some of the children mentioned were concerned about their adoptive status. He regarded this as natural, but several of his colleagues doubted whether this would occur where the child's family relationships were happy.

At all other schools the head was seen alone and was asked to comment on the probable views of staff members. The general reaction was that children were treated on their individual merits and that family circumstances were ignored unless they obtruded forcibly. More specifically, illigitimacy was no longer seen by teachers as a stigma no matter how the child might feel about it.

However, there are reasons for supposing that this air of objectivity may be spurious. Few professional people will admit to prejudice in response to leading questions, whereas exploration of related issues may bring it rapidly to the surface. Even some of the head teachers themselves, for all their apparent sophistication, displayed evidence of preconceived ideas about adoption. This is hardly surprising considering that the topic is apt to arouse deep feelings on a basis of superficial knowledge.

A secondary school head thought that problems of one kind or another were bound to arise in the adolescence of adopted children; and whilst some of his comments were shrewd, it was not always clear whether the problems he mentioned were specific to the adoptive situation. In his experience the difficulties of adopted children were of two kinds; either the child would assert himself as if to convince the teacher of his individuality, or he would withdraw from the rest of the class. He readily conceded, however, that all adolescent difficulties could be polarised in this way, and that the adoption aspect might be largely incidental in any given case. Similarly, a junior school head on the verge of retirement suggested that there was nearly always a social problem associated with adoption, though she was convinced that the great majority of adopters did their level best for their children and did not bring them up in an atmosphere of mystery or evasion. Exactly how she construed this social problem was hard to determine, since her concept of adoption was clearly favourable. In one of the examples she quoted a mother had farmed out her young adopted son with relatives or friends when she found herself unable to cope with the added burden of her newborn child, and he had reacted badly to the separation. Even where the adoption had taken place in earliest infancy this teacher was accustomed to finding signs of insecurity. She had no explanation unless it was that children disliked the sense of deviating from the norm, especially where there was no other adoptee in the family. And if a child with anxieties about his adoptive status was also inclined to be aggressive, the problem was liable to be intensified by the reactions of other children.

We are left with the impression that head teachers get to know about most of the adopted children in their school, and usually from the parents. Once declared the fact is unlikely to be forgotten and may figure prominently in the teacher's interpretation of the child's behaviour. This over-valuation of adoption as a source of difficulty is by no means confined to teachers, since magistrates, psychiatrists and social workers are in the same position of focusing mainly on children who have become troublesome or disturbed. As Miller (1966) has pointed out, adoption can all too easily become a 'ticket of admission' to the psychiatrist, who may be tempted to look no further for an explanation of the presenting disorder. Teachers are less heavily blinkered, yet it is still possible to find members of the profession who have themselves been discouraged from adopting by their experience of troublemakers in the classroom.

Yet even if with any ordinary luck the adopted child has an excellent chance of a healthy development, the possibility remains that adoptive parents as a class are over-anxious. More than one head teacher in my small sample had come to this conclusion, which seems reasonable enough. The process of learning to live with reproductive failure, and of having one's fitness for parenthood submitted to official scrutiny, is hardly calculated to put a couple at their ease; and when the child too has been carefully vetted the burden of expectation may be high indeed, with the result that trivial problems are magnified in their effects. It has even been suggested that this may be one reason for the excessive psychiatric consultation (Stone, 1969).

But these teachers did not appear to have singled out adopted children for psychiatric help, and if there is any pressure towards seeking professional advice it is more likely to come from the adopters themselves. This does not mean, of course, that the teacher has no responsibility in the matter. Cases will arise from time to time where the need for intervention is obvious – the mother who complained that her son had 'never been the same' since learning of his adoption for the first time at the age of eleven is a classical example. Yet once again each case must be treated on its merits, and the question of psychiatric referral must be decided on the same criteria as apply to all children.

It is perhaps worth adding that if adoption is compared with other forms of atypical home, as when a child is brought up by grandparents or foster parents or is in residential care, the picture becomes increasingly optimistic. Step-children also are exposed to greater complexities in their family relationships. And as at least one of my informants pointed out, the child who is most likely to become a cause for teachers' concern is the victim of a broken home or the butt of quarrelsome parents who remain together. Whatever the hazards of adoption, a sense of proportion is essential.

Developmental aspects

These visits made it possible to consider the adopted child's development in relation to the different stages of school life. Adoption is seldom a realistic issue in the infant school, but this is a good time for parents to confide in the head teacher – which means not only revealing that the child is adopted but giving some idea of his present grasp of the situation. Some children may be far more confused than their parents realise, and some parents may try to impart too much information too soon. The teacher may occasionally be able to intervene helpfully in this matter while taking care not to usurp the parents' role. In the junior school period – typically around the age of eight or nine – there is a heightening or reawakening of the child's curiosity about his origins and more generally about the facts of birth and sexuality. If the current B.B.C. film strips are widely shown in schools the adopted child's extra needs may have to be considered. Some concern has been expressed about the impact of new methods of sex education, and the implications for children whose family circumstances are in some way peculiar will need to be faced.

Adolescence is characterised by problems of identity in all children (Erikson, 1963) and by 'genealogical bewilderment' in children with substitute parents (Sants, 1964). The secondary school teacher will receive some of the backlash, and my visits to two senior schools were of special interest in this connection. One of these was in the so-called 'stockbroker belt', where material affluence is not necessarily matched by emotional spontaneity in the home. Here the headmaster, speaking from many years of experience, suggested that identity crises might be more important in adolescent girls because they were more mature and their thoughts were already centred on marriage and parenthood. There is probably some truth in this. The girl who is adopted will be concerned with the meaning of this fact for her future husband and children, and perhaps also with her reproductive capacity. Those who remain with their natural parents are apt to take their fertility for granted, whereas those who have been reared by a childless couple will grow up more aware that some marriages are infertile. Sexual development may be more anxiety-provoking, especially if the adopters start wondering whether their daughter might make the same mistake as her original mother.

In conclusion, it seems reasonable to accept that adopted children may be exposed to extra developmental hazards. At the same time an attitude of constant vigilance is clearly undesirable whether on the part of teachers, parents or other influential adults. Children must be allowed to be themselves. The fact of having been adopted in early infancy will be outweighed by other far-reaching events in the child's life. Healthy growth and social adjustment are governed by the interaction between his constitutional make-up and his experience of life. If we exclude pathological conditions such as autism or severe brain damage, even the most difficult temperament will prove responsive to sympathetic nurture. Yet while every effort is made to select the best available adoptive homes, good parenthood is not a sufficient guarantee of the child's welfare. Ultimately it is society itself that must take care of his future.

Acknowledgements   I am grateful to all the teachers who agreed to discuss adoption with me. Mr S. J. N. Friend, Headmaster of Chipstead Valley Primary School, was particularly helpful in also providing introductions to other schools.

THE IMMIGRANT (WEST INDIAN) CHILD IN SCHOOL

Waveney Bushell

Since the mid-fifties there has been a steady increase in the number of West Indian children attending English schools. A few of these children came with their parents from their native lands, many others joined one or both parents already settled here, some were born here. Today children of West Indian parents are easily identified throughout the English school; for some, adjustment has been easy, others have shown signs of considerable stress, particularly when first introduced to school; with others, stress signals become evident during the adolescent years.

Historical and sociological background of West Indians

The West Indies are small groups of islands scattered along a great arc of more than 2,000 miles in the Caribbean Archipelago. These islands, Jamaica, Trinidad, Tobago, Barbados, the Leeward and Windward Islands, share, with the rest of the Caribbean, the experience of colonialism, slavery and the plantation. The term 'West Indian' therefore extends beyond the frontiers of the islands; it denotes an underlying similarity, a characteristic way of life, grown out of historical events. For the three and a half million English-speaking West Indians these events have linked them with Britain, and because of this relationship social and legal institutions are essentially British.

The West Indian society comprises an upper and middle class with a family structure based on formal marriage, and the mass of the population with a family unit based on the matrifocal household group, resulting from unstable or 'visiting' relationships and common law marriages. Such a household is mother centred, with a close bond existing between mother, daughter and granddaughter, the man's status depending largely on his ability to provide financial support. The foundations for this type of organisation seem to have been laid during slavery. As a slave the man was forbidden to marry, though he was free to mate, this freedom lending itself easily to the establishment of unstable relationships. The children of such relationships were the lawful property of the owner of the slave mother, who with her child could be disposed of at will by her master. It is easy to see how, under these circumstances, the woman acted as the sole permanent element of the slave family, a position existing in many West Indian households today.

Education

The colonial policy of education, when this was provided, was that for the masses education should be limited to the elementary stage. As secondary education had to be paid for, it was available for a small elite only. Education became, therefore, a divisive instrument, keeping rigid barriers between primary and secondary levels, at the same time providing on the one hand an inferior type of education up to the elementary stage for the masses, and on the other an education oriented to the English public school system extending through the secondary school years for the elite.

For the masses, therefore, the educational system, though following the English pattern, seemed never to have been revised during the colonial days. The pupil-teacher system which ensured the provision of cheap labour has been replaced in recent years by a local teachers' training system, under which teachers are exposed to and trained in modern teaching methods, though often after training they are faced with the difficulty of adjusting to existing classroom situations.

Classes are very large, averaging about sixty or seventy; schools are usually overcrowded, particularly those controlled by religious bodies, although those more recently built compare favourably with the modern type in this country. The older schools are generally the dormitory type buildings, which permit children of one class to see, hear and even touch those of another. It is easy to appreciate why in this type of environment children are encouraged to speak in class only when spoken to. Teaching usually takes the form of group instruction, with the whole class representing the group, often repeating in unison as required by the teacher.

Few classes have access to more than one reader a year. This text is bought by the parent, and it is not unusual for some children to go without the text book for the school year in any one class, because of the parents' inability to buy this book. The absence of supplementary readers implies that:

1   The class moves ahead methodically as a group from lesson 1 to the end of the book, no consideration being given to the individual differences. This method could create boredom for the child whose reading ability and rate of progress exceed that of the rest of the class.
2   The child's vocabulary is limited to that provided by the one book used in class.
3   Reading can hardly take place for pleasure.

Teaching of reading is therefore rather formally carried out, and often the main method used is repetition by the children of the teacher's example in class. Very little use is made of the phonic method but the alphabet method is popular as a means of facilitating spelling; the use of this method has no doubt been noticed by teachers of recently arrived West Indian children.

In these large schools education depends largely on reproduction of examples set by the teacher to her class, rather than encouragement of thinking or the production of ideas on the part of the child. Reproduction of work is encouraged by parents at home, where often the child is required to repeat an example of the day's work for their approval. Educational standards vary from territory to territory.

Language

In addition to the standard English spoken by the upper and middle classes, each island has its own creole language; the word 'creole' being used to denote belonging to the island. The particular type of creole spoken on an island depends largely on the country of origin of the earliest colonists and slave owners. In Trinidad, for example, the creole language is strongly influenced by Spanish and French, the popular creole construction 'It have a shop down the road' being reminiscent of the French construction.

Many old English words survive in the creole language, for example 'fowl' for 'chicken', 'beast' for 'mule' or 'horse', 'breadkind' for 'food', 'to carry one along the way' for 'to accompany'. Other words not in modern usage are retained as well. The West Indian child would mean 'tap' if she says 'pipe', she means 'puddle' if she says 'pool', 'grip' would be used instead of 'suitcase', 'waiter' instead of 'tray', 'rap' instead of 'knock'.

The other main influence on the structure of the creole language was African, but this influence seems to have varied with the size and physical features of the island. For example, in small compact Barbados, in which there was a relatively large group of white servants who came into contact with the African slave, the influence of African on the creole language was not as pronounced as in Jamaica. In this larger mountainous island contact between the black and the relatively small number of poor whites was less easy, and the influence of the African language on the spoken creole was much stronger. In addition to the vocabulary, the African language affected pronunciation and grammar, and influenced the character and mood of the creole language, sound playing an integral part, and gesture concretising thought as well as supplementing a limited vocabulary.

For these reasons, for the child recently arrived from a rural area of any of the West Indian Islands where creole is the most common and sometimes only means of verbal communication, comprehension of the English spoken in the classroom here as a means of instruction would at first be difficult. Gradually, as time passes and the child grows accustomed to this new speech pattern, it becomes easier for him to follow instruction and so assimilate knowledge.

Stresses of the newly arrived child

Stresses related mainly to school

Perhaps of greater concern to a teacher of West Indian children is the boy or girl of about nine or ten years of age who arrives in England to begin or continue his schooling here. Given the difference in educational systems the child who has attended school regularly and shown steady progress in the West Indies should, all things being equal, be able to apply himself intelligently to mechanical problems in arithmetic, and to read and spell adequately; however he would find it difficult to express his thoughts freely in written form, because this particular area is often neglected in the West Indies. For such a child the transition period at school varies according to his ability to adapt to the new situation and unfamiliar requirements; adjustment to the new educational system slowly takes place. But the child who had been previously exposed to little or no formal education in the West Indies, who has come from a rural area where the creole language is the most common and perhaps the only means of communication, would experience extreme difficulty in understanding the English spoken at school and great anxiety in trying to cope with this new means of communication. In this situation learning is intimately related to and highly dependent on the ability to interpret what is heard, think about it and then translate his own answer from the creole to the formal English required in the classroom. The sudden change from thinking in terms of the creole language to thinking in terms of formal English makes this process slower and creates for the child the type of anxieties which could affect his own communication. Teachers of West Indian children will no doubt recall to mind the child who, soon after joining the class, spoke very little or not at all. An example of such a case was Elaine who came to join her mother here after an absence of about nine years. She had very little previous schooling when she first attended school here, was placed with a group of six weak readers every morning in the care of a sympathetic teacher. For months her reaction to school was one of complete silence, even though she seemed more relaxed in the small group. In the parent class she was seen not to smile or talk to anyone. Gradually Elaine began to whisper to her friends in the small group, and finally spoke to her teacher after months of silence. She described in detail her experience on arriving in England, how she was told that she was coming to join her mother here, how utterly confused she felt when she could not identify her mother when two women approached her. It is significant that the first time Elaine spoke to her teacher, she mentioned what had bothered her from the time of her arrival here. What seems even more significant is the fact that, although she needed to talk about her anxieties to someone she saw as a friend, she dared not speak until she was sure that her attempts would be acceptable. However once this venture was made Elaine gained more confidence and was seen to speak not only in the small group, but in the larger class as well.

Stresses related mainly to the home environment

Although adjusting to school may in most cases be stressful, the newly arrived child can also experience many anxieties relating to the home situation. No two children's situations are the same, but a common factor among West Indian children is overcrowding. Parents tend to live in multiple-occupied houses where some facilities have to be shared. If the families occupying these houses are on very friendly terms, the child has to adjust to the behaviour of this 'extended family' within a new setting. If the families are not friendly, the effects of adjustment to the negative attitudes of his immediate neighbours could be damaging, and affect his work and relationships at school.

Many children come to join a mother whom they have not seen for years, or rather have never known (some were sent photographs). In many cases adjustment to reality could be stressful; expectations having been idealistic and totally different. Situations like these could be further complicated by the presence of a new father who is seen as a powerful stranger, unlike the indulgent grandfather left in the West Indies. The greatest threat to the newcomer however could be the younger children who are usually more secure in their relationship with their parents and whose very self assurance and security arouse jealousy and dislike in the newcomer. An example of the struggle for adjustment was seen in the behaviour of Michael. He joined his mother after an absence of about eight years, during which time he lived with his grandmother in Jamaica. His mother, now married, had four younger lively boys; Michael, having joined the family whose varying roles had already been established, felt a misfit when at home, where he gave no indication of his feelings until he disappeared one Saturday afternoon, later being returned home by the police. His relationship with his mother quickly deteriorated because of this behaviour and gradually the effects of his unhappiness at home were seen at school, where hitherto he had shown signs of settling down. In contrast to his silent withdrawn behaviour at home, Michael now displayed at school unsolicited anger which later gave way to violent temper tantrums. Eventually as the tantrums became more frequent, Michael was withdrawn from school and placed in a small unit for maladjusted children, where after a year he returned to normal school.

Poor adjustment to the home does not involve only the newcomers' attitude to the established family: that of the family to the child just arrived is of equal importance. Parents who are unaware of the importance of the child's emotional needs could do much damage, and we shall see later how the West Indian mother, quite unwittingly, gives the impression of depriving the growing child of the affection he grew accustomed to accepting as a matter of course. For the newcomer, the home, and more often the school, becomes the focal point for the release of tensions which result from the combination and interaction of frustrating experiences – disorientation, absence of those he loves, loneliness and loss of friends, change of climate, bewilderment at being in a new school with its strange language sounds, fear of the future. All these considerations crowd the mind and in his total confusion the child seems unable to talk of his feelings.

Let us now consider the child who does not overtly show signs of emotional stress, but who nevertheless must experience extreme stress in the classroom because of his gross retardation. Many West Indian children join the English school at the junior school age having had little or no previous schooling in the West Indies. Unlike his more literate counterpart who would be required merely to accommodate to a different educational system, he would have no academic foundation on which to build; reading particularly would be very poor. Most local authorities now run reception centres where newcomers attend classes for a given period of time; but unless the function of such a class is clearly thought out, the newcomer gains little or no help academically. Such classes should aim at bridging the gap created by the child's loss of schooling over the years, as well as fitting him to take up his position in his own age group at school; failure to achieve this merely helps to create pockets of semi-literate West Indian children throughout the English school. Ideally language classes should be set up to run concurrently with the child's parent class, children being withdrawn at certain intervals for individual help, and at the same time being able to participate in class activities such as games, music, singing, painting, etc. Tape recorders would be of great help in pointing to the difference in intonation and speech pattern of the new arrivals. For the teacher who has to help such a child within the classroom it is important to remember that the new word taught should always be reinforced with a drawing or picture of the object representing the word. The writer found that even with children who have lived here for some years the word 'coal' is almost always misunderstood for 'cold'. This is because in the West Indies 'coal' is a plural noun (coal(s)) and again 'd' at the end of the word is not often sounded.

Stress of the infant school child

Stress related to the cultural background of the parent

The West Indian family arriving in Britain is usually received by relatives and friends who tend to live in twilight areas; families move about from one such area to another, often because of opportunities for employment, sometimes in search of better accommodation and cheaper rents. Children, especially the newly arrived, could be exposed to stress as a result of frequent movement from one area to another; in many cases previous adjustment to school achieved over a long period could be affected by such a move, causing a regression in behaviour. Children seem to experience the same effects of disorientation in moving from one area of a large city to another, as from the West Indies to England.

West Indians tend to be unaware of the importance of the emotional needs of the growing child. Children are fondled and fussed over while they remain babies; as the child makes his first step across the room or utters his first word the entire family rejoices with him, and he is the recipient of love and affection. But as he leaves the stage of babyhood behind and approaches his school age, the affection he had hitherto accepted as part of his right is seen to be suddenly withdrawn and bestowed on the new-born baby. It seems therefore that with the West Indian mother the degree of affection shown to her child varies with the amount of physical care the child requires, the fast growing child being pushed out from the inner circle of love which includes mother and baby only. In the West Indies the matrifocal family organisation caters for this dilution of relationship, some of the growing child's emotional needs being met by another member of the extended family, particularly the maternal grandmother and an aunt. In England, in the nuclear family organisation, children are made more aware of what may appear to them a reduction of their mother's affection and even before starting school tend to make more demands for her attention and love. The mother's inability to understand the need for these demands could lead to a breakdown in relationship between herself and the growing child, whose behaviour therefore reflects that of the emotionally deprived child. Conditions of living tend to accentuate what would be regarded by the mother as bad behaviour, and slapping becomes the only form of correction. One calls to mind the case of Winston, born in London to West Indian parents; he started school after his mother had given birth to her second child. At school, he was immediately seen to be a source of trouble, unable to cope with the free activity in the classroom. He tended to snatch toys away from the other children, rush about disturbing others, and generally disrupted the class. A visit to Winston's home revealed that he was expected to accept replacement by the young baby without question and that he had spent all of his life in conditions which did not permit him to learn to play without arousing anxiety in the household. After some months he settled at school, a change in his behaviour coinciding with removal from the flat his family occupied to better accommodation.

How could the teacher meet the needs of a child coming from such a home environment?

In some infant schools there is more opportunity for teachers to discuss difficult cases with health visitors who visit the homes. Children who come from homes where the value of play is unknown to parents could be introduced to school gradually, spending one or two afternoons only during the first week in which they start school. Parents should be encouraged to attend with their children on these days; in this way they could be helped towards changing their attitude towards play.

Stresses related directly to baby-minding conditions

The research by Pless and Hood (1967) pointed to the fact that a higher proportion of West Indians relied on substitute care for their children from an early age. The Gregory study in Paddington, 1967–1968, found that West Indian mothers tended to make use of both registered and unregistered baby-minders for their children; that generally the latter were more poorly housed and had more domestic commitments, though a number of the former lived in more crowded and unsatisfactory circumstances. Few of the unregistered minders provided stimulating care and some of the registered minders provided no toys and had nowhere for the children to play. Generally the impression gained was that quite a large number of children were confined to the one room used by the minder.

The West Indian mother's reasons for using substitute care for her child at an early age are closely related to her own home circumstances; if she is the sole supporter of the home it is necessary for her to earn: if there is a father in the home, she must try to add to his contribution if better living accommodation is to be obtained. Her choice of a minder is determined largely by proximity to her own home, the price charged and willingness to fit in with her long working hours. Very little importance is attached to the number of children the baby-minder has in her care, and all that this implies; reliability and personal cleanliness are her main considerations. Because she herself is unaware of the importance of stimulation, derived verbally and through the use of toys, she does not regard this as part of the function of a baby minder.

Baby-minding conditions therefore have far-reaching results on the child's future progress at school; poor verbal stimulation limits the child's vocabulary and lack of play leaves a gap in the child's imaginative experience. The passivity encouraged during the pre-school years by the baby-minder of the many children in her care does not prepare the child for the spontaneous investigation of ideas and acquisition of concepts in the classroom at the age of five. The West Indian child who spends his pre-school years under these conditions represents the culturally deprived children mentioned by Pringle (1969) who 'have lost the educational race long before starting school'. Often these children find themselves at a loss to comprehend what is taking place in the classroom.

But if inadequate intellectual pre-school stimulation places the child at a disadvantage when he starts school, lack of emotional stimulation is an even greater hazard for children of West Indian parents. A report by Dr Prince at a conference held in London, organised by the World Organisation for Early Childhood Education, drew attention to the fact that an increasing number of immigrant children, mostly of West Indian parents, were referred to the psychiatry department of Kings College Hospital and other child guidance clinics, suffering from a condition which at first sight resembles autism. Further investigation of the condition showed, however, that the symptoms of aloofness, apathy and little or no speech reflected maternal deprivation and lack of emotional and intellectual stimulation. What was common among the cases was the fact that the children lived with mothers who felt homesick for their own country as they felt depressed and isolated in their neighbourhood and disillusioned about life in this country. In many cases children were separated from an early age for varying lengths of time during the day from their mothers who worked long hours and who, on returning home, were too exhausted, depressed or busy to give some emotional support to their children. Often parents supported other children left in the West Indies, and so problems of finance were severe. Keith's case is a classic example of the effects of maternal deprivation and limited early stimulation. He was minded out on a daily basis from an early age as his father was a full-time student so his mother had to go out to work. By the time he started school at the age of five it was evident that he was 'different'; he merely sat in class, saying nothing to the other children, not wishing to participate in the classroom activity, verbally or otherwise. On referral to the school psychological service for assessment the possibility of autism or even mental defectiveness was raised. However he was given a place in a small diagnostic unit where he spent more than three years. During this period Keith gradually became less withdrawn and more aware of his surroundings, and at last began talking to his peers and taking a great interest in books and started responding to reading sessions with his teacher. By the time he was eight he was able to take his place in a class for normal children, laughing and talking as children do, an achievement which three years previously one would not have dared hope for. Keith's mother did experience at about the time he was born a feeling of intense loneliness and depression, having had to spend most of her free time alone at home while her husband attended lectures. It seems that during this period she was unable to give adequate emotional stimulation to her child, this deprivation being closely followed by separation, as he was minded out on a daily basis from a very early age.

The behaviour of children who are handicapped because of limited pre-school intellectual stimulation seems to represent one end of a continuum, the other end representing that described by Dr Prince of the child who, because of an absence of emotional stimulation as well, is aloof, almost unable to speak, apathetic, reflecting perhaps the emotional climate in which he lives. Teachers, health visitors and other social workers could assist greatly if they were able to detect this type of behaviour as a reaction to the stress to which the child is exposed, and help not only the child by referral to the local clinics, but the mother or guardian.

Stresses of the adolescent related to continuous retardation in school and a breakdown of relationship with parents

Many West Indian children now attending secondary school are grossly retarded educationally, and are experiencing the effects of continuous retardation at school. Generally they are those who, having joined their parents when of junior school age with little or no previous formal education, have coped with the painful period of adjustment to a previously unknown parent and a new family, while trying at the same time to become a member of the school community. Few children who find difficulty in settling at home are able to show progress at school at the same time, and given the educational gap between them and their contemporaries at school, and the lack of facilities existing in schools for coping with the educational problem that they present, they tend, by and large, to occupy positions at the bottom end of the class. Most of these children are lively, intelligent youngsters, who would be capable of learning at the same rate as their English counterparts, but for the fact that they lack the basic skills in reading and numbers. By the time they reach secondary school and become aware of their continuous failure, they begin to doubt their own ability to improve, and so lose the will to attempt anything new. In some cases school becomes a place they would prefer not to attend.

In most cases realisation of their failure at school is combined with an awareness of their parents' disappointment in their lack of progress. Many West Indian parents send for their children mainly because of the educational opportunities, and so find it difficult to hide their feelings of disappointment and even their criticism as the child's performance at school falls below expectation. In this way they show little or no insight into the difficulties which the child must overcome before he becomes adjusted to school.

The case of Frank comes to mind. His uncle, having lived here for some years, felt that he could be of some help to his sister in the West Indies by sending for one of her sons. Frank was chosen to attend school in England, to avail himself of the educational opportunities. Unfortunately no thought had been given to the fact that Frank would have had to adjust to the life in England, one which was far removed from that which he was accustomed to, one which involved the absence of all his loved ones. Frank had had little previous schooling, and was attending a secondary school when I saw him; attendance at the remedial class in school had helped to raise his reading age to about eight years, but he showed no desire to participate in school activities. His uncle was extremely critical of the fact that he had shown little progress after nearly two years at school and seemed to place little importance on the fact that in strong contrast to the West Indian situation, Frank now lived an extremely lonely life, often returning home to an empty flat in the evenings, and sometimes retiring at night without seeing his uncle or communicating with anyone else in the house.

Lack of parents' awareness of the need for adolescents to conform to the group norm would lead to disapproval on the part of the West Indian parent, and even a breakdown of relationship between parent and child. Parents tend to remain West Indian in outlook, particularly with regard to the authority they seek to exercise over their children and the standards of behaviour expected of them. Relationship between parent and child could sometimes be reminiscent of the Victorian era, with the former giving the impression that the latter should 'love, honour and obey' a severe and chastising parent. In the West Indies this type of upbringing, though regarded by the adolescent as harsh, is accepted as part of growing up; but in this society the adolescent, realising that his English counterpart is not subject to such treatment, objects strenuously, and a clash of personality follows. The West Indian adolescent seems to be caught between identifying with a world belonging to his parents and with one which he regards his own. Most adolescents, in their bid to assert their independence, experience a period of poor relationship with their parents, but with the West Indian in England this experience is made more crucial by the clash of the two worlds of which he is a part, particularly since he is aware that as a West Indian acceptance by the group with which he identifies is limited to a few rather than the wider more general adolescent world.

The stresses of the West Indian child are closely related to the conditions under which he lives, his parents' cultural background, and his own attempts to come to terms with these, first within the framework of the English educational system, and later as one of a minority group within the wider adult community. Any attempt to help the child to make full use of his potential at school should take this socio-cultural background into consideration. There is no doubt that for the child of three to four years, we should think in terms of offering him an opportunity to enquire more of his immediate environment, to acquire concepts, and to learn to enjoy play experience without arousing anxiety in himself and others around him; in this way we could help to prepare him for the type of education to which he would be exposed at the age of five. This immediately suggests the need for more nursery classes in the twilight areas. For the newcomers there should be a more positive attempt on the part of local authorities to integrate children into the school system; this could only be achieved through the establishment of well-planned language units with facilities for providing for children for at least a year, and opportunity for them to continue to attend after this period if necessary, while attending ordinary school. Without such an establishment we run the risk of exposing children to complete bewilderment throughout their school life, or of effecting a hasty and often unnecessary transfer to a school for the educationally subnormal and creating maladjustment in this way. We also need to think in terms of planning for the children now in the lowest stream at secondary school, the type of curriculum which would aim at exploiting their particular interests, with emphasis on subjects like woodwork, metalwork, handicraft, art, so that through these subjects the basic skills in reading, writing and numbers could be acquired. For this group particularly we would need a reorganisation of the traditional remedial class within the school, if we hope to sustain their interest in class, and reduce the degree of difficult behaviour seen at school. If we accept unreservedly that the West Indian child is capable of good intellectual functioning, in spite of his sometimes seemingly gross retardation, we could help him to overcome his feelings of intellectual inadequacy which he must experience after long-standing retardation at school. Unless we plan in this way, and aim to succeed, we run the risk of sending out of school into the adult world adolescents whose limited education may well make it more difficult for them to bear the frustration that they could experience as a result of living in a society in which they are not wholly accepted.

INJURY-PRONE CHILDREN
Lindy Burton

Occasionally teachers are confronted with a child who, though apparently reasonable and intelligent, nevertheless shows a persistent tendency to injure or destroy himself. Such children get caught up in frequent minor accidents, for example catching their fingers in doors and windows, falling in the play-ground, or running into obstacles. Sometimes they engage in brawling and fighting, getting bruised and scarred in the process. From time to time more serious disasters occur, such as falls resulting in fractured limbs, or road accidents necessitating in-patient treatment in hospital.

To some extent minor accidents are common to all children and indeed few of us have escaped into adulthood without the odd scar as a reminder of our own early exploits. Childhood is undoubtedly the time when the individual is most injury prone, probably as a result of his own neural, motor, and intellectual immaturity.

What then makes an injury-prone child so special? I would suggest that it is not the type of injury he sustains, nor the circumstances in which he sustains it; rather it is the persistence with which he is able to hurt himself bodily, even when placed in a well controlled environment. In contrast to the majority of children who suffer only the odd scratch or bruise, the injury-prone child regularly presents an array of self inflicted hurts.

Factors contributing to injury proneness

Many factors may contribute to a child's tendency to accidental self-injury. Sometimes he may be placed in an environment which is so hazardous that despite himself he will sustain hurt. Imagine, for example, a pre-school child who is regularly left alone in a room with an unguarded fire, a stove with projecting pan handles, and a cupboard full of interesting and toxic substances. The possibility of his sustaining harm will be much greater than that of a comparable child, carefully supervised, in a home from which all obvious dangers have been excluded.

Sometimes a child's injuries may stem from his inability to appreciate normal hazards or overcome them on his own. Inherent factors such as impaired coordination, inadequate perception or general intellectual retardation may contribute to this. Most usually such handicapped children receive education in special schools or centres, where school buildings and services are adapted to meet their special needs. At home extra supervision is essential.

At other times a tendency to accidental self-injury is only explicable in terms of the child's general unsettledness and underlying personality needs. Such children may be quite capable of caring for themselves, intelligent enough to perceive danger, and placed in a fairly well controlled environment – such as a school classroom – yet repeatedly they manage to hurt themselves. The injuries stem directly from their need to assert themselves, often in the face of adult authority, or conversely from their desire for sympathy and attention. Often such children are constitutionally hyper-active, over-responsive to stress of even the most trivial nature, and display an inordinate need for stimulation and an impulsive lack of concern. Understandably they are difficult children to teach and, whilst normal in intelligence, may well be retarded in basic school subjects.

When a careful assessment of such children is made, it is often found that they have stressful home backgrounds. Their parents are frequently over-burdened by their own problems, and consequently have little time to consider their children or assist them in their general development. As a result these children injure themselves in an attempt to gain the sympathy necessary for their personality growth. Alternatively the accidents may form part of a retaliatory pattern against a generally unsympathetic environment. Repeated accidents express the child's own frustration, and his preoccupation with personal problems. When placed in difficult circumstances such children fail to perceive danger simply because they are too busy thinking of other – to them, more essential – things.

Accident-proneness therefore represents a temporarily variable state of mind in which the individual becomes so absorbed in his personal pre-occupations that he fails to take care in difficult circumstances. When the accident occurs he is given the opportunity to assuage both his need for attention and also for retaliation against uncaring authority. In addition the incident affords him an opportunity for escaping, albeit only for a short time, the problems which confront him.

Theories relating to injury proneness

The concept of injury proneness resulting from personality problems is not a new one. As early as 1914 Freud (*Psychopathology of Everyday Life*) made the suggestion that an accident might not be due solely to unpredictable and uncontrollable external forces but rather to unconscious psychological factors subserving deep-rooted personality needs. He quoted numerous examples of accidents sustained by adult patients, which could only be regarded as 'unconsciously purposive' (Menninger 1936). Later in his *Collected Papers* (Volume III, 1925) Freud described an accident as an 'in-direct attempt at suicide'. Freud, and other psychoanalysts writing at the time, offered no explanation of the personality mechanisms underlying these indirect attempts at suicide. But from the examples they cited it seems reasonable to suppose that they viewed the root cause as guilt produced by non-permissible longings – for example, for sex or aggression – ameliorated only by self-punishment. In other words, the individual, wishing to do something which he felt was wrong, punished himself for this guilty longing by hurting himself.

Karl Menninger (1936) added to this theory by stressing the notion that frequent involvement in accidents may be a periodic payment for the continued indulgence in forbidden erotic and aggressive tendencies. In addition, Menninger suggested that accidents might be caused by a desire for sympathy.

Eighteen years after Freud's initial consideration of the subject Melanie Klein (1932) suggested that accidents in childhood might also be motivated in the same way. She quoted the case of a three year old girl called Trude who, following the birth of a baby sister, was burdened by sexual and aggressive longings directed at her parents. Trude exhibited aggressive behaviour towards her parents, coupled with extreme fear of retribution, and 'used to manage to hurt herself in some way almost every time before she came for her analytic hour'.

Ackerman and Chichester (1936) extended the idea of purposive accidents in childhood. They stressed the notion that such children are not fearless children who can see no purpose in caution, on the contrary 'they often have more fear, but also more unexpressed hatred and guilt than the average child'.

These authors advanced the idea that accidental self-injury fulfils two functions in the economy of the child's personality. Primarily, it serves to disguise the child's own hostility towards another person, and the guilt occasioned by this hostility. They argue that children learn very early on that it is not permissible to strike out directly against others, and they argue that such impulses are often converted into self-attacks. Secondarily, they reason that accidents enable the child to gain some sort of reward, for example, avoiding an unpleasant task or gaining a special treat or attention and sympathy. In most cases of self-injury they suggest that more than a single motive or purpose is served – the injury meeting several personality needs.

They quote the case of a twelve year old socially maladjusted girl, educationally retarded, with a history of sexual misdemeanours, an arm badly scarred from an accident, and deserted by her mother at six years of age. She hurt herself daily at school.

'She frequently injured herself as an expression of her anger toward another person. She did to herself what she wished to do to another. In addition the self-injuries appeared to be a punishment for her sexual phantasies for which she felt overwhelmed with guilt. Her conscience would not permit her any form of sexual indulgence without coincident severe punishment.'

Flanders Dunbar (1944) put forward the theory that accident-prone persons have great difficulty in coming to terms with authority. She emphasised that such individuals are essentially striving for independence and autonomy outside authority relationships and they attempt to avoid conflict with authority wherever possible, although not by submission.

She studied 1,600 adults who had sustained fractures as a result of accidents and found that eighty per cent of these cope with day to day problems '. . . by focusing their values on immediate concrete experience, striving to find satisfactions and security outside the authoritarian hierarchy and avoiding any marked submission or domination in vocational or social roles . . .'. When however these '. . . defences fail and conflict with authority becomes unavoidable, the accident happens. Aggressiveness may break out in an act which appears to punish the victim or those responsible for his frustration or both. Or it may come near enough to the surface to cause the kind of confusion which leaves the person defenceless in the danger situation normally encountered from day to day'.

In summary, we may say that the theories constructed to explain accident proneness repeatedly stress the existence of an inordinate need for aggression or self-assertion in the individual's personality structure. It is suggested that the individual's need to react aggressively against authority is accompanied by a fear of reprisal, a feeling of personal guilt, and a need to make retribution.

Consequently, the accident-prone child is thought to be a fearful child, obsessed with the problems of maintaining a truce with hated authority figures. An accident is thought to occur when open conflict appears inevitable. The injury sustained serves both to punish the guilty aggressor and symbolically to punish the authority figure against whom his aggression is directed. Secondly, it enables the child to gain attention, sympathy or other rewards.

Whilst no mention is made in the theoretical literature of the parents of injury-prone children, the repeated stress on the punitiveness of the authority figure would suggest that there may well be much amiss in the parent-child relationship.

Previous studies of injury-prone children

By comparison with the vast number of studies relating to injury proneness in adults, there exist relatively few objective assessments of injury-prone children.

Perhaps this paucity of observations is due to the fact that children's injuries are rarely as socially disruptive as those of adults and are consequently more easily ignored.

Also, because of his dual existence at home and in school, the true extent of a child's injury proneness may never be detected. Teachers may dismiss cuts and bruises sustained at home as being caused by careless parents, whilst parents may attribute injuries sustained at school to the pugnacity of other children. Neither side may stop to total up the true extent of the injuries or appreciate how remarkable they are.

A further explanation may lie, as Finch (1951) points out, in the fact that for the adult means of dealing with inner and outer drives and needs have become much more rigid and unchanging than for the child. Consequently adults may be more easily recognisable as injury-prone due to personality difficulties.

The first empirical study of injury-prone children was made by Elizabeth Mechen Fuller in 1947. She observed sixty one children attending the University of Minnesota Nursery School. From her observations she was able to establish the fact that a small percentage of both boys and girls are significantly more injury-prone than their peers. She noted a direct relationship between children who got hurt and those who inflicted injuries on other children. She concluded '. . . part of the proneness pattern is the habit of getting into certain injury laden situations which the non-prone child would avoid'.

The children were compared with one another using the Haggerty–Olson–Wickman Behaviour Rating Schedules. An analysis of the results suggested that the injury-prone child was more impulsive, obstinate, highly strung, overactive, dare-devil, assertive and insolent than other children of his age. He was also a child with slightly more than average problem tendencies.

Four years after her first study Fuller, working with Helen Baune, assessed the injury proneness of a class of seven to eight year olds in the University of Minnesota Elementary School. They found that as a class these children received five times as many injuries as any other class in the same school. Many of the injuries involved conflicts with other children, and the authors were forced to conclude that the class group structure was incompatible with and reflecting unhappiness in the school environment. The unhappy atmosphere within the class was undoubtedly an important factor in the injury proneness syndrome.

When the authors considered individual children they noted that usually the least popular children – the 'fringers' – with the highest behaviour problem tendency were most prone to injury.

To some extent these results must be viewed with caution because adequate control subjects were not used and the authors freely admit that the group chosen was non-normal both in terms of intelligence, and in socio-economic status, both of which were well above average.

Another school study made by Birnbach in 1948 compared fifty five accident-repeating children with forty eight accident-free children, both from a junior high school in New York. Birnbach found that the accident-prone boys were more aggressive and exhibited a greater tendency to control situations by force. They were described by their teachers as less polite, less reliable, less hard working and generally more inadequate than the accident-free group. Accident-repeating children were physically stronger and with a better health record than the control group, but their knowledge of safety precautions was less, and twenty per cent of them came from broken homes.

Vita Krall (1953) compared a group of thirty two five to eight year old accident-prone children with a group of carefully matched non accident-prone children. Both groups were asked on two occasions to make up a story about a doll family living in a doll's house. Both their behaviour and their use of words were noted.

The results suggested that accident-repeating children displayed more aggression – particularly verbal aggression – than accident-free children. They were also less inhibited and expressed aggression more quickly than accident-free children. The accident-repeaters showed more commands, threats and prohibitions and more affection seeking behaviour than their age mates. They also displayed more activity. In addition they were more often from larger families and broken homes. They tended to be somewhat later in birth order and showed more school transfers than usual. Also they were more frequently known to home and school counsellors, suggesting more previous problem behaviour.

Krall concluded that her findings agreed with the clinical assumption that accident-repeating children tended to come from homes where there is more parental dominance, less affection and more evidence of physical strength.

A pilot study of nine accident-repeating children completed by Langford in 1953 suggested that the accident-repeaters seemed unable to face up to or deal with problem situations, and after the accident showed a surprising lack of concern regarding their injuries. Langford suggested that accident-involved children might have faulty parental relationships and might be used to searching for substitute affection.

He suggested that there might be three types of accident-prone child:

1 An impulsive, overactive child, who reacts poorly to stress, becoming disorganised. When stressed, he disregards, or fails to recognise, danger signals. This type of child is often more popular with adults than with other children, and over-asserts himself to achieve his ambitions;

2 Also an assertive child, but this time one who is emotionally immature. Lacking supervision from his parents, he gangs up with other children and becomes involved in dangerous escapades;

3 A child who is hostile and resentful towards his rejecting parents.

In 1957 Stiles, in an unpublished doctoral thesis, concluded that accident-repeating children could be distinguished from accident-free children by their general impulsiveness, and tendency to motoric response. She also discerned a decided, though unmet, need for love and affection amongst them, produced, she felt, by poor parent-child relationships. She concluded that accidents might be reduced if parents and children were helped to accept each other.

The parental situation was further examined by Backett and Johnston in 1959. They compared a group of 101 children involved in road accidents with a non accident-involved group and looked into family structure, size and organisation. Several factors were considered significant in determining accidents. They were:

1 maternal preoccupation of some kind – work, children, or pregnancy;

2 illness in the mother or in a near member of the family;

3 overcrowding, less protection during play and possibly even an absence of elementary play facilities.

They concluded that where the domestic standards of the parents were low, accidents were more likely to take place.

Further emphasis was placed on the faulty parental relationships of accident-involved children by Marcus and his colleagues, working in 1960. They compared three groups of carefully matched children aged six to ten years, one of which was accident-prone, one accident-free, and one enuretic.

They concluded that the accident-prone children were involved in fewer family activities than the other two groups of children, and their parents were often anxious and insecure. All the accident-prone children had problems in adjustment, and Marcus concluded that they displayed 'a hyperactivity which may be constitutional, and a tendency to express tension through physical activity, and disturbed family relationships'.

In 1967, Salwen found that boys of seven to eleven who were frequently involved in accidents tended to be impulsive, and also performed erratically on motor tasks.

Mannheimer and Mellinger (1967) confirmed this finding, when comparing four to eighteen year olds with high accident liability, with classmates with low accident liability. They showed that the higher a boy's accident liability, the more likely he was to be considered daring, active, exploring and extraverted. All these characteristics would increase his exposure to potential hazards. Equally, boys with high accident liability tended to have characteristics that impared their ability to cope with hazardous situations, for example, a general lack of self-control, and a tendency to be careless, inattentive, and easily distracted. In addition, such children tended to be hostile to parents, teachers and peers, were thought of as show-offs, who always wanted to win, and tended to be impulsive and angry when frustrated. They were often maladjusted, and had frequently been referred to school counsellors or psychiatrists for help.

Mannheimer and Mellinger found that for girls accident liability was often related to a desire for attention, and in contrast to the boys, they were not over-rebellious.

My own study of children involved in road accidents (1968) bears out many of the findings of these previous studies. I should emphasise that I made no attempt to establish a proneness pattern (that is, a pattern of regular accident involvement) on the part of the children I studied. I was content merely to investigate the personality factors underlying even a single involvement in a road accident. However there is some evidence (Dunbar, 1944) to support the assumption that individuals sustaining one major accident are statistically more likely to have another, and the personality dynamics precipitating one accident are essentially the same as those observed in people who are injury-prone. My own study offered some degree of validation for this assumption.

I compared twenty accident-involved children, with peers matched carefully in terms of intelligence, attainment, socio-economic background and position within the family. Both groups were tested with a projective personality test (the T.A.T.) and teachers were asked to assess the children's classroom behaviour, using Bristol Social Adjustment Guides. Mothers of all the children were seen and answered questions relating to their behaviour at home, and their early developmental history. They were also assessed in terms of their own personality and their attitudes to child upbringing.

The accident-involved children were more assertive and unsettled than their peers. In school they tended to be more restless, more easily distracted from school work, and they behaved inconsequentially. They were often attention-seekers, both towards adults and other children, and they showed a greater degree of hostility than their peers.

At home, the accident-involved children had always appeared problematic. During infancy they tended to sleep badly, they cried excessively and they were apathetic feeders. Later they appeared prone to temper tantrums, they tended to roam or wander away from home and they got up to all kinds of escapades and fighting. At the time of their accident the most significant problem behaviours reported at home were impatience, temper tantrums, and inordinately demanding behaviour.

In terms of their underlying personality needs, the accident-involved children displayed a greater need for assertion than their peers, and also a significantly greater fear of domination. The stories they recounted in response to the thematic pictures shown to them suggested that they viewed their parents as threatening and punitive. They often exhibited a wish to escape from the parent-child situation, and showed evidence of considerable, but often repressed, hostility.

It was possible to establish a direct relationship between the child's need for assertion, as measured by the personality test, and the general level of frustration in the home. The more frustrating the domestic environment, the more assertive was the child. There was evidence of considerable stress in the accident-involved children's backgrounds. Significantly more of their mothers had rejected their pregnancy, and had been more frequently sick or emotionally disturbed during it. To some extent these disturbances were explicable in terms of the stresses with which the mothers themselves were coping. Some of them showed evidence of chronic – often nervous – illness, which had been present before the child's conception and might well have made them unwilling to conceive. Some homes were without a father – due to death, separation or distant employment. In many cases the mothers compensated for these stresses by becoming over-dominant themselves. Their personal hardships heightened their own level of frustration and consequent irritability. When faced with an irritable, stressful baby their initial attitude of rejection was accentuated, and mother and child became linked in a spiral of unsatisfactory relationships.

In these circumstances, the children often felt unwanted and actively sought out substitute relationships. Many accidents were preceded by events which might well have diverted the mother's attention yet further from the child, and consequently increased his feeling of rejection. Accidents therefore might well represent attempts at wresting sympathy and the required love from an indifferent environment.

Equally the accident might represent an attempt on the child's part to cope with feelings of hostility. These children felt hostile towards those in their environment and at the same time felt unable to express their feelings openly. Consequently they may have directed their hostile feelings inwards, a 'trend commonly evident in small children' (Ackerman and Chidester, 1936). They punished themselves in lieu of someone else. Indeed, in a subtle way, the accident afforded the child a means of punishing the unloving parent, by further adding to her stress – and in a manner which was beyond her remonstration.

Sometimes the accidents seemed to occur as attempts to avoid conflict or open hostility with the parents. The accident diverted the parents' attention away from a childish transgression, which would otherwise have been punishable.

Finally, it was possible to detect some evidence of constitutional hyperactivity and slight neural impairment in the accident-involved children. Such impairment might well have been caused by the high degree of maternal stress in the later stages of pregnancy. Such stress supposedly produces excessive emotion, and this in turn is thought to cause secretions which produce an imbalance of chemical agents, which 'may cross the placenta and, though causing no microscopic abnormality may somehow affect those developing neural tissues of the foetus which govern behaviour in later life.' (Leading article, *British Medical Journal*, April 1964.) Environmental stress would undoubtedly heighten this constitutional restlessness, producing the impulsive, demanding, inconsequential behaviour noted in the children at home and in school.

The stresses underlying injury proneness in childhood

From the studies cited above there appears a fairly comprehensive description of the stresses underlying injury proneness in childhood. Quite obviously each child will present a unique constellation of such stresses. The degree of importance which may be attributed to any one causative factor will, therefore, vary from individual to individual, and within the same individual from time to time.

Briefly, however, the essential elements underlying injury proneness would seem to be:

1 A constitutional hyperactivity or a restlessness which is apparent from birth. Such children tend to be poor sleepers and given to excessive crying. They may crawl and walk earlier than average and when fully mobile, show a tendency to wander from home. In school they will be easily distracted, and display only limited powers of concentration. They may show little reasoning ability, particularly in terms of their own actions, and tend to be impulsive and inconsequential.

2 These children may appear over-reactive to environmental stress. Again, this tendency may be inherent rather than acquired. Consequently even minor frustrations may produce excessive behavioural responses.

3   Injury-prone children may view themselves as unloved and may actively seek out substitute affection from teachers and other pupils. Such attention seeking may take the form of accepting dares or endeavouring to prove their strength and courage. As a result these children may be lured unthinkingly into injury-laden situations. In addition, indulgence in injury may produce the longed-for sympathy and attention.

4   Such children may appear unduly assertive, possibly because of their need to overcome the frustration of feeling unloved, and also because of their inherent restlessness. The assertiveness may also stem from anger engendered by an unaccepting domestic environment. They may wish to hit back at adults and other children.

5   The dominance so frequently displayed by parents of injury-prone children may make the children fearful and apprehensive of retribution. When conflicts with teacher or parent are imminent they may tend to injure themselves, as a means of circumventing the expected punishment.

6   Finally, one may deduce that injury-prone children come most often from stressful domestic backgrounds. They may lack proper supervision and training, have mothers who are coping with personal ill-health, or are rearing their families without the support of a father within the home. Accidents may occur when domestic circumstances become excessively stressful, diverting the mother's attention still further from the child.

Perhaps these points are best illustrated by some short case histories.

History 1

James was a ten year old boy of normal intelligence who appeared very much on the fringe of classroom activities, and somewhat retarded in basic school subjects. He tended to have few friends, and he was constantly at war with those he had. After each fight he blamed the other child, cried profusely, and endeavoured to elicit sympathy from the teacher by showing any cuts or bruises he had sustained. He tended to hang round the teacher and on his 'good' days would constantly bring drawings and work to be looked at. In addition, in school, he was frequently falling in the playground or getting splinters embedded in his fingers or knees.

At home James was a tearful and resentful child, rarely at peace and frequently shouting at his younger sisters for trivial offences. His relationship with his father appeared poor. He was cowed by his violent temper, and seemed fearful of approaching him. With his mother he seemed more ambivalent, sometimes approaching her with his models and drawings, and sometimes weeping and shouting criticisms of all around. He was constantly getting hurt and crying for sympathy – only to be cuffed and then cuddled.

James had been conceived premaritally and understandably his mother had been distressed during her pregnancy. She was uncertain whether she should marry, and when in fact she did, things were by no means smooth. There were financial problems and she became sick and tense. After James's birth she became depressed, and retreated within herself so that she rarely heard his crying. This tendency persisted throughout his childhood, and from time to time when things became too stressful for her, she withdrew into her own world of silence. At the time of the study she was extremely nervous and heavily sedated. She was coping with severe marital problems, her husband's persistent unemployment, and consequent financial distress. James's proneness to injury appeared a direct means of attracting attention and sympathy from those around him.

History II

Maurice was a thirteen year old boy, of low average intelligence, attending an intermediate school. He was placed in a slow-learning stream. I first met him after he had been knocked down by a car, thereby breaking both legs. This was his second major road accident. The first occurred at the age of eight, when he was run over by a van, fracturing both legs. At the same age Maurice had fallen into a large river, whilst still unable to swim. A passer-by had fished him out.

Maurice was the first of three children conceived shortly after his parent's marriage. The pregnancy was unwelcome, and Maurice's mother had all manner of domestic problems during it. She discovered that her husband was an alcoholic and this, in addition to financial stresses, produced a depression, and later a 'nervous illness' for which she was given sedatives. A kidney infection and, later, high blood pressure disturbed her pregnancy and Maurice was induced three weeks before term. During infancy he was 'cross and gurney. He cried all the time, and never settled. The least noise disturbed him'.

This restlessness and bad temper persisted throughout his childhood. In addition, he tended to roam far and wide and at three years of age was found five miles from home. His sleep habits showed considerable disturbance, and he tended to shout and scream in bed at night.

Maurice's mother was excessively stressed by her husband's alcoholism. He was rarely at home yet 'he neither works nor nothing'. Money was short and she was tired by the effort of bringing up three sons virtually on her own. She and her husband quarrelled constantly, but she knew she could not leave him for she had nowhere else to go. Maurice's accident-proneness seemed to stem from a constitutional over-activity exaggerated by parental stress.

Reducing the stresses of injury-prone children

Every conscientous teacher who is faced with an injury-prone pupil must attempt to assess the stresses underlying the syndrome, and then ameliorate them. Neither task is easy, but genuine attempts to understand and assist may well prove rewarding to both child and adult.

Perhaps the first step should be a proper psychological examination by an educational psychologist. An assessment will be made at this stage of the child's personality needs and his attitudes to home and school. This may well be followed by an interview with the parents, from which a case history will be derived. If the child's behaviour is suggestive of contributory constitutional defect, he may be referred to a child psychiatrist or a neurologist for a complete physical assessment. When the results of all these tests are known it should be possible to understand the child's injury proneness, and devise a programme to counter the stresses underlying it.

Obviously any such programme must take account of the specific factors involved in each individual case, and no two programmes will be exactly alike.

However, in general, one may say that where there seems to be an underlying constitutional element, the child will need as peaceful and as orderly an environment as possible. Sudden changes and over much freedom should be avoided. Consistent discipline is essential. A reasonable communicative attitude on the part of the teacher will go a long way to avoiding overt temper tantrums or other exaggerations of behaviour.

The hostile child should be befriended, and his assertiveness channelled into helpful duties and responsibilities. Anything too onerous should be avoided, but he should be given a regular job and some semblance of prestige for it. Encouragement and praise is essential.

Equally the attention-seeking child should be encouraged to assist the teacher and praised for help given. He should be included in all group activities and if he tends to appear a 'loner' the teacher might well ask another, more mature, child to make a special effort to befriend him. Encouragement should be given to the child to join clubs, both inside and outside school. Whenever possible, attention should be directed towards socially acceptable behaviour and ministrations necessary for wounds, scratches, etc., kept to an absolute minimum. Without neglecting the injury, it is usually wise to pass over it without undue fuss or comment, confining sympathy and friendship for other more acceptable occasions.

An effort should be made to praise the child consistently, although his restless nature may understandably stress the adults around him. The restlessness or variability of mood will only remit when he is really secure.

Finally, it may be most advantageous to befriend the parents, and encourage them to discuss the child's progress. When a trusting relationship is established, it may be possible for the tactful teacher to suggest safety precautions, or through listening to the parents own problems, to lower the general level of frustration in the child's home.

BLIND CHILDREN
Myfanwy Williams

This chapter considers what harmful effects upon a child's all-round development can stem from blindness, the stresses that can arise, and how these can be counteracted. Society's attitude towards those who are blind is examined and found to be charitable but lacking in understanding of their need to be accepted into the community as respected and contributing members. Family stresses are explored: the initial shock to parents at the birth of a baby who cannot see, the suspense of a long-drawn out medical diagnosis, the distorted family relationships that can occur. The implications of blindness for child management are considered, and emphasis is placed on the vital role that the pre-school counsellor has to play in helping a mother to fill adequately her blind child's basic needs and maximise his opportunities for learning during the crucial early years of his development.

Those stresses that the blind child himself is likely to encounter before adolescence and those he may meet during adolescence are treated separately, although there is no break in the experiences of a child. Stresses for a blind child during his earlier years are likely to be those resulting from his separation from home, which may be for hospital treatment or for educational reasons. The careful preparation required to help to make such experiences as joining a play group, going to a local nursery school or boarding at a blind school, pleasurable and rewarding is considered in detail. The stresses that the blind adolescent has to face are likely to occur in social situations, in situations involving physical independence, in sex relationships and in career ambitions, so each of these areas is explored for its possible stresses. Various aspects of the curriculum are examined to try to discover the most effective measures whereby the blind adolescent may be helped to gain sufficient confidence in himself to cope adequately with some of life's exigencies in a sighted community.

Introduction

Total blindness, i.e. absence of response to any visual stimulus at all, is comparatively rare; it is much more common to find that there is sufficient sensitivity left in the retina of the damaged eye for response, at least, to light. In *The Handicapped Pupil and Special School Regulations* (1959) and the *Amending Regulations* (1962), blind pupils are defined as 'pupils who have no sight or whose sight is, or likely to become, so defective that they require education by methods not involving the use of sight'. It follows that many of the pupils attending a blind school do have a little residual vision. In accordance with this ruling, throughout this chapter the term 'blind' often does not denote complete absence of sight.

In common with other categories of the handicapped, a substantial number of blind children suffer from more than the one handicap but, though much of what follows applies to them, their specific stresses are not considered.

According to Fine's results given in Education 4 (Department of Education and Science, 1968) of 817 children in blind schools in England and Wales as high a proportion as thirty six per cent were thought by their teachers to be emotionally disturbed. If, as Wolff (1969) suggests, 'children are usually identified by their teachers on the basis of overall global judgements, these being influenced by the degree of tolerance on the part of some of them of various kinds of deviant behaviour', this high percentage needs to be taken with caution for it may, to a certain extent, reflect rather a low measure of tolerance on the part of individual teachers of 'naughty' behaviour. Even so, the figure indicates the need for an examination of the stresses to which blind children may be subjected to find out how they may be lessened.

Society's attitude towards blindness

How does the community at large view blindness? Do stresses arise because of the attitudes generally adopted towards blind individuals?

Hayes (1941) draws attention to blindness as a condition very little understood and appreciated and about which much that is erroneous has been written. It could be said that nowadays blindness is not regarded so calamitously as it was; after all, blind workmates and blind colleagues are to be seen efficiently coping with life; but blindness still carries implications of darkness and blankness. The actual condition, as blind people themselves would substantiate, is vastly different. With concentration and trained awareness each new situation confronting an observant blind person is examined for cues which pour in from all sides, enabling him to build up a mental picture. (Compare, though, how quickly vision takes in the whole of a situation in a single glance.) Blindness necessitates an increased use of the other senses, which explains their higher efficiency. Their heightened sensitivity is thus acquired and not, as often described by the public, a compensatory mechanism. To help a blind child to acquire the fullest potentiality of his other senses is one of the underlying principles of his education. Much more needs to be done to promote a better understanding of blindness on the part of the public by articles in newspapers and magazines, programmes on radio and television, plays and films, lectures, talks and discussion.

Because some of the implications of blindness are misunderstood, the handicap evoked a great deal of pity from the public, a response not always appreciated by a blind individual and one that can engender stress. This was illustrated by an article in the *Sunday Times* (8 December 1968) deprecating existing attitudes which the writer declared 'turns blind people into second-class citizens' and further on added 'the blind want understanding, not charity'. A few minutes' consideration would lead many readers to agree that to extend pity *vis-à-vis* another individual tends to engender in the recipient a feeling of inferiority, for it is not the currency exchanged between equals. It is possible for pity to breed resentment, producing a 'touchy' individual, always on the defensive, or to produce one too pliant and flabby.

Blind people share in a universally felt need of the handicapped for acceptance by the community as ordinary members of society, possessing their own unique qualities and having their own contribution to make to the common good. Blindness, probably more than some handicaps, mitigates against this acceptance for it strikes the public forcibly and is often singled out in an individual as a distinguishing mark, categorising him into a class, 'the blind'. He is thus stereotyped; a certain sort of behaviour is expected of him and what he says and does judged accordingly. But blindness does not automatically bestow upon its possessors common characteristics and a group of blind people are as heterogenous as any comparative sighted group.

Personal knowledge of blind individuals will be the key factor in changing these mistaken attitudes and prejudices of the public. Current trends to educate some blind children in ordinary schools are to be welcomed for the contribution that would thus be made towards greater mutual understanding between blind and sighted children thereby laying a foundation for unprejudiced attitudes in adulthood. In parts of the United States the practice of sending blind children to public school is almost universal. Bateman (1962) found in her study of 232 sighted public school children that those children who had known blind children perceived them as being somewhat more capable than those who had not, and that sighted children's perceptions of the abilities of blind children became more positive as the number of blind pupils in a school increased.

As many ways as possible of fostering contacts between blind and sighted must be sought. A few clubs for seeing members already accept blind members, as do associations such as Guides and Scouts. More could follow their examples. It is likely that there will be a need for special schools to cater for some blind children, at any rate, in the foreseeable future. Such schools should establish as close contacts as possible with ordinary schools in their areas. In the pre-school period parents should be encouraged to let their own blind child mix as much as possible with seeing children. During holidays blind and sighted should join in activities such as drama, swimming, dancing, etc. Care should be exercised that those who are blind are not always at the receiving end of favours: it is reciprocal giving and receiving that will lead to the acceptance of blind individuals within the community.

Family stresses

There is a sad note of truth in the comment of a mother of a handicapped child that 'truly a handicapped child is a handicapped family' (The National

Bureau for Cooperation in Child Care, 1970). In the case of a blind child one handicap for his family, and a source of stress, could be society's attitude towards blindness. Even nowadays complaints are heard from mothers about the way they are shunned by some of their neighbours when out with their blind child. It may be that the mothers are too sensitive, that they are projecting on to others their own guilty feelings at having produced a less than perfect baby, but that there should be a chance of such a rebuff is surely an indictment on society in these supposedly enlightened days.

The initial shock to the parents at the birth of a blind child cannot help but be very great and can have traumatic effects. The manner of imparting such sad news is crucially important and is best undertaken by a sensitive person, skilled in psychological awareness and with an understanding of the implications of blindness. Both parents will need opportunities to talk out their possible secret feelings of blame, guilt and shame, and to get over their disappointment at the arrival of this maimed child instead of the normal healthy baby expected. They need support and wise counselling to bring them to accept their handicapped child just as he is, with his limitations, not wishing him to be different, not harbouring the thought 'if only he were like other babies'. Gradually, it is hoped, they will come to look upon his rearing as a challenge.

More often than an outright diagnosis of blindness, the baby's eye condition is such that there is indication of a defect which might or might not lead to eventual blindness. A period of suspense for the parents is thus inaugurated with, probably, intermittent visits to hospitals. Or onset of eye trouble may not occur until later; but whenever during infancy an eye condition requiring ophthalmological diagnosis occurs, it is of the utmost importance for help to be given to parents immediately as Langdon (1968) bears out in his survey of services for blind children and young persons. He found that the most frequently and vehemently expressed complaint of the parents he interviewed was about the lack or inadequacy of counselling either at or immediately following the diagnosis, shown by his verbatim reports of parents' experiences such as 'You need help and encouragement. When you first realise this [the child's disability] it's a very black time', and another 'You need someone to talk to; to tell you what's going to happen'. Langdon's suggested procedure, that the first qualified person to diagnose a visual defect should, after asking the child's parents to authorise him, inform the local welfare authority, would go far to avoid such stress at a critical juncture, by setting in action machinery for a prompt offer of help by a specially qualified counsellor.

It is important that the blind infant does not become the pivot around which family life revolves, for this would distort family relationships, provoking situations in which stresses due to jealousies could easily develop. A blind baby requires more than the usual amount of time and attention from his mother if he is to develop into a lively, active, mobile youngster. His successful rearing, demanding as it does stimulation and much opportunity for new experiences, is a challenging task. At the same time a mother's need for leisure in company with her husband must be safeguarded and, also, the interest of other members of the family. Any other siblings are sometimes pushed into the background or too heavy demands are made on their time. Domestic help for a mother should be available, if required, as should baby-sitting services. Holidays should be made possible for the family by the offer of the particular assistance required, and, in cases of need, financial help extended to offset a mother's inability to leave her handicapped child for gainful employment.

It is being increasingly recognised that pre-school counselling for parents of blind children is essential, and this is a service that will lessen stress, not only for the family, but for the child himself, particularly by preparing him for entry to school. A blind child's basic needs are the same as those of every other child: affection, security, new experiences, independence and recognition, but his handicap makes it just that little bit more difficult to meet them adequately. For instance, blindness, by interfering with the usual facial interplay between mother and child, blocks one of the first ways of establishing rapport. This may cause a mother to feel defeated in that her baby seems so unresponsive, but advice from a counsellor will give her fresh incentive to seek other ways of expressing mutual affection, and she will find that her baby, with a little more than the usual amount of cuddling, more mutual laughter (rather than mere smiles), more audible murmurings, will soon respond to the sound of her approaching footsteps with gurgles of satisfaction, demonstrating the close, affectionate tie between them. To be able to give security to her baby a mother needs to feel confident in her handling of him. But blindness is likely to be strange to her as probably neither she nor any others in the family circle will ever have met with a blind baby. Naturally she will need support from some outside source to enable her to gain confidence in rearing her child.

A young blind child is more dependent on others for stimulation than is one with sight, for he cannot see the attractive objects around him. If left untended in his cot he is likely to develop such habits as hand flapping or head rocking, the so-called 'mannerisms' of blind children. Suggestions from a counsellor are needed about suitable toys, about the need to bring everyday objects for the child to explore, about the need for his mother to chat to him about her household tasks. (There are pamphlets to be obtained from the Royal National Institute for the Blind giving advice to parents on the rearing of a blind child.)

The quest for adventure, once a seeing infant is able to propel himself about, comes naturally and he finds the world a friendly and enticing place to explore, thus learning for himself a great deal about it. A blind infant's environment, on the other hand, is limited: to venture into the unknown can bring bumps and bruises, and if he does not in the meantime give up the struggle, what he gathers from experience needs to be described to him if he is to learn very much about his world. Guidance from a person with know-lege of blind children is required in order for a mother to encourage her child to be as mobile as possible, at the same time reducing unpleasant experiences to a minimum.

Independence in everyday skills is not gained without a great deal of effort on the part of a blind child, for sight plays a significant role in guiding and controlling hand movements, and an easy way of learning, by visual imitation, is closed to him. A mother will need endless patience to encourage her child to perform a task for himself, and she should have guidance on what can be reasonably expected of him at certain stages of his development. She needs to understand, too, the significance for the child of praise from the people who matter to him, praise for effort as well as results. But the praise should have been earned, not given indiscriminately whether or not there has been genuine effort.

Sommers (1944) found that of the parents in her sample some over-protected their child, some rejected him, and some denied his blindness; only a few seemed to have adjusted to the realities of the situation and accepted their child's blindness. Gomulicki (1961) found that the blind children in his sample who performed best in the practical tests administered were those with parents who had deliberately encouraged them to be active and self-reliant and provided them with ample opportunities to develop the use of their other senses. To enable as many as possible of today's parents to provide their blind child with such ample opportunities, pre-school counselling services must be available in every Local Authority area.

Childhood stresses

All children have to cope with stresses, for they are inherent in the growing-up process; situations inevitably occur from time to time that give rise to anxiety. One of the effects of blindness is to heighten any anxiety that a situation might ordinarily present. A blind child is likely to be placed in such situations more often, partly because blindness creates more situations containing an unfamiliar factor, and the unknown tends to give rise to fear, and partly because it increases his general level of fatigue for, as mentioned earlier, without control from the eye, everyday tasks require greater concentration. Wolff (1969) says that events occurring during childhood are harmful when they arouse more anxiety than can be coped with. Whether a situation is stressful for a child depends upon his stage of development. For example, how he interprets the event depends upon his stage of intellectual development. If he is at Piaget's animistic, egocentric stage he is likely to explain an event in terms of motivation and intent, a 'bad' happening, such as an illness, being seen as a punishment for what he himself has done wrong. Feelings of guilt thus arise. How he reacts to his experiences depends on his social and emotional development, the significant factor being the quality of his relationships with the people that matter at the time of the event. If it occurs during the first year of life, when the baby's dependence on his mother is almost total, and disturbs the relationship, it is likely to be specially traumatic.

One of the prerequisites for a child to be able to cope adequately with stress is a healthy self concept. From the consideration already given to general attitudes towards blindness and blind people it will be realised that this is not always easy for a blind child to gain for 'we know ourselves by how people behave towards us'. Undue significance is often given by the sighted to his handicap, he is pitied instead of being treated by them first and foremost as a child. It is only with closer and more frequent contact with blind children and adults that this situation will improve.

Much has been written about the possible stress that a young child may undergo during a stay in hospital away from his mother since the film 'A Two-Year-Old Goes to Hospital', made in 1952, demonstrated the typical reaction of such a young child to hospital routine. In 1959 the Platt Committee recommended that mothers should be admitted to hospital with their young children and that all parents should be allowed unrestricted visiting, recommendations repeated in 1966 and yet again in 1971, but many hospitals still allow parents to see their children only during set visiting hours. A child with a handicap is particularly liable to have to undergo treatment involving a stay in hospital, and to many psychologists treatment of the eye carries an undue risk of emotional disturbance, because they believe the eye to have symbolic sexual significance. Blindness intensifies the fear of the unknown, too, for every sound can take on an ominous significance if it cannot be interpreted aright. It should certainly be recommended most strongly that a young blind child has his mother or mother-substitute with him during his stay in hospital, for it is only her actual presence that can alleviate his anxiety.

An experience that the majority of blind children in Great Britain today have to face is going away from home at the age of five years to boarding school. This is not the place to go into all the pros and cons of what is known as 'open' or integrated education – educating a blind child at an ordinary school with his neighbourhood peers. But mention must be made of the growing recognition of the importance for the foundation of a child's mental health of a warm, loving continuous relationship with his parents in his early years. It is when a child can carry with him the image of good parents with whom he has established a relationship of trust that he is likely to be able to adjust favourably to changed circumstances and not find a temporary separation from them too stressful to be coped with. The gain in mutual understanding resulting from blind and sighted children playing and working together at one and the same school has already been mentioned; however it may be that there are certain advantages to be gained for the blind child in attending a boarding school for those similarly handicapped at certain stages in his education. Certain stresses may be removed by so doing. For instance, at such a school he will find himself able to compete in games and other activities on a similar footing, in respect of vision, as the others in his group. His defect will be less conspicuous, and he is likely to feel less need to 'prove' himself. Because he will be one among many with similar, if not worse, handicaps than himself, he will have ample opportunity to render, rather than receive, help, and learn the meaning of reciprocal giving. Also, the special school may make learning conditions less of a strain by gearing them to his particular needs, for it is able to provide trained teachers, expert in braille and in techniques and methods appropriate for blind children, consciously aware of the importance of calling into service the remaining senses and ingenious at planning experiences and situations in which learning through these other sensory channels can take place.

Increasingly more often, nowadays, a blind child has the opportunity of joining a play-group or attending a nursery school in his own locality before leaving to go to a residential school. This is excellent, but adequate preparation beforehand is a prerequisite for this to be a happy and rewarding experience for him rather than an experience to cause stress. First, the head and members of staff who will be closely concerned with the blind child must be eager to have him and look forward to the challenge. Naturally, the teacher will want suggestions on a number of matters from someone with knowledge of young blind children. A preliminary visit by some such person will afford opportunity for her to put forward any queries and to get information on suitable toys, games and other activities, on what can be reasonably expected from a young blind child in the way of everyday skills and on how to treat him. Emphasis will be laid on the importance of his being treated from the start as a member of a group, joining in with the others in as many activities as possible, rather than being over-protected and given special favours. It is likely that from time to time the teacher will welcome further visits from the counsellor, and the latter will wish to maintain contact with the child.

In the meantime, the counsellor should be looking ahead to the next stage in the child's education; probably this will be at a residential school for blind children. Parents should visit the school well before their child is due to be admitted, so they can be on friendly terms with the staff, assure themselves about house arrangements and meet the children at work and at play. The child himself should have visited his future school and played with his future companions. The coming experience should be looked forward to in a spirit of adventure and when he goes he should be able to depend to the uttermost on his parents' promises as to letters, telephone calls and visits. If at all practicable, boarding should be only from Monday to Friday, weekend visits home being regarded as routine. Holidays at home should be pleasant and rewarding experiences, times for renewing contacts with erstwhile neighbourhood friends and for participation in all kinds of ordinary social experiences. Some parents may need help and advice in planning activities for their blind child during school holidays, and this should be easily available.

Sometimes it happens that the parents of a blind child are able and willing to move nearer to a blind school so that he is able to attend daily. This can be one happy solution to the problem of separation, but it is imperative that close liaison between school and home is maintained so that parents and school staff cooperate together to bring about the fullest development possible of the child's potentialities.

The years from seven to twelve are usually passed in relative calm, and constitute a period during which a child becomes acquainted with an expanding world, is curious about everything, is gaining knowledge and skills, experiencing prowess in sports and establishing for himself a place within his own group of peers. Providing a blind child has enjoyed a favourable warm home environment, his blindness being accepted realistically by his parents, and has been given ample opportunities for active exploration he too will enter a similar phase of calm and enjoy his junior school years untroubled, except perhaps occasionally, by upsets and frustrations. It is important for the school to build solidly upon such good foundations, keeping close contacts with all parents, having as wide a curriculum as possible, a full programme of leisure activities and constant opportunities for mixing with schools and clubs in its vicinity. Above all, the school should be a happy community; the children, members of teaching and residential care staff and all who serve it in any capacity, working harmoniously together towards a common goal. An acceptance of a Christian interpretation of life would, some strongly believe, enrich the community life of any school (Children's Council, 1969).

Stresses in adolescence

Finally there are the stresses that the adolescent blind have to face. Erikson (1959) describes the main task to be completed during this period as 'identity formation, involving the definition of a working role, the acquisition of social attitudes, emotional as well as physical separation from the parents and the definition of a sexual role'. Confronted with such goals a blind adolescent will meet stresses common to all individuals who are handicapped and others that will arise from his particular disability. The latter are likely to occur in social situations, in situations involving physical independence, in sexual relationships and in career ambitions.

It is much more difficult for a blind than a fully sighted person to grasp the social implications of a situation, for he is not able, by glancing over his shoulder, to pick up unobtrusively from his neighbour cues on how to behave, supposing he does not know. Therefore he needs direct teaching on etiquette and social manners if he is to avoid the stress that can arise from an embarrassing situation. The learning of social skills should continue throughout a student's days, both for their value in outside contacts with the sighted and for their contribution in enabling a blind person to lead a full life after leaving school. Every little bit of knowledge that can help to give confidence to a blind person, however simple and trite it may appear to be, is precious and well worth time and trouble to impart if thereby he is better equipped to meet a new situation in a challenging manner, which will consequently be less likely to arouse anxiety within and leave him greater freedom to cope with its realities. By the time a young blind person is ready to take up employment, it is hoped that he will have at his command a working knowledge of, and an ability to execute, the accepted social patterns.

As the blind adolescent's social environment expands he will more and more come directly up against society's attitude towards blind people, its bias and prejudices. If, during his school years, positive feelings towards himself and his personal worth have been fostered, and developed throughout adolescence, there will be some chance of his being able gradually to tolerate the misunderstanding and ignorance he will sometimes meet, to accept pity imperturbably, knowing that behind it lies sympathy and kindness. It is hoped that his attitude towards others, blind or sighted, will be one of friendliness and cooperation and that he will have adjusted to society sufficiently to make life easy and will have accepted his blindness sufficiently to free him from having to struggle constantly against it.

Considerable attention should have been given to a blind child's mobility from infancy onwards, but during adolescence it is of paramount importance to develop his potentiality in this direction to the full. This is the time to give practice in specific techniques: use of long cane, use of sonic torch, guide dog training, etc. To be independently mobile gives a blind person great satisfaction by affording him greater choice of action than would otherwise be the case and thereby lessening frustration. However, allowance must be made for individual differences in this as in every other ability, as well as for the variety that exists in personality traits, otherwise there is a danger of too great a strain being imposed by setting an impossible goal for a particular individual. It should also be remembered that blind youngsters are more likely, in any case, to be under nervous strain and to be closer to fatigue than their sighted counterparts. It is important that fatigue be lessened as much as possible for it is at times of tiredness that emotional disturbances can occur, especially in conditions that place a blind person at a decided disadvantage among his sighted fellows. He is liable to feel that he is being watched by those with sight, and during adolescence this feeling is likely to be heightened. The expert in mobility training will guard against undue fatigue, and will discuss any problems with his pupil as they arise.

During adolescence relationships with members of the opposite sex assume significance. In this context blindness is apt to thrust itself into the forefront, causing upset and frustration. At the time when a young man wants to appear manly and virile, able to take the initiative, to be confident in relating to members of the other sex, he is hampered by blindness. A young woman wants, above everything, to look attractive in the company of men and to be at her best on every social occasion, but blindness makes her hesitant, doubtful of her charms. Facial interplay, so effective an introduction to a better acquaintance, leading perhaps to courtship, is debarred by blindness. Is it surprising that bitterness and resentment can arise? 'Why has this happened to me?' must surely be a question that has been asked by countless blind adolescents. A sympathetic wise friend who will listen to this and other such queries is invaluable at this time. Some believe that a Christian philosophy of life would provide an anchor in such circumstances or, at least, offer some light to lessen the gloom.

Sex education poses certain specific problems for teachers of blind children; for example, teaching has to be adapted so as to use models in place of pictures for concrete aids. However, much thought is being given to the subject and ideas are being exchanged with schools abroad in order to discover the most effective approach with blind boys and girls.

Greater uncertainty about his future working role will arise in the case of the blind than in that of the sighted adolescent, because of the limitations imposed by his disablement. Blindness restricts considerably the choice of employment open to him. Careful consideration needs to be given to the questions posed in 'Living with Handicap', 1970: 'When and how should youngsters be made aware of their limitations in the field of employment?' 'How can a young person's unrealistic career ambitions be discouraged without crushing his faith in himself and his future employment potential?' It is essential for the blind adolescent to have a friend to whom he can turn for guidance, someone who will listen to his hopes and fears. It may be that a friend who is blind himself, who has 'made the grade' as it were, will be the one to kindle his courage and fire anew his imagination, for adolescence is a time for hero-worship and ideals.

Consideration should be given to an adolescent's future working role by a knowledgeable and sympathetic team, and consultation with the parents take place two or three years before he is due to leave school. Employment opportunities in a pupil's home area will need to be explored for there is no more frustrating experience than to be trained for an occupation that cannot be followed. It should, however, be recognised that there is nothing to prevent a blind person seeking employment away from home if by doing so he will be able to practise the most personally satisfying skill that he is capable of acquiring.

There are two centres to which blind adolescents may go for assessment and vocational guidance. Courses in these are geared to social as well as practical needs, and every opportunity taken to prepare the blind student for the coming change from a place where his difficulties have been understood to the outside world of keen competition in which he will have to stand on his own feet. On leaving, students are recommended for employment, training or further education.

A strain is sometimes placed on the shoulders of a blind entrant to industry inasmuch as he is burdened with responsibility for others. He is told that he must succeed or he will spoil future employment prospects for blind persons in that particular factory, thus attaching to failure calamitous results. This is wrong psychologically, for failure should be an experience whereby learning can take place: neither should impossible standards be allowed to constitute another strain for a young blind person at the outset of his working life.

Blindness can bring stress, as shown in the foregoing pages, but it can, also, bring challenge: to the one who is blind, to minimise its handicapping effects on life; to the educationist, to circumvent the obstacles it presents by impeding visual learning. Provided that at each stage of his education these challenges are accepted, a student may emerge at the end, in spite of blindness, able to live a full and satisfactory life.

PARTIALLY-SIGHTED CHILDREN

J. Kell

Despite its official recognition as a handicap for which special educational help may be needed and its numerical supremacy over the more dramatic handicap of blindness – there are nearly twice as many partially-sighted children as there are blind children – partial sight is a condition to which comparatively little understanding is extended. This is not perhaps surprising since partial sight is a generic term covering many different aspects of defective vision. Most partially-sighted children live in an imperfectly defined world; a world in which objects and the movements of others are not clearly apprehended. They may see hazily or with fragmented vision, as one sees a jig-saw puzzle picture which has fallen apart, or with clarity over a very small area, receiving an image comparable to that conveyed through the wrong end of a telescope. Peripheral vision may be unaffected so that movement and recognition of large objects in the vicinity may be unimpaired but difficulty will nevertheless be experienced in identifying detail. The visual field may be affected over a large area, for example where there has been a lesion in the region of the optic nerve, the person affected may see only objects in the lower or upper half of the visual field, or in the left or right hemisphere. Reading presents problems in the last mentioned condition since the patient will lack the ability to scan in advance along the left to right line of printed matter.

The child whose vision is faulty in any of these, or other ways, is liable to feel unsure of himself and of his response to the actions of others. In communicating with each other we rely to a much greater extent than we realise upon impressions conveyed by facial expressions and bodily gesture. All this may serve to show why it is difficult for the layman to gain a clear concept of partial sight as a handicap. He may dismiss as a slightly clumsy oddity the person who moves or works slowly or awkwardly as a result of visual defects but who nevertheless manages the demands of everyday life with a reasonable degree of competence. On the other hand, the partially-sighted person whose handicap is recognised may be mistakenly placed in the near blind category because he holds small print close to his nose or fails to acknowledge a friend passing in the street.

Much valuable publicity has been given in recent years to the need for identification and understanding of a large number of conditions and defects which lead to physical and mental handicap. In many cases, the impetus for the growth of understanding has arisen from the efforts of the parents of handicapped children to create and maintain organisations which have eventually achieved national significance in the fields of welfare, research, education and training. The partially-sighted have lacked a parental pressure group of this kind. The Royal National Institute for the Blind has been sympathetic within the terms of its charter but has been unable to venture far beyond the legal definition of blindness in many areas where help is needed. The small but tenacious Association of Teachers of the Partially Sighted has been able to concern itself mainly with aspects of the work in schools. In surgery spectacular advances continue to be made and many patients who would have been condemned to a life of near blindness a few years ago have been able to function visually within near normal limits as a result of improvements in surgical techniques and advances in prophylactic treatment – advances disseminated by continued intercourse in the world of ophthalmology at international level. Similar advances have been made in the field of optics. Progress in the understanding and alleviation of social and developmental problems, however, has depended mainly upon the exercise of individual effort and initiative. The comparatively small number of people grossly affected, the varying manifestations of visual defect referred to above, and the absence of a powerful pressure group, have all contributed to the degree of apathy and lack of information which is often found in these areas.

The difficulties which beset the parents of very young partially-sighted children are to some extent shared with the parents of all handicapped children. Most parents of handicapped children are, to a greater or lesser degree, anxious parents, and their anxiety is inevitably to some extent communicated to the child. The numbing sense of unreality which follows the unexpected pronouncement of severe handicap in the clinical situation, the vain continuing search for sources of cure or alleviation, the refusal to accept the degree of handicap even when it is patently manifest, are features which may be found among all parents in this position. To the parents of a partially-sighted child, particularly when partial sight is the child's only handicap, the fact that they have a child who has a severe defect which cannot be cured, and may become progressively worse, often comes as a profound shock.

The parents of partially-sighted children when contributing to an unpublished survey which covered over a third of the children in this category in England and Wales, described graphically their feelings when awareness of the handicap made its impact.

'We could not believe it had happened to us.'
'I do not remember anything of my journey home from the hospital when I was told.'
'We continued to seek advice from doctors in several different countries. We could not accept that nothing could be done.'

These are phrases which, with minor variations, occur throughout the survey material.

Complete acceptance by the parents, even when the knowledge of the existence of the handicap is of long standing, may be slow in coming, and the need of parents to know and understand and accept the extent of the child's handicap is so often brushed aside by busy medical staff working under pressure. Even where there is provision for meeting this need it is not always possible for help to be coincident with the emotional readiness of parents to receive it. Many parents even when considerable care has been taken in the manner of conveying the final diagnosis are unable fully to comprehend immediately the nature of what is being imparted. One exceptionally enlightened ophthalmologist describes how, having given his private telephone number to a distressed parent, he awaits the call, which almost invariably comes within a few hours, in which re-affirmation is sought. To many parents the knowledge that a severe visual defect of an incurable nature is present may come completely out of the blue even after several months of careful preparation.

Visual acuity in the human infant is not developed at birth and it may be many months before a young inexperienced mother begins to suspect that her baby is not reaching out to grasp objects or responding to visual stimuli in the way that other babies of the same age are. Unless there is an obvious abnormality in the appearance or movement of the eye, and in many eye conditions abnormality is not easily detected by those unfamiliar with visual defects, it is possible that even where the baby has been under the skilled surveillance of auxillary medical personnel the presence of imperfect sight will remain unsuspected. It may not be realised that a severe defect is present until a baby reaches the toddling stage, or even later, especially if the birth has been a normal one and there is no history of visual defect in the family.

As the severely partially-sighted child reaches and attempts to pass the milestones of early growth and gradually becomes aware of his own identity, there appears the dawning realisation that he is somehow different. In the over-protective home this may take the form of 'I am different and important. I must be specially protected and taken care of. All my needs and desires must be given attention immediately.' On the other hand, one encounters the child who has become aware that he is different, but that, far from being important, he is an object of shame. He senses that one or both of his parents resent his presence as an imperfect member of the family. It is not infrequently found that intensely over-protective parents are attempting to meet needs and inadequacies in their own lives by concentrating too much on the handicapped boy or girl. Conversely, the child may be made the scapegoat for unresolved emotional difficulties present in the marriage, or the child's need to remain in proximity to specialised services may be made the excuse for failure to take up opportunities for promotion. Where the eye disease is inherited the parent who carries the defect may have powerful feelings of guilt. In some cases, the mother may ask herself quite irrationally whether she acted in a certain way during pregnancy which resulted in her child's sight being defective. If she is convinced rightly or wrongly that she did, the presence of the child in the family acts as a nagging reminder of this. Understanding of genetic inheritance of some defects is complicated, particularly when the defect is of a recessive nature. Parents may dredge around in their own backgrounds, and that of each other, for a defective relative extending back through several generations in an effort to place the blame for the visual defect. Sometimes a defect in an area quite unconnected with vision may be half-heartedly produced in an attempt to pin-point the source. When the child is an only son and likely to remain so, the father sometimes feels cheated in having a boy who seems unable to take part in masculine pursuits or follow him in his field of employment. If the father feels that he is to blame for the defect he may sometimes see this as an attack on his virility. He may attempt to hide his feelings by minimising the child's handicap or endeavour to equate it with a quite unrelated difficulty of his own. A father who tried to hide his feelings in this way, and who pushed his borderline blind son into a local grammar school where he was failing miserably, said 'He could overcome his eye trouble if he wanted to. I have overcome my deafness and he must overcome his partial sight.' A mature, partially-sighted young woman, when discussing the feelings of her parents towards her, referred to the irritation which her father's grossly over-protective attitude had engendered. She said that her mother had been unable to be completely assured in their relationship because it seemed as though the defect had been inherited from her mother's family. When it was indicated that her father had played an equal part in passing the defect and it might be helpful to her mother to know this, she thought for a moment and said 'My mother can cope, but if he thought he had handed it on it would shatter my father. He'd be worse than ever.'

The young partially-sighted child who feels himself to be an object of resentment or over-protection may react by withdrawing from contact with his environment into a world of his own. He may well be afraid to give expression to his normal urges to explore and to experience his own small adventures if, every time he reaches out to the world around him, he is told 'Don't touch that, you'll drop it' or 'Don't go there, you'll trip over' or hears himself spoken about in a disparaging way to visitors or neighbours. When near vision is particularly faulty, he may appear slow, stupid and clumsy.

When a partially-sighted child has a constant experience of failure a pattern is built up which is very difficult to alter at a later stage. A child in whom the expectation of failure is continually confirmed becomes less and less willing to participate in the delights and discoveries of early childhood. We often fail to realise in the case of unhandicapped children how much of their development is the product of an active creative learning process. The normal baby attacks his environment with an insatiable curiosity. He extends at an ever increasing rate his aggressive, restless search for form and pattern and meaning in all that goes on around him exercising all his senses in a variety of different ways as he does so. The synthesis of his sensory experiences enables him to structure his world. If, however, one of his senses is grossly impaired he is going to be retarded or muddled in his initial concepts. If the visually handicapped infant is to make sense of the 'booming, buzzing confusion' which is his world, it is essential to provide for him an environment which is stimulating and yet within his grasp. Beginning from the early months it is most important to verbalise and describe in language appropriate to the child's development just what our actions signify, to as it were carry on a constant running commentary on day to day activities in a way which will help the child relate what he hears and smells and touches with what he sees, however imperfectly. It is also important that the child is given every opportunity for experimental play of the sand and water, large building bricks, empty cardboard box kind, that he is encouraged to compare and classify, to test for movement and texture, to estimate, to ask himself and those around him questions about what he is feeling, touching and tasting. When natural development is frustrated and the young partially-sighted child becomes surrounded by a negation of his innate abilities he may become aggressive and give way to quite uncontrollable temper tantrums. Parents of partially-sighted children desperately need help in providing the right kind of play material and experience in the early years. It is unfortunate that they all too rarely get help of this kind. In the survey referred to previously only a very small percentage of those visited felt that they had been given any advice of real value. 'She just came once a year to tell us we were doing a good job and then went away again'; 'The social worker talked as though John was blind. I wanted to help him to learn to use his sight'; were remarks frequently encountered in the survey. It is to be hoped that the recommendations of the Committee of Enquiry into the Education of the Visually Handicapped will lead to a much greater emphasis on the provision of developmental advice by the Education and Social Service Departments of local authorities. Access to such a service is the right of all parents of handicapped children, but the advice and help given must be specific to the handicap and not consist merely of vague, irrelevant generalisations. The counselling given should also cover difficulties arising within the area of family relationships. Unfavourable comparisons with normally-sighted brothers and sisters, or too great a measure of concentrating on the needs of the handicapped child at their expense, apparent rejection by the family through the frequent periods of hospitalisation which some eye diseases necessitate, may all exacerbate symptoms of withdrawal or frustration or aggression. Having a child with a severe visual handicap can put a strain on the marriage itself, particularly if one or the other partner feels elbowed out by the excessive measure of attention given to the handicapped child. As one mother who had successfully come through a period of difficulty of this kind said, 'Having a handicapped child can make or break a marriage'. It is necessary for the worker visiting the home to be able to recognise the need for additional help to be given in such cases.

As the partially-sighted boy or girl nears the time when participation in playgroup or nursery activities or entry to the first school is contemplated further difficulties may arise. If the child has been cloistered within the family and never encouraged to undertake his own small adventurous expeditions, the adjustment process may be a painful one. Experience in a good playgroup or nursery setting can be invaluable for a partially-sighted child. It is re-assuring both to those dealing with the child and to his parents if some indication is given of the way in which his particular defect is likely to affect his activities and the areas of development to which special attention should be paid. The shortage of personnel experienced in the problem of partial sight as a handicap presents a real difficulty, but partially-sighted schools and classes will often prove helpful in the absence of an expert of this kind. It is important that the partially-sighted child is helped in the early years to make good use of strong visual, auditory and tactile clues if the synthesis of experience is to be achieved and if he is to explore the new wider environment which presents itself to him. It is at this stage that parents may become anxious and worried if they feel that their partially-sighted child compares unfavourably in attainment and social acceptance with his unhandicapped peers. Where the attention of the home is over-centred on the child his normal social development and more often than we realise perhaps also his cognitive development are impeded. It is not uncommon to encounter the five year old entrant to school who is dressed as though he is still at the toddling stage and who clings to the rudimentary speech patterns of early childhood. The children should be exposed to a continuing wide variety of sensory experiences though care must be taken not to confuse them with too many unrelated activities. At this stage they need above all to be able to correlate the impressions they are receiving – impressions which, because they may be ill-defined, distorted or inaccurately perceived, could well lead to the development of faulty or superficial concepts. It is of considerable value if the adult caring for young partially-sighted children carries out the running commentary on new activities previously referred to, verbalising and explaining the point and purpose of what is taking place.

Mobility should be closely linked with visual training. Large wheeled toys which are manipulated by the children's use of whole body movement can play a useful part in increasing confidence and spatial knowledge. Where children have been over-protected or otherwise restricted by an unfavourable environment it is important that they are encouraged towards the achievement of independence and responsibility. It is often necessary where development has been severely retarded to take them through the stages which have been missed in the earlier years. In addition to self-help in the sphere of dressing, feeding, washing and toilet training they should be shown how to use and care for and replace all the toys, materials and items of equipment which are presented to them. It is on the basis of this training in the early years that future development will take place; for it is only by fully comprehending and exploring the possibilities inherent in their immediate surroundings that children with severely defective vision will reach their ultimate potential. Left to themselves they will all too often curtail and circumscribe their experiences and fail to develop the instinct of curiosity and adventure which is natural to most handicapped children.

The attitude of many partially-sighted children towards a new learning situation is often one of what might be termed 'negative subterfuge'. They may be reluctant to approach anything new or exaggerate the difficulties they encounter. Above all, and often most dangerously, they may be quite emphatic that they understand when, in fact, no understanding has taken place. What do they mean by understanding? We may say that we understand something if we can talk about it, give examples of it, see connections between it and other ideas and make use of it in various ways. It is essential to find out what partially-sighted children really know as opposed to what they give the appearance of knowing. We must discover what has been their real learning as opposed to their apparent learning. It is all too easy to think that because learning opportunities are supplied, learning is automatically going to take place. This is particularly important in considering the progress of partially-sighted children placed in main stream schools. Wherever possible in such circumstances, it should be arranged for a member of the teaching staff to undertake responsibility for the partially-sighted child while he is placed in that particular school or department. The person appointed must be one who can forge a good relationship with the child and dig beneath the surface of an apparent learning blockage or negative exhibition of emotion. A severely partially-sighted girl was feverishly trying to finish a soft toy which she was making by the end of her first half term in a special school. When asked why she was so anxious to complete the toy she replied 'I want to take it to my other school [an ordinary school] and show it to the needle-work teacher there. She thinks I can't do things and I can'. When partially-sighted children are involved in learning situations outside the school – and this should be happening regularly, persistently and frequently – it can again be all too easy to over-estimate the visual input they receive. Any learning situation which takes place in unfamiliar surroundings must be carefully structured and programmed for partially-sighted children. The onset of visual fatigue is for them a process which can occur quite rapidly. It is often necessary to intersperse periods of intense observation with activities which are visually less demanding. It is all too easy for such children to appear stupid, uncomprehending or uncooperative when they are merely visually fatigued. Carefully planned practice in road safety training and the inculcation of confidence in the use of public transport can do much to allay the natural fear of parents who are reluctant to expose their children to the rigours of independent mobility. This will involve much patient planning in journeying to a variety of shops, libraries, factories, museums, cinemas and venues further afield in order to provide additional opportunities for the correlation of everyday experiences with an achievement of independence. School and the home should work together to ensure that sufficient time is devoted to this work.

Some partially-sighted children exhibit a chip on the shoulder in later years which can be traced to negative experiences in earlier childhood, re-inforced by a continuation of over-protective parental attitudes. A twelve year old girl referred by her mother because of behaviour difficulties in the home said bitterly 'Yes, I do get in a temper. She has never let me go any-where or do anything.' Exposure to the pity of well-meaning friends, relations and others unfamiliar with partial sight as a handicap may also threaten emotional well-being. In discussing her forthcoming transfer to a school for the blind with an intelligent ten year old whose sight had deteriorated, I referred to the fact that her sight would probably be better than that of most of the other people at the school and that she would find it necessary to adjust herself to this. She said rather fiercely 'I won't mind that, at least they won't pity me there.' Somewhat surprised I asked her 'You don't think anyone pities you here, do you?' 'No,' she replied, 'not here but they did at my other school [an ordinary school] and I hated it so. I hate being pitied.' This girl, who had been placed in a special school about a year before this incident took place, had previously been persistently absconding from schools and institutions to which she had been sent for treatment.

Continuing opportunity should be given to the parents of partially-sighted children to discuss their feelings and difficulties throughout the period of childhood. Parents need time to reveal their anxieties and it is often only after a considerable period has passed that their real worries begin to emerge. It can be a relief to the parents of quite young children to be able to see clearly the way ahead, to know that a handicapped five year old is likely to be employable and that further education and training facilities will be available at a later stage. Information of this kind is all too often not available. One parent contributing to the survey said 'Nobody tells you anything about what can be done. I only learnt about special schools from a chance conversation with someone in a cafe.' There are many times when those dealing with the parents of visually-handicapped children need to allow themselves to be used as emotional pincushions.

What can be done to help partially-sighted children achieve the right sort of self-respect? The over-protected egocentric child often gains a great deal when he joins a progressive school or playgroup at the early stage, by learning to contribute to group activities and to adjust his needs and desires to those of other children. When a child has missed the opportunity for early help of this kind it is often necessary to find an activity in which he is able to build up a good measure of personal satisfaction. It is then possible to build on the sense of achievement healthily acquired and to enable him to make adequate social adjustment to his handicap. This 'special activity' approach can also sometimes provide the key to unlock the personality of an inhibited, withdrawn child. A physically handicapped, bordering on blind and apparently sub-normal boy reached a special school after having somehow survived in an ordinary school until the age of fifteen. At first, he made only monosyllabic contact with both staff and children and it was not until his interest in stamp collecting was noticed – this was one of the pastimes encouraged in the school – that he began to reveal himself as a boy of character who, far from being mentally sub-normal, was able to participate in many activities both at school and outside. A specialised training centre which had refused his application on a previous interview, felt able to reconsider their decision as a result of the impressive change in attitude and the improvement in his grasp of the techniques of everyday living. This boy was able to attempt an elementary public examination in an academic subject and to pass a dancing exam at the end of his two years in the school concerned.

One of the difficulties in helping partially-sighted boys and girls is the striking of the right balance in giving support, encouragement and consideration when needed and in preparing gradually the boy or girl who is nearing school-leaving age for the less concerned attitude of the world of enjoyment. The schema of the partially-sighted boy or girl tends to be blurred at the edges emotionally, as well as visually, and he may dither or jump to the wrong conclusions in judging the actions or desires of those around him. It is significant that, when invited to discuss their experiences freely several members of a group of partially-sighted adolescents described situations in which they had apparently been brusquely checked or arbitrarily treated. The word 'shouted' was frequently used in their descriptions. 'The teacher at my infant school shouted at me.' 'A shop assistant shouted, "No, not that one, the one over there".' Partially-sighted youngsters tend to feel 'picked upon' when their difficulties are only imperfectly understood. There are activities which can be used to help them throw off this feeling. Participation in any free expression activity in which they can forget themselves and gain a sense of personal achievement and through which they can voice their difficulties is particularly valuable. They have a special need to know clearly what is being demanded from them and to be able to progress in a clear, unconfused framework. If the right atmosphere of mutual trust and respect is achieved between the partially-sighted adolescent and those dealing with him, and this is one of the strengths of a good school where the individual relationships make this possible, much can be done by group discussion or by apparently casual, but in reality carefully considered, conversational remarks to prepare the boy or girl for the demands of the work situation. For this reason the standard of tidiness, natural courtesy and clarity of expression in speech demanded of partially-sighted adolescents should be high. Reliability and working to capacity should be stressed. If we are to expect them to take their place satisfactorily in working life, we must not demand less than they are capable of giving or adopt a lax attitude towards their performance merely because they are handicapped. We are treating them as less than full human beings if we do so. Education must essentially provide a framework in which the partially-sighted child feels secure and wanted, but if the school organisation is too static and inflexible the opportunity will be lost for providing the situation and experiences which are sufficiently varied and open to stimulate individual development.

Intensive work with older children can pay dividends. It needs, however, to be constantly borne in mind that if the children are really to learn from what they are seeing and doing, they need in the initial stages to have their attention directed to what is actually there. I remember talking to an old pupil some two or three years after he had left school and had gone to work in central London. He said 'Do you remember not long before I left, taking us to Charing Cross station and making us give you details from the various timetables of trains to different places? I thought to myself at the time, Oh! They are at it again. I have reason to be very grateful since, however, since I know exactly where to go on the station to read the train timetable and I am not afraid to push in front of other people to get a really close look. Often I have been able to help strangers on the station enquiring about trains.' Older partially-sighted boys and girls are often diffident in strange situations. They do not realise the extent to which adults who are strangers in a strange place need to ask for information and help from those around them. It was reported a year or two before she was due to leave school, that an able but severely handicapped girl had spent half an hour hopping from one foot to the other in a very busy central London street not sure where she was going and afraid to cross a busy road in what might have been the right direction. This girl is now working very successfully on the child care staff of a large educational establishment but it needed several months of intensive work with her before she would happily travel alone and get herself from one place to another without fear.

It is very often necessary to push partially-sighted children in at the deep end where new experiences are concerned. It is only by so doing that they learn they can really swim. Another factor which must be borne in mind when a fresh learning situation is presented is their need to feel secure. There are many amusing instances in which children have tried to manipulate circumstances to force acceptance of a framework or programme with which they are familiar, and in which they feel sure of themselves, in order to side-step the challenge of a new situation. They must be helped to become accustomed to the unexpected. It can be very useful at the later secondary stage if they participate in a learning situation other than in their usual school or college. They often do not realise, particularly if they have been educated in small schools, that there are many different ways of teaching and many different ways of illustrating teaching points. If they feel unable to accept the challenge of a situation just because it is new and unfamiliar, then they are not going to make good employees when the time comes for them to venture into the working world. It is all too easy for a partially-sighted adolescent who has not gained the degree of confidence which comes through successful achievement to feel quite unable to face the demands of a work situation. It is particularly important where a boy or girl has not had special educational help to determine whether apparent failure has been caused by the difficulties of the learning situation proving overwhelming. A sixteen year old boy who was about to leave an ordinary school exhibited a somewhat patchy academic record. When I asked him why he had done so badly in a particular subject, he said 'I got fed up with asking Mr X to write more clearly on the blackboard. I thought I was being a nuisance. You can't go on asking.' This particular boy had lacked a sympathetic member of staff who would have been prepared to make his difficulties known to Mr X. He was able to achieve a good degree of success in the subject at which he had previously failed after a period of private coaching.

Careful placing in employment is necessary. The young partially-sighted employee does not realise what he cannot see and does not, in consequence, always appear rational in his interpretation of situations. It is not uncommon for a task to be carried out by a partially-sighted youngster, when the task was not in fact intended for him, because verbal directions have been imperfectly comprehended and the accompanying gesture has been missed. Partially-sighted young people, in common with most adolescents, do not like to feel different or to admit that they are confused or unsure of themselves. A quiet, stable, partially-sighted girl was placed in employment in a chain store. Early reports indicated that the placement was a successful one and for a while all seemed to be going well. The Youth Employment Officer concerned was, however, very worried when she suddenly started to receive bad reports. The girl, it was said, was rude and could no longer be offered employment in the store. On investigation it turned out that she had been assigned to the birthday card counter at which elderly ladies had asked her to read the verses on the birthday cards because they had forgotten their spectacles. Rather than admit that she could not see the words herself, the girl brushed requests aside discourteously. All was well when she was transferred to the hardware counter. As one partially-sighted young woman successfully bringing up her family said, 'Being partially-sighted involves playing a constant game of bluff.' When I asked her to elaborate this remark she said 'You are constantly bluffing other people that you can see what is going on even when you can't. If I am at the bus stop I cannot see the bus coming, but I pick up my bag when the other people in the queue do. If it's the wrong bus I put it down again. Life is a constant game of bluff.' That she was able to recount all this with a degree of good humour was a strong indication that this young woman had, in fact, come to terms with her handicap and was minimising its effect in her life.

In considering the factors which bring about healthy emotional adjustment, it is necessary to distinguish between the difficulties which arise directly from the handicap of partial sight itself and those which arise from the attitudes implied and feelings expressed by all those involved. Partially-sighted children can be helped to exercise insight in accepting their disability and to meet their difficulties with confidence.

Perhaps the situation in regard to both the young people and their parents and employers can best be summed up in the remark made by a twelve year old boy when I was dishing out the bedtime cocoa to a group gathered round a camp fire one evening. I had been discussing the problem of home sickness with another boy. The twelve year old chipped in 'I think it's all a question of practice.' I said to him 'What do you mean exactly?' and he replied 'Oh, I don't know, I suppose practice in finding out about yourself and other people. In finding out what you are made of, I guess.' These words of wisdom from a twelve year old offer a useful indication of the way in which partially-sighted young people can be helped. By encouraging them to explore their own potential in learning and social relationships and to experience a wide variety of challenging activities in everyday living, within a framework of gradually withdrawn support, the degree of stress imposed by the handicapped will be minimised for them and for their parents. They will then reach the stage when they are able to make a successful takeover bid for healthy adult independence.

DEAF AND PARTIALLY-HEARING CHILDREN

Lawrence Ives

Summary

1   The terms 'deaf' and 'partially-hearing' are defined and background factors which could result in stress in hearing-impaired children are set down in general terms.
2   A model of personality development in normally-hearing children is outlined in order to provide a frame of reference.
3   The role of language in social-emotional development is discussed.
4   Possible effects of sensory deprivation are suggested and discussed with reference to deaf infants.
5   Studies of adjustment patterns in deaf and partially-hearing children are reported and interpreted in the light of the model mentioned in 2.
6   Stress factors indicated by the behaviour of a group of deaf children with severe language problems are reported and discussed.
7   Attention is paid to research problems, in particular, the lack of an adequate frame of reference in order to guide studies of stress factors in hearing-impaired children.

Introduction

This chapter is concerned with stress factors, as indicated by deviant emotional-social and/or educational responses, in deaf and partially-hearing children. The psychologist views the degree of deafness as being critical when it precludes the normal acquisition of language. It is pertinent to note that in 1962 the then Ministry of Education defined 'deaf' and 'partial hearing' in terms of educational needs. The definitions are as follows:

a   deaf pupils, that is to say pupils with impaired hearing who require education by methods suitable for pupils with little or no naturally acquired speech or language;

b   partially-hearing pupils, that is to say pupils with impaired hearing whose development of speech and language, even if retarded, is following a normal pattern and who require for their education special arrangements or facilities, though not necessarily all the educational methods used for deaf pupils.

It will be seen that no attempt was made to give more than a broad classification and many factors must be taken into account when considering the pattern of general development in a hearing-impaired child. In fact, the Department of Education and Science (1968) Report 'The Education of Deaf Children: The Possible Place of Finger Spelling and Signing' lists twenty two factors likely to affect the adjustment and attainments of children with impaired hearing. Apart from hearing-impaired children within the range of normal intelligence, special problems are presented by deaf children with other additional handicaps, including relatively low non-verbal intelligence, and these difficulties will be discussed later in this paper.

The problems inherent in attempting to assess the significance of stress factors in hearing-impaired children are greatly increased by difficulties associated with their restricted linguistic development. These difficulties manifest themselves in two ways. Firstly, abstraction and generalisation from the concrete is severely restricted in the absence of language in young deaf children, so that many aspects of social concept formation are delayed and impoverished. Symbolic behaviour is much more tied to the 'here and now' of the situation and much intercommunication would take place by means of gesture and simple mime. Secondly, many investigators have attempted to look at adjustment factors in the deaf by means of tests which depend to a greater or lesser degree on the use of verbal exchanges: inevitably, this method leads to many problems of interpretation.

It is impossible to describe and discuss the evidence with reference to adjustment and stress patterns in hearing-impaired children in the absence of a model which illustrates the pattern of normal personality development in hearing children. There are children with normal hearing who show disturbed behaviour which seems to be the outcome of treatment by their parents. It seems probable that in children with impaired hearing, the additional strain and uncertainty experienced by their parents could aggravate any adjustment difficulties associated with the handicap. Of course, there is no black and white simplicity about this situation. There are examples of neurotic and/or socially incompetent parents who would produce a disturbed child, hearing impairment or not. At the present time we do not have sufficient firm information about the effects of parental reactions to a child's hearing impairment as a factor in making stressful reactions of relatively minimal significance (Oliver, 1965; Broomfield, 1967).

Personality acquisition and development in young children with normal hearing

These notes are concerned with the first six or seven years of life. They are based on a social psychological frame of reference (see Chapter 4 in Hall and Lindzey, 1970).

A number of writers have stressed the primary importance of creating a home environment in which the baby (and infant) acquires and develops the ability to form a reciprocal love relationship (Hadfield, 1950; Fleming, 1958; Bowlby, 1965). The infant receiving an adequate amount of love will begin to show the following aspects of development between one and two and a half years:

self-display;
curiosity and exploration;
imitation;
self-will.

Piaget and Inhelder (1969) have given an excellent account of the normal child's emergence from sensori-motor learning into the phase of symbolic behaviour. During the early period of imitation and self-will the infant is moving from a phase of overwhelming physical dependence to the stage of psychic dependence. This development is of greater significance during the phase from two and a half to four years, when the organisation of personality is taking place as impulsive behaviour is brought under some degree of control. This phase is marked by reality testing as the infant extends his knowledge of what is (or is not) socially acceptable. It is at this time that the *ego* is being formed (see Vernon, 1964). The process of *imitation* continues and because the child *identifies* with the actions and moods of his parents, he becomes *suggestible*. By the age of four years the normal infant will begin to have some primitive, intuitive concept of self and will form an *ego-ideal* based on his identification with significant adults. Because of his primarily *egocentric* motivation the incorporation of ego-ideal patterns into his personality will not take place without some difficulty and the function of verbal language will be of considerable significance at this point. Primitive introspections and comparisons of self with others will lead to self-criticism; the formation of duality in the personality; and the acquisition of self-control, along with the development of will. The last process will occur as the ego, which obeys a reality principle, matures so as to prevent a discharge of tension until an acceptable solution is discovered.

From these processes comes the beginning of *super-ego* function as the child internalises traditional values and ideals (in imitation of the model offered by his parents) and strives to release tension in a manner acceptable not only to himself but also to others. At this stage, which marks the growth from the initial period of personality organisation (two and a half to four years) to the period of loosely-knit group interaction (six to seven years), the child incorporates into a developing social conscience what is 'improper' (or punishable) and reinforces his tendency to seek situations in which he is rewarded.

It must be stressed that although the introduction of this outline model of normal personality development provides a necessary frame of reference, any attempt to over-simplify carries its own dangers. The reader is referred to Chazan's (1970) detailed review of the complex considerations which are encountered when attempting to identify and evaluate emotional and behaviour patterns.

Language and orectic development

Lewis (1963 and 1968) has used the term *orectic* to describe striving for a satisfactory degree of cognitive and emotional equilibrium. As long ago as

1932 Piaget suggested that a child first develops a 'schemata of motor adaptation' when he is progressing towards a functional equilibrium between himself and his social environment. This process is unconscious at first but later becomes conscious as the child acquires language and is able to symbolise past, present and future events. The role of language in developing and structuring a concept of self was described by Freud (1927) who wrote 'the ego wears an auditory lobe'. Isaacs (1933) has given many examples of the role of language in the orectic development of normally-hearing children. Lewis, in particular, has adopted the view that as a child acquires language, so he is able to differentiate a variety of diverse orectic attitudes in himself, and in others, and is thus able to modify his attitudes and behaviour.

Writing of the deaf, Myklebust (1964) notes the possibility that delays in the growth of an adequate degree of identification could be an outcome of restricted language acquisition. It seems likely that the instability of arousal and feeling in some deaf children, recorded by Pintner (1946), is an indication of the effects of impaired linguistic development on orectic behaviour. This same factor is probably responsible for the severely restricted role playing in young deaf children which was reported by Heider and Heider (1941). It is remarkable that their rich study of social interaction and play has not been repeated and extended with due reference to manual and oral modes of communication, and Piaget's developmental psychology.

Taylor (1958) has pointed out that the deaf infant does not hear the inflectional and intonational meanings which will have more significance than the words themselves during early development. This comment is important in the light of Bowlby's (1965) descriptions of the effects of a lack of stimulation and social communication on normally-hearing children. A child deaf from babyhood will have a long pre-language period during which it is necessary to establish and maintain adequate social relationships. Ewing (1957) has described

a   the problems involved in keeping the child informed of daily events and circumstances, and
b   the child's difficulty in monitoring his environment by means of hearing.

Some effects of sensory deprivation

Any discussion of the effects of deafness from birth or early infancy must recognise the fact that perceptual organisation will be affected to a considerable extent. The degree to which a young deaf infant may be helped so as to compensate for the loss of information gained from hearing is a factor of great importance.

Piaget (1950) has written '. . . every action involves an energetic or affective aspect and a structural or cognitive aspect . . . Affective and cognitive life, then, are inseparable although distinct. They are inseparable because all interaction with the environment involves both a structuring and a valuation, but they are none the less distinct because these two aspects of behaviour cannot be reduced to one another.' Because of severe linguistic deficiency the development of verbal intelligence is impaired in the great majority of deaf children (see Ives, 1968 and 1969). The deaf child will have limited experience of the regulatory function of language and will not be able to assimilate his auditory environment in the manner open to the child with normal hearing. His limited audition will result in restriction of the range of aural stimulation to which he is expected to respond. It is worth looking at the sensori-motor period in this respect. In normal child development the main cognitive characteristics at this stage include the gradual integration of reflex activity so as to develop motor habits in response to objects in the immediate environment and this, in turn, leads to a sense of object permanence, and crude concepts of space, time, causality and intentionality. There is a tendency to fixate on individual objects rather than relations between objects. The normal child can begin to imitate both visual and auditory models. With regard to non-verbal aspects of behaviour, it seems reasonable to suggest that in the absence of a general mental handicap the deaf infant would proceed through the six sub-stages detailed by Piaget and Inhelder (1969) at approximately the same rate as the child without impaired hearing. As far as the present writer is aware, there is no firm evidence on this point. In a study of older deaf infants Kendall (1953 and 1957) employed the performance version of the Merrill-Palmer Scale (Stutsman, 1931) in order to investigate the non-verbal development of hearing-impaired children in the chronological age range from eighteen to sixty five months. He found that the great majority of the deaf children were on a par with a control group with normal acuity.

At sub-stage three – the period of secondary circular reactions when achievements relate to reproductive, recognitory, and generalising assimilation – the infant attempts to maintain, through repetition, any interesting change in his environment adventitiously produced by his own actions. For example, the normal infant continues to strike and swing a rattle suspended in his pram. It is necessary to question the effects of a reduction in sound stimulation, as this factor adds interest to the repetition of exploratory behaviour.

The next point concerns the normal infant's use of signals in order to anticipate events. This appears at stage four (eight to twelve months) when the coordination of secondary schema takes place, e.g. the infant establishes a relationship between two objects – instead of simple and undifferentiated connections between an object and an action. Piaget does not infer complicated symbolic or imaginal processes as mediators of signal behaviour during this early period (see Flavell, 1963). Subsequent development at stages five and six takes the normal infant to the point at which he is able to imitate and insert events into play schemas. Although, hitherto, the infant has been able to show a kind of reference behaviour, such as treating a perceptual cue as a signal, the essential requirement for representation is, in Piaget's view, the ability to differentiate signifiers from significates and thus become able to evoke one to call forth or refer to another.

On the assumption that, at stages three and four, the foundations for the subsequent development of representation are being established, we have to consider the effects of a reduction of symbol acquisition on the deaf infant. As the deaf child grows older any deficiencies at this early stage will appear to be more pronounced. This is perhaps due to the possibility that later (and more sophisticated) representations, such as role playing, could be thought of as depending to some extent on flexibility and range in schemata which come about in part, and are stimulated by, verbal language acquisition.

The whole question of perceptual cues, as this relates to deaf infants (and older generally backward deaf children and adolescents), leads to many points concerning selective combinations of sensory information. In particular, we have little knowledge of the development of auditory-visual integration and decoding processes in the young deaf. Any adequate theory of personality development in the deaf must consider such factors. In addition, the likely effects of restricted linguistic growth on the area of self-concept form another key area for investigation.

It has been said that cognitive actions involve an energetic or affective aspect and comments have been made about the relatively limited frame of reference employed by the deaf child. There would seem to be reason to believe that limitations in the range of motivation, but not necessarily the depth, are inevitable in the great majority of cases.

These notes on some of the deeper issues in this field have been included so as to indicate the complex considerations which must be recognised when we attempt to interpret certain research findings. Much research into emotional-social adjustment factors in the hearing-impaired population is not open to anything more than a relatively superficial interpretation. The most notable contributions in future years seem likely to come from attempts to establish longitudinal studies of hearing-impaired children without additional handicaps, and other groups of dually and multiply handicapped deaf and partially-hearing children. Clinicians at the Department of Audiology and Education of the Deaf at Manchester University have completed a small study of such groups and are beginning a large survey which will lead to extended studies (Ives, 1972).

Adjustment patterns in deaf infants

Kendall (1953 and 1957) made a study of the behaviour problems shown by groups of deaf and normally-hearing children (180 in each group: C.A. range 18 to 65 months). His methods of observation included:

a   interviews with the parent(s);
b   direct observation of the child;
c   rating on the Bowley emotional development scale.

If a particular symptom
a   occurred frequently;
b   had persisted for some length of time; and
c   was thought to be disruptive of emotional security,

it was recorded as an item symptomatic of emotional stress. Many items of this nature were found to be more prevalent among the deaf subjects. Significant differences between the groups were found in respect of:

a   retarded general development;
b   toilet training (excluding all cases below 24 months);
c   nocturnal enuresis (excluding the 18 to 29 month group);
d   sleeping difficulties;
e   play difficulties;
f   temper tantrums;
g   over-dependence;
h   social withdrawal;
i   habits.

Kendall recorded that these symptoms tended not to decline with age among the deaf children.

This piece of research raises some interesting problems. For example, it would be reasonable to think of social withdrawal in a normally-hearing infant as being a stress factor. This same pattern in a deaf infant could be the outcome of little or no verbal language for which the child cannot fully compensate by means of simple gestures and/or mime. Such a pattern in deaf children, particularly when with normally-hearing age peers, need not cause an undue amount of stress. Inevitably, there must be a phase when the young deaf child is engaging in his own form of reality testing and is without the verbal resources of the hearing child. Thus he is going to develop within a relatively narrow meaningful environment and must learn by means of direct trial and error. This is, in turn, likely to result in a reinforcement of the concern which parents feel when told that their child is deaf, and this will tend to strengthen over-dependency – in the parent as well as the child. On the other hand, identification and consequent suggestibility, as these are extensions of the hearing child's involvement with the psychic aura which emanates from his parents, will not necessarily find the same depth and range in the deaf child's growing personality. In some (perhaps most) instances the deaf child will take much longer to pass through the phase of impulsive behaviour, as shown by primitive displays of self-will. Delay of this kind will make for erratic behaviour at a time when the hearing child is beginning to form (and have the verbal language to symbolise) an ego-ideal. Therefore Kendall's finding of a higher incidence of temper tantrums and play difficul-ties in his deaf sample is a not unexpected reflection of the rather different pattern of personality development which is a consequence of impaired com-munication. Many problems which arise from this different form of develop-ment need not become of such an order that the child is exposed to a serious amount of stress. The able parents will take every action to structure their deaf infant's experiences to the point at which social learning is successful within the limits of the controlled exploration arranged by parents and teachers. Not all parents will have the same ability to make skilled use of situational guidance in this manner. In some instances the parent-guidance worker will have to shoulder heavy responsibilities.

The reader will appreciate that the author is taking the view that although some aspects of the deaf infant's personality development will move at a much slower pace than would be commonly found in the hearing infant, and although the difficulties indicated by Kendall certainly exist in many instances, there is no reason to suppose that these problems cannot be made of minimal significance. Furthermore, it is very important to realise that developmental differences of the type outlined above do not in themselves suggest maladjusted behaviour. Although it is of value to compare deaf and normally hearing children, it could be unwise unless due attention is paid to the probable effects of a hearing handicap on a child's frame of reference. There is a good case for workers who are experienced enough to be aware of the range of major factors which indicate the existence of emotional-social hazard to concentrate their resources on the home situations of deaf children which are more risk-prone than the majority of family situations found in the field of the hearing-impaired. In other words, rather than ask the degree to which a deaf child differs from his normally hearing age peers, it would be more to the point to look for those deaf children and/or parents of deaf children who are experiencing greater difficulties than others in the same position. In this way it is possible to concentrate advisory work within a frame of reference which emphasises therapeutic approaches to adverse reactions to a hearing handicap, against a background of positive and successful reactions.

Emotional development and social adjustment in school age deaf children

L. J. Murphy (1952 and 1957) studied these factors in 300 pupils (C.A. range 6 to 10 years) in nine day and four residential schools for the deaf. No control group was used because, in Murphy's opinion, comparative studies of deaf and normal children are of little practical value.

The methods of investigation included:

a   sociometric ratings;
b   rigidity testing;
c   a qualitative assessment of affect shown during responses to cognitive tests;
d   an assessment of home adjustment.

The subjects were rated on a five point scale:

a   excellent adjustment;
b   very good adjustment;
c   average adjustment;
d   poor adjustment, needing additional support;
e   showing signs of serious instability, needing further psychological and psychiatric investigation.

The number of children in each category was as follows:

(a) 36; (b) 81; (c) 107; (d) 65; (e) 11.

Murphy concluded that one of the greatest needs in the education of teachers of the deaf was to give them skilled guidance in the problems presented by children in categories (*d*) and (*e*). This recommendation with regard to teacher training was repeated by a Working Party set up by the Child Psychiatry Section of The Royal Medico-Psychological Association (1962). The Memorandum which includes this suggestion contains a number of proposals for the setting up of diagnostic and treatment facilities. One notable advance was made in 1966 when Larchmoor School for Maladjusted Deaf Children was opened.

The adjustment of partially-hearing children attending ordinary classes

Fisher (1965) studied the adjustment of 83 children with impaired hearing attending ordinary classes (C.A. range from 5·4 to 16·0; 41 boys and 42 girls; mean C.A. 10·3 and 9·9 respectively). The degree of hearing loss ranged from 20 to 64db (mean loss 38db).

A control group was made up by asking teachers to select a child with normal hearing in the same class as the hearing-impaired subject. In each case the teacher was asked to select the next child of the same sex whose name appeared on the class register after that of the experimental group child.

Information obtained about both groups included a Bristol Social Adjustment Guide assessment (Stott, 1963). The BSAG is a widely used device for the assessment of a child's social-emotional adjustment to the school environment.

An analysis of the completed Bristol Guides made it possible to allocate the children to adjustment categories.

	NORMAL ADJUSTMENT	UNSETTLED	MALADJUSTED
Experimental Group	53%	27%	20%
Control Group	72%	15%	13%

The difference between the adjustment of the groups was significant at the 5 per cent level.

It is of interest to note that Johnson (1962) studied 68 children with impaired hearing attending ordinary classes and on the basis of a questionnaire, interviews, and discussions with class teachers, classified 53 per cent of the children as normally adjusted, 33 per cent as unsettled, and 9 per cent as maladjusted. The total within the unsettled/maladjusted groups is the same as that reported by Fisher.

A broad syndrome analysis was carried out. *Withdrawing* was used to describe sections of the Guide devoted to unforthcoming and withdrawing behaviour. *Demonstrative* referred to the externalisation of emotional disturbance of the type recorded in the sections concerned with anxiety/hostility in relation to adults and/or children, and evidence of moral impairment.

Mixed was used to describe a general syndrome in which neither of these patterns predominated. The normal expectation would be that a child's defence mechanisms would operate mainly in the direction of withdrawing or demonstrative behaviour. In the present writer's experience it is exceptional to find a mixed pattern in children unless they have particular learning difficulties.

Fisher's findings are detailed below.

	NORMAL	WITH-DRAWING	DEMON-STRATIVE	MIXED
Experimental Group	44	10	13	16
Control Group	59	5	15	3

The most striking feature of these findings is the much higher incidence of mixed behaviour found in the partially hearing children. The peak period for poor adjustment in this group was 8·0 to 10·11 years: the smallest incidence of disturbed behaviour was found in the 11 to 16 year group. It seems possible that this investigation shows that a relatively high incidence of personality immaturity is found in ordinary primary school partially-hearing pupils. This factor could be associated with the general tendency for there to be some educational retardation in such children (Fisher, 1965; Hamilton and Owrid, 1970; and Owrid, 1970). It would require a detailed clinical investigation in order to distinguish between children with mixed immaturity factors thought to be consequent on a partial hearing loss, and those children with definite signs of maladjustment. The latter group would almost certainly include a high incidence of children from disturbed homes but from time to time the writer examines a partially-hearing normal school child who although from a conventionally good home, is showing considerable stress reactions. Two types of problems crop up relatively often. The first concerns the partially-hearing child who is of superior general intelligence. Sometimes the parents of such a child set an unrealistically high academic goal and the child veers between over and under-aspiration. This type of difficulty requires therapeutic intervention in order to modify the child's self-concept, and to adjust relationships within the family group. The second type of problem concerns the child who rejects a conventional and relatively bulky hearing aid. In such cases the provision of a small ear-level aid is indicated.

In some instances it is possible for these problems to be anticipated and remedied by a peripatetic teacher of hearing-impaired children. Sometimes, particularly in the first type of problem, School Psychological Service and/or Child Guidance Clinic help is necessary.

Three Bristol Social Adjustment Guide studies of hearing-impaired children

Three studies are compared in this section. In addition to the findings reported by Fisher, investigations by Hine (1969) and Ives (1972) are reported here. Hine's study was undertaken with 104 partially-hearing children in a special school (C.A. range 7·8 to 16·5; mean C.A. 12·1). Ives' study was carried out with a sample drawn from two schools for the deaf. Forty four children were studied (C.A. range 6·11 to 16·5; mean C.A. 11·6).

	QUASI-STABLE*	UNSETTLED*	MALAD-JUSTED*	TOTAL
Fisher	44 (53·0%)	22 (26·5%)	17 (20·5%)	83 (100·0%)
Hine	46 (44·2%)	38 (36·5%)	20 (19·2%)	104 (99·9%)
Ives	25 (56·7%)	11 (25·0%)	8 (18·2%)	44 (99·9%)

As yet no device such as the Bristol Guide has been designed with a hearing-impaired population in mind. However, with a number of reservations, the BSAG appears to be a useful tool at a screening level (Reeves, 1969).† The BSAG studies mentioned above have been selected as being of interest, particularly in view of the degree of agreement about the incidence of maladjustment found in three hearing-impaired samples drawn from very different settings, but it must be stressed that a BSAG investigation would be no more than a very small part of a detailed single case study.

Hine (1970) has reported the eight most frequently marked BSAG items in respect of his sample. These included several items which could be thought to reflect a partially-hearing syndrome, or in other words behavioural patterns common to partially-hearing children which do not necessarily indicate emotional disturbance. For example, both the following items had a frequency of occurrence of 27·9 per cent.

Sometimes eager to answer teacher, sometimes doesn't bother.

On the fringe, somewhat of an outsider.

As with other measures, it is necessary to consider whether adjustment should be assessed with primary reference to other hearing-impaired children, or by means of comparison with normally-hearing children. If the latter course is adopted and BSAG quantification is employed, there would seem good reason to expect an inflated proportion of hearing-impaired children to fall in the unsettled or maladjusted categories. In the former case the incidence of adverse pointers should be obtained and the record for any single child should be evaluated with due reference to the number of adverse indications reported for other children in the same school or unit. If a proper allowance is made for the descriptions which characterise at least the majority of the hearing-impaired children in the same setting, then this should result in a realistic employment of the BSAG device.

Deaf children with additional difficulties

One alternative to the BSAG method is the more time-demanding technique of time sampling a deaf child's social-emotional behaviour, including forms

---

Quasi-Stable: 0 to 9 adverse pointers; *Unsettled:* 10 to 19; *Maladjusted:* 20 plus.
†Meredith (1971) has produced a promising adaptation of Stott's Adjustment Pointers (1963, page 9) for use in schools for the deaf. Contact the present writer for full details.

of communication, during 'free' classroom periods. The present writer organised a pilot study of two groups of deaf children in which observations were recorded on a sheet of items which described aspects of aggressive, withdrawing, and constructive behaviour. Each group consisted of 11 children (C.A. range 6·50 to 16·08). Group A children were considered by their teachers to be within the normal deaf range (mean C.A. 11·04). Group B children were put forward as deaf children with additional language difficulties (mean C.A. 10·98).

Statistical analysis showed a significantly higher incidence of withdrawing behaviour in group B (1 per cent level). There was a significantly higher incidence of constructive behaviour in group A (5 per cent level). There was no significant difference between the groups in terms of aggressive behaviour.

A detailed examination of these children showed a significantly lower level of non-verbal intelligence and linguistic attainments in group B (respectively, 5 per cent and 1 per cent levels). A number of the group B children displayed autistic-like behaviour which took the form of stress reactions to gross communication problems. The difficulties encountered by such children require extended investigation and there is considerable need for special class provision for deaf children with additional handicaps (Ives, 1972).

Final comments

Some of the factors associated with stress in hearing-impaired children have been considered in this chapter. The author has taken the view that some patterns of behaviour in the hearing-impaired, although not the same as those seen in normally-hearing children, do not necessarily indicate any more than a somewhat different personality structure consequent on deafness. On the other hand when hearing-impaired children are compared with each other a number seem to have markedly more adjustment difficulties than their deaf age peers. Sometimes these problems are caused by adverse home management but in some instances they appear to be the outcome of complex communication difficulties, for example, as seen in some dually/multiply handicapped hearing-impaired children.

There has been considerable growth in the provision of advisory services made available by peripatetic teachers of the deaf. The range of facilities made available to school-age deaf children with adjustment difficulties needs to be extended and there is an extreme shortage of suitably trained and experienced staff. Some of the problems mentioned in this chapter require detailed investigation and lengthy remedial help. Work in this field is made more difficult because of our lack of a wholly suitable frame of reference when examining stress factors in hearing-impaired children. However, the slow but steady growth in special facilities for deaf and partially-hearing children with adjustment difficulties is helping us to gain a fuller understanding of ways in which we may be of service.

The author would be pleased to enter into correspondence about any of the points made in this chapter.

CHILDREN WITH PHYSICAL HANDICAPS
Joan Reynell

The term 'stress' is often used rather loosely to mean either a factor which disturbs, or the resulting disturbance. It is important to distinguish these two conceptions because each involves a different orientation for help. Factors which disturb involve preventative measures, and the resulting disturbances require a therapeutic approach.

In order to clarify the ideas presented here, stress is defined as a force acting in opposition to healthy development, particularly emotional development. Stress may arise from the social-emotional or physical environment, including the child's own body. Such forces, unless circumvented or overcome, may prevent children from realising their full potential in many areas of development.

The effects of stress are not necessarily adverse, but it is the more damaging aspects of stress which will be discussed here.

No attempt will be made to cover the psycho-dynamics of childrens' response to stress, as these are psychiatric problems outside this author's competence, but the interested reader is referred to Graham and Rutter (1968).

The subject of this chapter is the mechanism of adverse stress experienced by children with physical handicaps.

Investigations of stress in physically handicapped children

Stress arising from reactions of parents and family

The distress of the parents at having a handicapped child is probably the earliest and most persistent stress that a child with a congenital physical handicap has to experience. Goldie (1966), studying the psychiatry of the 'handicapped family', says 'the whole family, and particularly the parents, are living with a dual problem. On the one hand they are attempting to accept, love and live with their handicapped child, while at the same time they are mourning the normal child whom they had hoped for, and of whom the handicapped child is a perpetual living reminder'. He makes a plea for psychiatric help for such families right from the start.

Creak (1960), in an article on the emotional implications of cerebral palsy, discusses the parents' reactions to their handicapped child, pointing to the distorting influence this may have on the child's early development. She comments on the parents' feelings of guilt at having produced a 'damaged' child, and their tendency towards over-protection. This produces a dependent attitude in the child which 'may make children afraid to try new things, which in turn will close to them many avenues of learning'.

Although most authors writing about such parental difficulties have had considerable first-hand experience with the problem, there are few studies which make any attempt to identify and quantify this type of stress. Cockburn (1961) has attempted this in her study of cerebral-palsied children in Dundee. She used two five-point rating scales for parental attitudes. The first was concerned with understanding of the handicap, and the second with its acceptance. She found that homes which were rated as of above average mental status were better able to understand the handicap, but not better able to accept it. She also found that understanding was greater when the handicap was severe, but acceptance greater when the handicap was mild.

Reports to the Carnegie Trust (1964) shows that stress arising from parents and family is not all emotionally determined, but may have a physical basis. Poor living conditions are referred to by Curran and Swann in the Glasgow study (1964), who report 'so great was the complicating effect of the bad environmental conditions in which many of the children lived, that it was well-nigh impossible to study the problems inherent in the defect itself, for these were often obscured by superimposed difficulties and side-effects resulting from the conditions in which the family lived'. There is a suggestion here that some of the problems attributed to handicaps may in fact bear no direct relationship to them. The suggestion that difficulties related to handicaps may be obscured by more general environmental problems carries a warning to investigators.

Curran and Swann also comment on the poor health of the parents often resulting from the excessive care needed for the handicapped child. This in itself becomes further stress to the child. All three of the reports to the Carnegie Trust comment on the parents' inadequate understanding of the problems concerned with physical handicaps, and on the paucity of advisory services to help them.

In summary, stress arising from the parents and family seems to centre around (a) the parents' emotional reaction to having a handicapped child; (b) a failure of understanding of the implications of the handicap and acceptance of this; (c) difficult physical conditions exacerbated by the extra time and care needed for the handicapped child. Without help, such a situation may well create a tense and insecure early environment, with limitations of early learning opportunities.

Stress arising from other environmental factors

Although stress arising from parents and family may be very great in the early years, other environmentally determined stress is less great in younger than in older children. Most of the literature on this type of stress is concerned with school age children and young adults.

Creak (1960) points out some of the stress affecting very young children, including the administration of 'too-ardent physiotherapy'. A study of cerebral palsied children's response to physiotherapy (Reynell, 1963) supports this as a cause of stress in some cases. This study suggests that some children were so distressed and unhappy during their physiotherapy sessions that they were unable to benefit from it. The first concern of the physiotherapist in such cases needs to be to befriend the child and make him happy, so that physiotherapy can be introduced gradually without arousing a negative response.

d'Avignon *et al* (1967) in a study of thalidomide traumatised children, pointed out some common-sense early difficulties, which are not always recognised or allowed for, and so could constitute early stress. Children with short arms have to be too close to their work so that they cannot look at it properly. This could affect all early hand-eye learning. The authors suggest that the child's need constantly to position himself so that hand-eye work is possible necessitates tiring activity and adjustment which prevent him from keeping up with school work, of which he may be intellectually capable. In addition to the usual obvious self-help problems of dressing, feeding and toiletting, they point out such difficulties as an inability to break a fall with their arms. Of the children with more than one handicap they write '. . . combination of two or more handicaps, even if each defect in itself may seem trifling, constitute a considerable hindrance. This hindrance must be overcome at school daily and many times a day.'

Freeman (1970), discussing the stresses in adolescents with cerebral palsy, points out the following: (a) possible deterioration in the physical condition; (b) the need for the child and his parents gradually to give up the fantasy of being cured 'some day'; (c) peers become acutely aware of differences, so that the child may feel increasingly left out; (d) exclusion from certain social activities, and awareness of their physical unattractiveness; (e) difficulties associated with sexual maturation and limitations of expression; (f) difficulties concerned with leaving school necessitating adjustment to a new set of circumstances which may be less tolerant and accepting than a special school.

Stress contingent upon leaving school and seeking employment has a good coverage in the literature. Stephen (1961) estimates that 'we must expect at least 70 per cent of cerebral-palsied adults to be unfit for open employment'.

The magnitude of the problems on leaving school is born out by other workers and is described in some detail by Ingram *et al* (1964). These authors claim that many young adults with cerebral palsy are more dependent and less mature than they need be, as a result of inadequate preparation for leaving school and over-protection by parents. It seems, then, that in attempting to protect children from stress in the school years, we are adding to the stress they experience on leaving school.

Studies of childrens' response to stress

Most studies of so-called stress in physically handicapped children have been concerned with assessment of the childrens' response to stress in terms of emotional disturbance and immature personality development. The studies can be separated into those concerned with behaviour, and those concerned with deeper investigations such as psycho-therapy and projection techniques.

STUDIES OF BEHAVIOUR   There are many references to the high proportion of physically-handicapped children showing disturbed behaviour, but only a few studies in which there has been any real attempt to carry out a planned investigation. Among these should be mentioned Gardner and Johnson's (1964) study of children undergoing a long-term assessment programme and Bowley's (1967) follow up study of children from a special nursery school.

Gardner and Johnson used a rating system to study forty one cerebral-palsied children in a residential setting. They reported that 'The majority of the forty one children showed such disturbances in their social and emotional life on entry, with periods of excessive anxiety, over-dependence and inhibition on the one hand, or defiance, tempers or aggressive behaviour on the other, that the staff had difficulty in making a normal relationship with them.' On entry, and at intervals afterwards, the children were rated on adjustment scales by the teacher, psychologist and psychiatrist.

The authors found that the proportion of disturbed children was sixty one per cent on entry, falling to forty five per cent when the initial trauma due to separation from home was overcome. By the end of their stay at the assessment centre this proportion was reduced to twenty per cent. The authors considered their techniques of measurement to be crude but valid. They attributed the improvements to many factors, including psychiatric help, satisfying constructive experiences in the classroom, and skilled house parent care.

Bowley (1967) presents a preliminary report of sixty four cerebral palsied children originally assessed at a nursery school and followed up on further placement. Assessment of the children's emotional reactions were made by the teachers, who were asked to mark a list of 'symptoms of stress' noted in school. The list is a long one, including such behaviour manifestations as 'restless and distractable', 'depressed and tearful', 'discouraged', and 'lethargic'. Commenting on the follow-up Bowley reports 'It is encouraging to find that, despite quite severe handicaps . . . the majority of the intelligent children are working up to capacity and show few signs of stress and strain.'

These studies highlight the difficulties of gathering truly objective data in this rather nebulous area of research, difficulties which confine most authors to opinions and subjective interpretations of observed behaviour. As Freeman (1970) comments concerning emotional problems of handicapped children 'There are no studies using sophisticated methodology, and the reports which are available seldom agree.' There remains a need for someone to work out a really scientific method for the assessment of stress, emotional response to stress, and its behavioural correlates.

PERSONALITY STUDIES   Few people undertake psychotherapy with children who have severe physical handicaps, and fewer still publish their findings. Wainer (1965) reports on the psychotherapy of an eighteen year old girl severely handicapped with cerebral palsy. The report is short, and contains little information about the psychodynamics of the girl herself. The author concludes that 'every handicapped patient needs psychotherapy', and recommends group therapy, because 'it offers them the opportunity of elaborating the anxiety and delusions of persecution which such a situation creates for the group'.

Francis-Williams (1968) reports on studies of projective techniques with cerebral-palsied children. Although mainly concerned with her own Rorschach studies, the volume also contains useful references to studies using other projective techniques. She writes 'There have been few published studies of attempts to understand the problems of inner personality growth which these children must have to meet. It was in order to try to elucidate some of these problems that I used the Rorschach method for cerebral palsied children who had sufficient speech to be capable of responding'. She studied thirty two children from eight and a half to eleven years, and with Stanford Binet I.Q.'s 52 to 120. She found perceptual distortions so common that it was difficult to separate these from emotional factors, but those with relatively unimpaired perception showed protocols resembling those of emotionally maladjusted children. The records suggested some responses directly related to the handicaps in the high proportion of 'mutilated' responses. 'Out of 32 records . . . 29 give at least 3 responses in which they see torn or mutilated objects or figures'.

A study by Cockburn (1961) is more directly concerned with children's awareness of their own handicaps. She asked 128 children with cerebral palsy to express three wishes. She found that wishes related to handicaps were expressed only by the older children. Only ten per cent of the sample expressed this type of wish, and of these, the mean age was fifteen years eight months, and only three of these were under eleven years of age. This finding lends some confirmation to the experience of most people who work with physically handicapped children, that their awareness of their own handicap, at least as a permanent disability, does not usually come until early adolescence.

In a small unpublished study of the author's, parents of cerebral-palsied children, and therapists working with the children, were asked to note any references to their own handicap made by the children. Comments occurred occasionally from three years, and more frequently from six years, and referred mainly to the handicap as some sort of a nuisance.

Examples are:

Karen, aged six and a half years: 'B's lucky, she's got a good hand'.
Catherine, aged seven years: 'I can't skip like the others'.

Many mothers commented that the children seemed to know they were handicapped, but to accept it as part of themselves. Older children often seemed to go through a stage of denial of the handicaps, with unrealistic ambitions, before the true implications of permanent handicap could be accepted.

Examples are:

Janet, aged eleven years: 'Do you think anyone will marry me because my teeth stick out', with no mention of her hemiplegia.

Julie, aged eleven years, and severely handicapped with quadriplegia: 'We're going to live in a bungalow, not because of me but because of Lucy [normal younger sister]'.

Studies which attempt to reveal the child's awareness of, and attitude to his own handicap are just as difficult to carry out as studies of any other aspects of stress. There are so many defences at work within the children, that what they say or do may be far removed from their true feelings. Studies of normal child development, indicating the increasing self-awareness which comes with adolescence, suggest that this is a crisis period for physically handicapped children. Reported studies of handicapped children tend to support this, but most of the data still depends on a certain amount of subjective interpretation.

Gray (1964), writing about himself as a handicapped person, reveals a curious unawareness of certain aspects of his handicap, even as an adult. He was only aware of his odd gait, for example, when other people commented on it. 'I was never able to overcome that lurching at the knees, which I still have, but neither then nor now have I ever been conscious of it . . . as far as I am concerned I walk as normally as anyone'.

AUTOBIOGRAPHIES   Autobiographies are useful sources of information abut the actual experience of stress in handicapped people. Some references are contained in a short article by Oliver (1970). Such reports have the inevitable disadvantage of being retrospective, but can be helpful in that they show how the mature handicapped person sees the stresses he has had to experience.

A sensitive autobiography by Thomassen (1957) illustrates many of the reactions reported in the literature and observed in our experience with handicapped children. For example, he reports his fear of being above floor level. 'To fall down on the floor or anything else I am sitting on seems worse than endangering my life'. This same fear was shown by some of the children studied during physiotherapy when treated on the plinth (Reynell 1963). Physiotherapists who are aware of this possibility treat these children on the floor.

Thomassen also reports on hopes raised by operation, followed by overwhelming depression at the disappointing outcome. This sort of unrealistic hope was illustrated by Julie (quoted above) at the age of twelve years, talking of what she would do when she grew up. 'I'd like to be a shorthand typist, but if I'm normal after my operation I'd like to be a hairdresser'. This attitude indicates the need for very careful preparation before an operation, in order to avoid the appalling 'let down' that so many of the older children and adults feel.

Thomassen also talks of his own desire to live among disabled people, as a way of lessening environmental and social stress. As a young adult he was for a long time only happy when in hospital, or when in a 'home' for disabled people, despite an apparently happy home and devoted family. This seems a reflection of the enormous amount of stress involved in competing with 'normal' people in everyday living.

No attempt has been made to give a full coverage of the literature, but rather to give examples of the different approaches to the study of stress in children with physical handicap. Further references can be found in a recent report by the National Bureau for Cooperation in Child Care (Ed. Younghusband *et al*, 1970).

A model illustrating areas of stress at different ages

Studies which have been carried out, and the experiences of those who work with handicapped children suggest that the pattern and intensity of stress in a child's life varies with his age. The following diagram is an attempt to illustrate this changing pattern of stress throughout the childhood of a

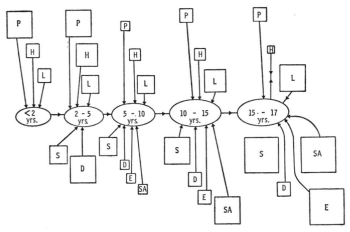

P... Stress arising from parents' reaction to child's handicap.

H... Stress arising from hospital visits, hospitalisation, physiotherapy, and operation.

L... Stress arising from limitations of activity.

S... Stress arising from social limitations and difficulties in social relationships.

D... Stress arising from dependence on others.

E... Stress arising from educational or employment demands.

SA... Stress arising from self-awareness. Realisation of own handicap.

FIG. I   *Stress in children with physical handicaps*

cerebral-palsied child who goes to a special school. The pattern is likely to be slightly different for a physically handicapped child who goes to ordinary school, and so has to meet competition with non-handicapped peers at an earlier age. It is also likely to be different for physical handicaps other than cerebral palsy. It should be emphasised that this is a hypothetical scheme, and is not based on quantitative studies. It is suggested as a model upon which to base help for the children.

The total amount of stress, illustrated by the combined area of the individual squares at each age, is much greater at school-leaving age than at any earlier age. The pre-school years, two to five, and the early secondary school years, ten to fifteen, are periods of relatively high stress, whereas during the first two years, and the primary school years, stress is not so great. The number of sources of stress increases with age.

Stress arising from parents' reaction to child's handicap

In the first two years the greatest stress arises from the parents' distress at having a handicapped child. It usually takes some time to work through this first traumatic experience. Their tension, anxiety and 'mourning' (Goldie, 1966) can create a disturbing early emotional environment for the child. This often continues to be a considerable source of stress during the pre-school years, when the child is no longer a baby and yet continues to be helpless. Anxiety about his mental state is often apparent during these years, and worry about what school he will go to. There may be pressure to show him off as more 'clever' than he is, while at the same time treating him as a baby and not letting him attempt to do things for himself.

During the primary school years stress from parental anxiety is usually much less. The child is now settled at school, where his daily needs are cared for and where he and his handicaps are accepted and understood.

In the secondary school years, as the child becomes heavier and more difficult to manage, his permanent disability now has to be faced. Stress from overtired parents may increase a little at this time, particularly as school-leaving age approaches, but this particular stress is not likely ever to be quite so great or disturbing for the child as in the early years.

Stress arising from hospital visits

In the first two years there is likely to be some stress from hospital visits, when the child is taken for examination and physiotherapy. His daily routine is upset, he is handled by unfamiliar people, in ways which may seem to him uncomfortable. This stress is obviously much greater in these early years for children with spina bifida, who often have to spend much of their time in hospital, often undergoing a series of operations.

During the pre-school years two to five, stress from hospital visits, hospitalisation and operations becomes greater. Children are often separated from their parents during physiotherapy, at an age when even such short separation is distressing to a child still so dependent on his mother for every need. Demands made by the physiotherapist may interfere with the child's chosen activity. He may see this as deliberate opposition, and resent it bitterly. In a study of response to treatment in cerebral-palsied children (Reynell and Martin, 1965a) it was shown that children under the mental age of three and a half years cannot cooperate, and will only respond positively to the physiotherapist if she so adapts her handling that she uses his own chosen activities rather than imposing a specific pattern of activity on him.

Physiotherapists with an understanding of young children discover this for themselves, so that treatment sessions can become less disturbing to the child. This also applies to examination by doctors. An impersonal, hurried examination can be very disturbing to children of this age, and may be accompanied by screams. Doctors who understand children are able to carry out much of the examination by making it seem like a game to the child. Certain types of examination, such as measuring heads and looking at fundi seem to be particularly resented by young children, and need a very careful approach.

If admission to hospital becomes necessary at this age, the stress can be very great indeed. There is plenty of evidence from research to show that emotional upset can last for many months after the child leaves hospital, and constitute a major disturbance even if the stay in hospital is short (Robertson 1958).

If an operation is necessary the disturbance is greater still. A study of post-operative disturbances in cerebral palsied children has been carried out using a timed observational technique (Reynell, 1965b). The children were observed regularly during their physiotherapy sessions before and for some time after operation. During these sessions the child's emotional state was rated on a five point scale as follows: (1) excited and boisterous; (2) laughing or smiling; (3) quiet; (4) fretting, grumbling, whimpering; and (5) crying, screaming. A percentage time score was calculated for each child for each treatment session, as a measure of his emotional state. The findings showed a very dramatic emotional disturbance which lasted for four to five months after operation. This is illustrated in figure 2. The observed disturbance over four months coincided with reports from mothers of disturbed behaviour at home, lasting about the same length of time.

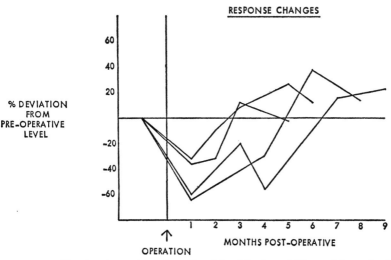

FIG. 2   *Showing depression of emotional level in four children with cerebral palsy, following orthopaedic operations*

It is easy to underestimate the amount of stress young handicapped children have to go through, in situations which may appear relatively unstressful to adults.

In the school years hospital visits are often less frequent. Physiotherapy may be carried out as part of the daily routine at school, and regular medical checks will also be carried out at school. At this age children often enjoy their physiotherapy sessions (Reynell, 1963). Hospitalisation is less disturbing (Illingworth and Holt, 1965) because children are better able to tolerate short separations from home and family. Operations are still very disturbing, and continue to be so throughout childhood and into adolescence (Thomassen, 1957).

At school leaving age young handicapped people usually transfer to an adult hospital for their medical care. This can be disturbing to immature, retarded children, but on the whole reports suggest that such visits are often not only tolerated but regarded as a certain relief from the demands of everyday living. Thomassen, quoted above, was for a long time happier in hospital than at home.

Limitations of activity

Stress arising from limitations of activity is the earliest stress directly related to the physical handicap itself. This is relatively small in the first two years and increases progressively as the children increase their range of interest and want to do more. Thomassen expresses the increase in intensity of frustration as follows, 'The worst thing was that this misery increased with the years, as I got more understanding', and 'the fact that I cannot run, or joyfully jump around or look as I would like to look is bad enough, but bears no comparison to the fact that I cannot develop the gifts of abilities given to me'.

Children vary considerably in their desire to achieve. Frustration increases with drive, for physically handicapped children, but so, ultimately, does success. One has only to watch an intelligent athetoid child trying to achieve some normally simple hand-eye task, to understand the tremendous effort and frustration involved.

The task of those who care for, and work with handicapped children must be to help them find the best ways of achieving a desired aim, rather than doing it for them. All children have some abilities, physical and intellectual, which can often be used to find ways round difficulties which may otherwise make certain tasks impossible for them. This particular stress arising from limitations of activity can be considerably reduced if educators and therapists help the children to work out ways of solving tasks rather than concentrating on the difficulty itself and trying to improve the handicap by practice. For example, if a child has a visual perceptual difficulty, it is better to help him translate perceptual tasks into verbal tasks (for example by verbalising the movements he needs to make in copying a model) rather than by endless 'training' in his area of particular difficulty.

Stress arising from social limitations, social relationships, and self awareness

Under the age of two years, stress arising from social relationships is much the same for handicapped children as for normal children, apart from that related to hospital. Parents do not usually mind taking their handicapped child out at this age, while he still passes for 'normal', and can be pushed around in a pram or sit on his mother's knee. Social difficulties appear from about two years, and increase enormously at school age. There is first an awareness of comments made by other people (Thomassen, 1957), then a realisation of being left out of games and expeditions. By school age children become more aware of themselves in relation to other children, and start to make comparisons. For example, Eileen (aged six and a half) complained that she could not run about like the other children. The earliest awareness of being different seems to arise more from the comments of other people than from the actual disability. For example Karen (aged six and a half) said 'People at school are always asking me how I got a poorly leg'. John (aged six) has begun to comment on being different since the birth of a normal brother. He was unfortunate enough to overhear his mother say to a neighbour, in response to enquiries about the baby, 'and this one's normal'.

It is difficult to see how this dawning awareness of being different can be other than traumatic for the children. It can be explained gently and kindly, but the situation is a reality, and must be faced. They continue to be limited in social activities, to be subjected to stares, comments and other hurtful responses from other people. Children at special schools are to some extent protected, as their handicaps are understood and accepted, and they are amongst others similarly afflicted. This temporary protection may save children some present stress, but may make it more difficult for them to face the world at school-leaving age. It seems that children cannot be protected from this type of stress, but they can be helped to face it, and to work through it as each crisis arises. Parents and teachers are necessary counsellors at such times.

With adolescence, self awareness and the desire to be physically attractive increases. For physically-handicapped children this is often a time of particular crisis. Many of the normal teenage social activities are denied them, and there are few outlets for sexual feelings. Freeman (1970) points out that 'the normal adolescent can get away from prying eyes to experiment, but the handicapped teenager is likely to be closely supervised and may have little, if any, privacy'. Gray (1964), speaking of his own feelings, wrote 'I was not immune from a desire for a partner of the opposite sex . . . but I could not even make a date with a girl'.

During adolescence and after, stress arising from social limitations and from self awareness is probably greater than any stress that any physically handicapped child has to face at any other time.

Stress arising from personal dependence

Dependence becomes a source of stress after the first two years, when children need to assert themselves as individuals. To be dependent on others for everyday needs, such as feeding, washing, toileting, fetching toys, and even a change of position in some cases, are recognised trials for the physically handicapped. Less often recognised, but probably equally stressful is the fact that severely handicapped children can never get away from a situation. They cannot run away from a threatening stranger, a cross mother, or teasing sibling. They must resort to other forms of isolating or protesting behaviour such as hiding their faces, screaming or vomiting. Parents, teachers and therapists need to be sensitive to such needs in handicapped children, and arrange situations in which they can withdraw if they need to. On the other hand some dependent children may panic when left alone, if they are physically helpless, so judgement of the right response is important.

Dependence is not a major source of stress at a special school, because the whole situation is geared towards the childrens' needs, and the teachers are experienced in communicating with the children. Stress increases again as the child gets older. He is expected to attempt more for himself and some of the props are withdrawn. Ingram *et al* (1964) have shown how unprepared young handicapped people are for some of the responsibilities they are expected to undertake for themselves as adults.

Stress arising from the demands of education or employment

Educational pressures do not usually arise until the age of five years, and even then they are often not severe for the child at a special school, but they increase towards school-leaving age. In an ordinary school physically handicapped children meet educational pressures earlier, but Bowley's studies (1967) suggest that even at ordinary school these pressures are well within the childrens' tolerance. The increase in stress at school-leaving age, particularly for those who are able to attempt open employment, is probably more sudden and more intense than at any other time. The very helpless are protected from this stress, at the expense of social activities, but those who are employable often face difficulties that they had never imagined when, for the first time, they find themselves competing with 'normal' peers on very unequal terms and without the familiar protective environment.

Conclusions

It seems inevitable that physical handicaps in children mean additional stress in a number of areas of experience. This is particularly so for children with congenital physical handicaps who experience a changing pattern of stress at every stage of development. The pattern and balance of stresses change, but there is an overall increase in intensity so that the change from leaving school to emergence into adult life is the most difficult and stressful time of all. The resources which such a youngster may have, to deal with and overcome the stress, will depend partly on his own personality (which will in turn depend a great deal on previous experiences), partly on support and encouragement from others, and partly on the opportunities life offers him. How can he be helped?

First by the offering of support in the form of counselling to the whole family right from the start, as suggested by Goldie (1966), and by a continuance of this support throughout childhood and adolescence along the lines suggested by Freeman (1970). Such help would be needed particularly at times of crisis such as change of school, leaving school and starting work. Such changes should be prepared for realistically so that the child does not build up false hopes and so does not constantly have to fail.

Alongside this all-important counselling should go material help as and when needed. In the early years there is a need for a home help (Carnegie Report, 1964) to relieve the strain on parents, and enable them occasionally to go out. At school age there is a need to enable children to make full use of such ability as they have, both in school work and in self help. The survey by Ingram *et al* suggests that physically handicapped children often achieve far less than their optimum in this respect. A system of incentives linked to realistic goals is needed.

Finally, at school leaving age, if Stephen (1961) is right in her estimate that seventy per cent of those with cerebral palsy will be unfit for open employment, there is clearly a need for more sheltered workshops, 'niche' employment, and hostel accommodation, if the almost inevitable stresses associated with physical handicaps are to be reduced.

NOTES AND REFERENCES

Psychotic children

Further Reading

The following are selected from an enormous number of books and papers on the subject of autistic children, published over the years. The list is intended only as a starting point for further reading. A complete bibliography is obtainable from the National Society for Autistic Children, 1A Golders Green Road, London NW11.

ELGAR, SYBIL and WING, LORNA (1969) 'Teaching Autistic Children', *Guidelines for Teachers*, London: The College of Special Education and the National Society for Autistic Children. A brief introduction to the method of teaching autistic children developed at the Society School, Ealing.

ITARD, J. M. G., trans. HUMPHREY, G. and M. (1962) *The Wild Boy of Aveyron* New York: Appleton-Century-Crofts. Itard wrote this book in 1799. It is a fascinating description of how he tried to educate a boy of about twelve, found wandering wild in the woods of Aveyron, whose behaviour was that of an autistic child. The film *L'Enfant Sauvage*, directed by Truffaut, is based on this book.

PARK, CLARA CLAIBORNE (1969) *The Seige* Gerrards Cross, Bucks.: Colin Smythe. The story of an autistic child, written by her mother. It is a most moving account of the problems faced by her parents, and the way in which they helped their handicapped daughter.

WING, J. K. (ed.) (1966) *Early Childhood Autism – Clinical, Educational and Social Aspects* London: Pergamon Press. This book contains chapters by eleven different authors and much of the work mentioned above is described in it, including the Middlesex survey by Dr V. Lotter and the follow-up study by Dr M. Rutter.

WING, LORNA (1970) *Children Apart* (A Family Doctor Booklet) London: The British Medical Association and National Association for Mental Health. A short booklet for parents and other lay people to help them understand the problems of autistic children.

Slow-learning children

References

BOWER, E. (1969) *The Early Identification of Emotionally Handicapped Children* (2nd Edition) Springfield, Ill.: C. C. Thomas.

CASHDAN, A. and WILLIAMS, P. (1972) 'Maladjustment and Learning', Units 11 and 12 of *Personality Growth and Learning* Bletchley: The Open University Press, 41–5.

CHAZAN, M. (1964) 'The Incidence and Nature of Maladjustment among Children in Schools for the Educationally Subnormal', *Br. J. educ. Psychol.*, 34, iii, 292–304.

DEPARTMENT OF EDUCATION AND SCIENCE (1967) *Children and their Primary Schools* (Plowden Report) London: H.M.S.O.

EVANS, K. M. (1962) *Sociometry and Education* London: Routledge and Kegan Paul.

PEAKER, G. F. (1967) 'The Regression Analysis of the National Survey', in *Children and their Primary Schools*, Appendix 4 of Vol. 2, London: H.M.S.O.

RUTTER, M. (1967) 'A Children's Behaviour Questionnaire for Completion by Teachers', *J. child Psychol. Psychiat.*, 8, 1–11.

SCHOOLS COUNCIL (1969) *Field Report No. 6* 'Project in Compensatory Education', London: H.M.S.O.

STOTT, D. H. (1963) *The Social Adjustment of Children* (2nd Edition) London: University of London Press.

WICKMAN, E. K. (1928) *Children's Behaviour and Teachers' Attitudes* New York: The Commonwealth Fund.

WISEMAN, S. (1967) 'The Manchester Survey', in *Children and their Primary Schools*, Appendix 9 of Vol. 2, London: H.M.S.O.

YULE, W. (1970) 'Reading Retardation and Antisocial Behaviour. The Nature of the Association', Ch. 14 of Rutter, M., Tizard, J. and Whitmore, K. (1970) *Education, Health and Behaviour* London: Longman.

Delinquent and maladjusted children

References and notes

In addition to the books and articles referred to in the text of this chapter, students who would like to know more about the relationship between educational experience and delinquency and maladjustment could not do better than to refer to Dr W. D. Wall's book, *Education and Mental Health*, Unesco/ Harrap, 1955. This book, which is a report upon the work of a European conference called by Unesco in 1952, is the best single statement of the subject that has yet been published on this side of the Atlantic.

1 Phillip Taylor, *Society, Social Education and the Young*, the 15th Charles Russell Memorial Lecture, published by the trustees, 17, Bedford Square, London WC1. This paper is an indictment of many aspects of the English educational system which is condemned for its failure to promote creative and critical minds. It expresses a tentative hope, however, that a new generation of teachers may arise who will be able to sharpen social awareness of the crucial moral and human values which should underlie a truly just and democratic community life.

2 Hilde T. Himmelweit, 'Socio-economic Background and Personality', *UNESCO International Social Science Bulletin*, 7, i, 1955, 107–8.

3 D. H. Stott, *Thirty-Three Troublesome Children*, National Children's Home, London, Convocation Lecture 1964. In this book Stott advances his thesis concerning the neurally impaired child and his proclivity to maladjusted and delinquent behaviour. In general this essay is of interest because it is an attack on the sociological interpretation of juvenile delinquency as predominantly a product of environmental influences. On pp. 113–14 he reproves the present author as an exponent of the latter viewpoint.

4 *Children and their Primary Schools*, A Report of the Central Advisory Council for Education (England), H.M.S.O., 2 vols, 1967. This famous report of the committee which worked under the chairmanship of Lady Plowden is a source book for a great deal of information about primary schools today and above all about their relationship with homes and parents. Amongst its many recommendations that for the establishment of Educational Priority Areas is perhaps the most novel. The Report, however, has certain intellectual shortcomings and it is advisable that students should read, in conjunction with it, the series of essays edited by Professor R. S. Peters, *Perspectives on Plowden* London: Routledge and Kegan Paul, 1969.

5 See the *British Journal of Educational Psychology*, 34, iii, 1964, for details of this study.

6 Harmondsworth, Middlesex: Penguin Books, 1956.

7 L. D. Weatherhead, *Prescription For Anxiety* London: Hodder and Stoughton, 1956, p. 44.

8 R. S. and C. M. Illingworth, *Lessons From Childhood* Edinburgh: Livingstone, 1966.

9 Emile Durkheim, *Moral Education, A Study in the Theory and Application of the Sociology of Education* New York: The Free Press, 1961. This book should be studied together with Durkheim's *Education and Sociology*, also published in translation by the Free Press in 1958. These two classical series of essays expound Durkheim's concept of education at length and reveal how much he relied upon sound educational practice to bring about the social regeneration of France after the disasters of the Franco-Prussian War of 1870.

10 F. Musgrove and P. Taylor, *Society and the Teacher's Role* London: Routledge and Kegan Paul, 1969. This essay is especially useful since it raises in an extreme form the nature of the relationship between a school and its surrounding community and suggests that society has given to the teachers too much freedom and responsibility to shape children's personalities and future destinies.

11 R. Havighurst *et. al. Growing Up In River City* New York: John Wiley, 1962. The authors conducted a longitudinal survey of a representative group of children as they grew up in a typical mid-western community of the U.S.A. Their findings impressively reveal the extent of potential alienation that exists in a modern industrial urban society and shows how education unintentionally reinforces social divisions and helps to turn its 'drop-outs' into social outcasts.

12 See 'Neighbourhood School' by A Schoolteacher, *New Society*, 23 June 1966.

13 John Partridge, *Middle School* London: Gollancz, 1966. This book, like the article referred to in the preceding note, is written by a member of the teaching profession and offers a first hand account of the organisation of an actual school. Its damning indictment of the inhuman results of certain aspects of our secondary educational system has not yet been adequately answered by any other author.

14 D. H. Hargreaves, *Social Relations in a Secondary School* London: Routledge and Kegan Paul, 1967. This study of the fourth year pupils in a northern secondary modern school for boys examines the relations between pupils and pupils and between pupils and staff. The author identifies two different and conflicting groups: the academic high streams and the non-academic low streams. He shows how the way in which the school operates tends to divide the 'good' from the 'bad' boys and how denigration in school seems to lead the D streamers into delinquency outside. His findings are of particular interest at a time when perhaps too much emphasis has been placed upon home background and parental influence in considering how a child succeeds or fails in school life and how and why a boy comes to fall foul of the law. His demonstration of the strong influence of the peer group upon unsuccessful pupils is of especial significance, illustrating, as it does, the pull of the lower class subculture on specific types of children. Moreover, in demonstrating how schools themselves actively help to produce delinquency, Hargreaves has gone some way towards finding an explanation of what we mean by 'delinquency areas' and why some schools, even in areas of high delinquency, have low crime rates.

15 M. J. Power, M. R. Alderson, C. M. Phillipson, E. Schoenberg and J. N. Morris, 'Delinquent Schools', *New Society*, 19 October 1967. This preliminary report endorses Hargreaves' findings and suggests, but does not prove, by empirical evidence that schools with high delinquency rates are seriously failing in the task of social education. A future report from this Social Medicine Research Unit of the Medical Research Council at the London Hospital will no doubt illustrate this thesis in greater depth and detail when it appears.

16 Alec Clegg and Barbara Megson, *Children in Distress* Harmondsworth, Middlesex: Penguin Books, 1968. Massive support for Sir Alec Clegg's point of view has come from an impressive American research report on the work of 490 schools in 41 large American cities. See Robert E. Herriott and Nancy Hoyt St. John, *Social Class and the Urban School, The Impact of Pupil Background on Teachers and Principals* New York: John Wiley, 1966. The research workers, making use of a sophisticated quantitative methodology, show that in slum and down-town schools most especially the administrative ability of the head teacher and his qualities of leadership exert a crucial influence on every aspect of the pupils' achievements and behaviour.

17 Alfred J. Khan, *Planning Community Services For Children in Trouble* New York: Columbia University Press, 1963. The author discusses general principles of the community's responsibility for the development of large scale programmes to prevent and treat social deviance and the book is especially valuable in that it offers a number of examples of practices in the New York area which show how general principles can be applied in specific localities. Any student who wishes to compare the magnitude of the American problem presented by delinquent and neglected children with our own situation could usefully take this book both as a measure of the problem and the differential resources that have already been deployed in such projects as Mobilization for Youth to cope with them. For a study of the philosophical and political obstacles which lie in the way of such attempts to deal radically with both delinquency and poverty in the U.S.A. students should consult P. Marris and M. Rein, *Dilemmas of Social Reform* London: Routledge and Kegan Paul, 1967.

18 D. H. Stott, 'The Prediction of Delinquency from Non-Delinquent Behaviour', *British Journal of Delinquency*, January 1960, 202–10. This paper is also reprinted in Johnston, Savitz and Wolfgang (eds) *The Sociology of Punishment and Correction* New York: John Wiley, 1962.

19 A recent report of a conference held in Exeter is H. Lytton and M. Craft, *Guidance and Counselling in British Schools* London: Edward Arnold, 1969. Papers deal with such varied topics as 'The School Counsellor and the Child Guidance Service' and 'The School Counsellor from the Local Education Authority's Viewpoint'.

20 Parent/Teacher Relations in Primary Schools, Education Survey No. 5, Department of Education and Science, H.M.S.O., 1968. A wide-ranging symposium covering the whole area of parent/teacher relations will be found in M. Craft, J. Raynor and L. Cohen, *Linking Home and School* London: Longman, 1967. Among many interesting contributions will be found A. Dawson on 'The Education Welfare Officer', and Margaret Auld and A. R. Chorlton on 'Attaching Social Workers to Schools', which offer reports on experiences in parts of the country as different as Glasgow and Oxfordshire. Another small book which gives the record of one school's achievements in this field and which exemplifies the faith of one headmaster is Lawrence Green, *Parents and Teachers, Partners or Rivals?* London: Allen and Unwin, 1968.

21 Charity James, *Young Lives At Stake* London: Collins, 1968, p. 173. Students will find this a lively and original essay and Part I, 'Education for a Well-spent Youth' will be of particular interest in outlining the moral, political and pedagogical bases of child-centred teaching and collaborative learning theory which is, of course, of special significance for the prevention of early maladjustment at school level.

Bereaved children

References

ANNUAL ABSTRACT OF STATISTICS NO 105 (1968) Tables 26, 28–36 London: H.M.S.O.

ANTHONY, SYLVIA (1940) *The Child's Discovery of Death* London: Routledge and Kegan Paul.

BETTLEHEIM, BRUNO (1955) *Truants from Life* London: Collier Macmillan.

BETTLEHEIM, BRUNO (1965) *Love is not Enough* London: Collier Macmillan.

BETTLEHEIM, BRUNO (1969) *Children of the Dream* London: Collier Macmillan.

BOWLBY, J. (1951) *Maternal Care and Mental Health* Geneva: W.H.O.

BOWLBY, J. (1960) 'Grief and mourning in infancy and early childhood', *The Psychoanalytic Study of the Child*, 15.

BOWLBY, J. (1961) 'Processes of mourning', *International Journal of Psychoanalysis*, 42, iv and v.

GORER, G. (1965) *Death, Grief and Mourning in Contemporary Britain* London: The Cresset Press.

GOULD, JONATHAN (ed.) (1968) *The Prevention of Damaging Stress in Children* London: Churchill.

GROLLMAN, EARL A. (ed.) (1967) *Explaining Death to Children* Boston: Beacon Press.

MILLER, DEREK (1969) *The Age Between* London: Cornmarket/Hutchinson.

MITCHELL, M. E. (1966) *The Child's Attitude to Death* London: Barrie and Rockliffe, in association with Pemberton Publishing Co.

MORRIS, DESMOND (1969) *The Human Zoo* London: Jonathan Cape.

REGISTRAR GENERALS RETURNS FOR 1967.

TOYNBEE, A. (ed.) (1968) *Man's Concern with Death* London: Hodder and Stoughton.

WOLFF, SULA (1969) *Children under Stress* London: Allen Lane The Penguin Press.

Books of particular importance to parents and teachers

TOYNBEE, ARNOLD (ed.) (1968) *Man's Concern with Death* London: Hodder and Stoughton. A symposium compiled by Arnold Toynbee with a team of seven other specialist contributors. Simon Yudkin's chapter 'Death and the Young' is particularly useful for those in charge of children. The book is in three parts dealing with definitions and concepts of death, attitudes and speculations.

GROLLMAN, EARL A. (ed.) (1967) *Explaining Death to Children* Boston: Beacon Press. An anthology edited by Dr Earl A. Grollman with a valuable introduction by Louise Bates Ames, the well-known developmental psychologist associated with the Gesell Institute. The authors include religious leaders of different denominations as well as contributors from the fields of psychology, sociology, anthropology, biology and literature.

The material is concerned with childrens' concepts, attitudes and experiences of death and valuable suggestions for dealing with the bereaved child are included.

MILLER, DEREK (1969) *The Age Between* London: Cornmarket Press. The subtitle 'Adolescents in a Disturbed Society' suggests that parents, teachers and others must take on responsibility for distorted adolescent behaviour, and the author believes that the degree of disturbance in this young generation is great. Chapter 9, 'Death and separation', stresses the danger of distortion or destruction of the child's identification image and regards the teacher as one who can help during this crisis. It is important to read the book in its entirety. Miller is a clinical psychiatrist who was formerly Chairman of the Adolescent Unit at the Tavistock Clinic and is now at Michigan.

WOLFF, SULA (1969) *Children under Stress* London: Allen Lane The Penguin Press. Sula Wolff, in this excellent survey, stresses the importance of recognising the occurrence of 'a critical life situation' in the developing child and the importance of dealing with it. Bereavement is one of these situations, and, if untreated, may lead to persistent disturbance and damaged personality. She includes retrospective studies as well as direct observations of stressed children and gives comprehensive references to the work of Michael Rutter, Marris and others who have made major contributions to studies of bereavement.

GOULD, JONATHAN (ed.) (1968) *The Prevention of Damaging Stress in Children* London: J. and A. Churchill. This paperback was published for the World Federation of Mental Health's 'coming of age' congress in 1968 and includes memoranda from contributors to United Kingdom Study Groups. 'It is intended as a plain man's guide to the topic of its concern'. The chapter on bereavement by Dr Felix Brown is invaluable to guardians of children and for those who want to pursue the subject further there is an excellent bibliography. Felix Brown's contribution is based on first-hand researches by himself and others and he makes clear the dangers to personality that may result from childhood bereavement and also suggests therapeutic treatment.

Apart from this particular section the book should be read as a whole in order to get a comprehensive picture of damaging stress in children. The summary by the editor, Jonathan Gould, contains some very clear and useful statistics.

The adopted child at school

References

ERIKSON, E. H. (1963) *Childhood and Society* (2nd edn.) New York: Norton (Penguin, 1965).

HUMPHREY, M. E. (1969) 'The adopted child as a fertility charm', *J. Reprod. Fert.*, 20, 354–5.

HUMPHREY, M. E. and OUNSTED, C. (1963) 'Adopted children referred for psychiatric advice: I. The Children', *Br. J. Psychiat*, 109, 599–608.

KADUSHIN, A. (1966) 'Adoptive parenthood: a hazardous adventure?', *Social Work*, 11, 30–39.

KIRK, H. D. (1964) *Shared Fate. A theory of adoption and mental health* New York: Free Press of Glencoe.

KORNITZER, M. (1968) *Adoption and Family Life* London: Putnam.

MCWHINNIE, A. M. (1967) *Adopted Children, How they Grow Up: A Study of their Adjustment as Adults* London: Routledge and Kegan Paul.

MILLER, D. H. (1966) 'Some psychological problems of adoption', paper read at British Psychological Society's annual conference, Swansea.

PRINGLE, M. L. K. (1961) 'The incidence of some supposedly adverse family conditions and of left-handedness in schools for maladjusted children', *Br. J. educ. Psychol.*, 31, 183–93.

RAYNOR, LOIS (1970) *Adoption of Non-White Children* London: Allen and Unwin.

SANTS, H. J. (1964) 'Genealogical bewilderment in children with substitute parents', *Br. J. med. Psychol.*, 37, 133–41.

SEGLOW, J., PRINGLE, M. L. K. and WEDGE, P. (1972) *Growing up Adopted* Slough: NFER.

STONE, F. H. (1969) 'Adoption and Identity', *Child Adoption*, 58, 17–28.

WITMER, H. L., HERZOG, E., WEINSTEIN, E. A. and SULLIVAN, M. E. (1963) *Independent Adoptions* New York: Russell Sage Foundation.

Further reading

HUMPHREY, M. E. (1969) *The Hostage Seekers: A study of childless and adopting couples* London: Longman. An enquiry into factors associated with the decision to adopt, with chapters on the special characteristics of adoptive families.

KORNITZER, M. (1959) *Adoption* London: Putnam. A useful introductory guide.

PRINGLE, M. L. K. (1967) *Adoption – Facts and Fallacies* London: Longman. A critical review of adoption research undertaken in Britain, Canada and the U.S.A. between 1948–65.

ROWE, J. (1969) *Yours by Choice* London: Routledge and Kegan Paul. Revised edition of a primer for adoptive parents which is also of more general interest.

The immigrant (West Indian) child in school

References

CARROLL, JOHN B. (1964) *Language and Thought* Englewood Cliffs, New Jersey: Prentice-Hall.

GORDON, S. C. (1963) *A Century of West Indian Education* London: Longman.

HALL, STUART (1967) *The Young Englanders* London: National Committee for Commonwealth Immigrants.

H.M.S.O. (1971) 'Potential and Progress in a Second Culture', *Education Survey 10* London: H.M.S.O.

KELLMER-PRINGLE, M. L. (1969) *Caring for Children* London: Longman.

PLESS, I. B. and HOOD, C. (1967) 'West Indian one-year olds: a comparative analysis of health and service utilisation', *The Lancet*, 24 June.

SHERLOCK, PHILIP (1966) *West Indies* London: Thames and Hudson.

STEWART, PRINCE, G. (1969) 'Mental health problems in pre-school West Indian children', paper given at a conference organised by the World Health Organisation for Early Childhood Education.

Further reading

CLARK, DAVID STAFFORD (1967) *Prejudice in the Community* London: National Committee for Commonwealth Immigrants.

COARD, B. and COARD, P. (1971) *Getting to know ourselves: How the West Indian child is made educationally subnormal in the British school system* London: Bogle l'Ouverture Publications.

EVANS, P. C. and LE PAGE, R. B. (1968) *The Education of the West Indian Immigrant Children* London: National Committee for Commonwealth Immigrants.

GORDON, S. (1968) *Reports and Repercussions on West Indian Education 1835–1933* London: Ginn and Co.

HASHMI, FARRUKH (1969) *Psychology of Racial Prejudice* London: National Committee for Commonwealth Immigrants.

Injury-prone children

References

ACKERMAN, N. W. and CHIDESTER, LEONA (1936) ' "Accidental" self injury in children', *Archs Pediatrics*, 43, xi, 711–21.

BACKETT, E. M. and JOHNSTON, A. M. (1959) 'Social Patterns of Road Accidents to children. Some characteristics of vulnerable families', *Br. Med. J.* 1, 409.

BIRNBACH, S. B. (1948) *Comparative Study of Accident Repeater and Accident Free Children* New York: New York University Press.

BRITISH MEDICAL JOURNAL (1964) 'Prenatal Shaping of Behaviour', Leading article, 25 April 1964.

BURTON, LINDY (1968) *Vulnerable Children* London: Routledge and Kegan Paul.

DUNBAR, FLANDERS (1944) 'Susceptibility to accidents', *Med. Clin. N. Amer.*, 28, 653.

FINCH, S. M. (1951) 'Psychosomatic Problems in Children', *Nerv. Chi.*, 19.

FREUD, SIGMUND (1914) *Psychopathology of Everyday Life*, 198–209.

FREUD, SIGMUND (1925) *Collected Papers*, Vol. III London: Hogarth.

FULLER, E. M. (1948) 'Injury-Prone Children', *Am. J. Orthopsychiat*, 18, 708.

FULLER, E. M. and BAUNE, H. B. (1951) 'Injury Proneness and adjustment in the second grade', *Sociometry*, 14, 210–25.

KRALL, VITA (1953) 'Personality characteristics of accident-repeating children', *J. abnorm. soc. Psychol.*, 48, 99–107.

KLEIN, M. (1932) *Psychoanalysis of Children* London: Hogarth.

LANGFORD, W. S. *et al.* (1953) 'Pilot Study of Childhood Accidents', *Pediatrics*, 2, 405–13.

MENNINGER, K. (1936) 'Purposive accidents as an expression of the self destruction tendencies', *Int. J. Psycho-Anal.*, 17, 6–16.

MANHEIMER, D. and MELLINGER, G. (1967) 'Personality Characteristics of the Child Accident Repeater', *Child Dev.*, 38, *ii*, 419–513.

MARCUS, *et al.* (1960) 'An interdisciplinary approach to accident patterns in childhood', *Monographs for Research in Child Dev.*, 25, *ii*.

SALWEN, L. H. (1967) 'Personality Factors in The Accident Repeating Boy', *Dissertation Abstracts*, 28, 5B, 2149–50.

STILES, G. E. (1957) 'Relationships of unmet emotional needs to Accident Repeating Tendencies in Children', *Dissertation Abstracts*, 17, 2942.

Blind children

References

BATEMAN, S. (1962) 'Sighted children's perceptions of blind children s abilities', *Exceptional Children*, 29, 42–6.

CHILDREN'S COUNCIL (1969) *Seeing in the Dark* Church of England Board of Education.

ERIKSON, E. H. (1959) 'Identity and the Life Cycle', *Psychological Issues*, 1, Monograph 1.

FINE, S. R. (1968) *Education Survey 4* Department of Education and Science, London: H.M.S.O.

GOMULICKI, B. R. (1961) *The development of perception and learning in blind children* Private publication, Cambridge: The Psychology Laboratory, University of Cambridge.

HAYES, S. P. (1941) *Contributions to a psychology of blindness* New York: American Foundation for the Blind.

LANGDON, J. N. (1968) 'A Matter for Concern', *New Beacon*, 52, 619, 282–6.

NATIONAL BUREAU FOR COOPERATION IN CHILDCARE (1970) *The influence of parental attitudes and social environment on the personality of the adolescent blind* New York: American Foundation for the Blind.

WOLFF, S. (1969) *Children under Stress* London: Allen Lane The Penguin Press.

Deaf and partially-hearing children

References

BOWLBY, J. (1965) *Child Care and the Growth of Love* (2nd ed.) Harmondsworth, Middlesex: Pelican Books.

BROOMFIELD, A. M. (1967) 'Guidance to children of deaf parents – a perspective', *Br. J. Dis. Comm.*, 2, *ii*, 112–23.

CHAZAN, M. (1970) 'Maladjusted Children', in Mittler, P. (ed.) *The Psychological Assessment of Mental and Physical Handicaps* London: Methuen.

DEPARTMENT OF EDUCATION AND SCIENCE (1968) *The Education of Deaf Children: The Possible Place of Finger Spelling and Signing* London: H.M.S.O.

EWING, A. W. G. (ed.) (1957) *Educational Guidance and the Deaf Child* Manchester: Manchester University Press.

FISHER, B. (1965) 'The social and emotional adjustment of children with impaired hearing attending ordinary classes', M.Ed. thesis, Manchester: Manchester University Press.

FLAVELL, J. H. (1963) *The Developmental Psychology of Jean Piaget* New Jersey: Van Nostrand Reinhold.

FLEMING, C. M. (1958) *Teaching: A Psychological Analysis* London: Methuen.

FREUD, S. (1927) *The Ego and the Id* London: Hogarth Press.

HADFIELD, J. A. (1950) *Psychology and Mental Health* London: Allen and Unwin.

HALL, G. S. and LINDZEY, G. (1970) *Theories of Personality* (2nd ed.) New York: John Wiley.

HAMILTON, P. and OWRID, H. L. (1970) 'Reading and impaired hearing', *Reading*, 4, *ii*, 13–18.

HEIDER, F. and HEIDER, G. M. (1941) 'Studies in the Psychology of the Deaf, no. 2', *Psychol. Monog.*, 53, *v*, Am. Psychol. Assoc.

HINE, W. D. (1969) 'The abilities of children with partial hearing', M.A. thesis, University of Liverpool.

HINE, W. D. (1970) 'The social adjustment of partially hearing children', *Teacher of the Deaf*, 69, 5–13.

IVES, L. A. (1968) 'Proposals for a British Learning Aptitude Scale standardized on deaf, partially hearing and hearing children', *Teacher of the Deaf*, 66, 171–84.

IVES, L. A. (1969) 'Verbal language development and concept formation in the deaf child', *Teacher of the Deaf*, 68, 111–28.

IVES, L. A. (1972) 'A psychological study of children described by their schools as deaf or language disordered', *Proceeding of the International Conference on Education of the Deaf, Stockholm 1970*, vol. 1

ISAACS, S. (1933) *Social Development in Young Children* London: Routledge and Kegan Paul.

JOHNSON, J. C. (1962) *Educating Hearing Impaired Children in Ordinary Schools* Manchester: Manchester University Press.

KENDALL, D. C. (1953) 'The mental development of young deaf children', Ph.D. thesis, University of Manchester.

KENDALL, D. C. (1957) 'Mental Development of Young Deaf Children', in Ewing, A. W. G. (ed.) *Educational Guidance and the Deaf Child* Manchester: Manchester University Press.

LEWIS, M. M. (1963) *Language, Thought and Personality in Infancy and Childhood* London: Harrap.

LEWIS, M. M. (1968) *Language and Personality in Deaf Children* Slough: National Foundation for Educational Research.

MEREDITH, K. N. (1971) 'Free and controlled drawing responses by stable and maladjusted educationally deaf children', Dip.Aud.Dis., University of Manchester.

MURPHY, L. J. (1952) 'Assessment of the abilities of deaf children', Ph.D. thesis, University of Manchester.

MURPHY, L. J. (1957) 'Tests of Abilities and Attainments', in Ewing, A. W. G. (ed.) *Educational Guidance and the Deaf Child* Manchester: Manchester University Press.

MYKLEBUST, H. R. (1964) *The Psychology of Deafness* (2nd edn.) New York: Grune and Stratton.

OLIVER, R. M. (1965) 'The families of young deaf children: an experience of research in an unfamiliar field', *Br. J. psychiat. soc. Wk.*, 8, 11.

OWRID, H. L. (1970) 'Hearing impairment and verbal attainments in primary school children', *Educ. Res.*, 3, 209–14.

PIAGET, J. (1932) *The Moral Judgement of the Child* London: Routledge and Kegan Paul.

PIAGET, J. (1950) *The Psychology of Intelligence* London: Routledge and Kegan Paul.

PIAGET, J. and INHELDER, B. (1969) *The Psychology of the Child* London: Routledge and Kegan Paul.

PINTNER, R. (1946) *The Psychology of the Physically Handicapped* New York: F. S. Crofts.

REEVES, K. (1969) Personal communication to the author.

ROYAL MEDICO-PSYCHOLOGICAL ASSOCIATION (1962) 'Memorandum on the Psychiatric Needs of the Deaf', reprinted in *The Psychiatric Problems of Deaf Children and Adolescents* London: The National Deaf Children's Society.

STOTT, D. H. (1963) *The Social Adjustment of Children: Manual to the Bristol Social Adjustment Guides* (2nd edn.) London: University of London Press.

STUTSMAN, R. (1931) 'Mental measurement for pre-school children: Merrill Palmer', *Am. J. Orthopsychiat.*, 3, 181.

TAYLOR, I. G. T. (1958) 'Basic problems in mental health of children during pre-school years', in Ewing, A. W. G. (ed.) *The Modern Educational Treatment of Deafness* Manchester: Manchester University Press.

VERNON, P. E. (1964) *Personality Assessment* London: Methuen.

Children with physical handicaps

References

D'AVIGNON, M., HELLGRUN, K., JUHLIN, I. M., ATTERBACK, B. (1967) 'Diagnostic and habilitation problems of thalidomide traumatised children with multiple handicaps', *Develop. Med. Child Neurol.*, 9, 707–12.

BOWLEY, AGATHA (1967) 'A follow up study of 64 children with cerebral palsy', *Develop. Med. Child Neurol.*, 9, 172–82.

CARNEGIE TRUST (1964) *Reports to the Carnegie United Kingdom Trust on the Problems of 600 Handicapped Children and their Families.*

COCKBURN, JUNE M. (1961) 'Attitude to handicap', *Educ. Rev.*, 10, *i*, 35–41.

CREAK, MILDRED (1960) 'Emotional implications of cerebral palsy', *Spastics Quarterly*, 9, *iv*, 16–22.

CURRAN, A. P., and SWANN, E. (1964) 'Glasgow study', *Reports to the Carnegie United Kingdom Trust on the Problems of 600 Handicapped Children and their Families.*

FRANCIS-WILLIAMS, JESSIE (1968) *Rorschach with Children* London: Pergamon Press.

FREEMAN, ROGER D. (1970) 'Psychiatric problems in adolescents with cerebral palsy', *Develop. Med. Child Neurol.*, 12, 64–70.

GARDNER, L., and JOHNSON, J. (1964) 'Long term assessment and experimental education of retarded cerebral palsied children', *Develop. Med. Child Neurol.*, 6, 250–60.

GOLDIE, L. (1966) 'The psychiatry of the handicapped family', *Develop. Med. Child Neurol.*, 8, 456–62.

GRAHAM, P. and RUTTER, M. (1968) 'Organic brain dysfunction and child psychiatric disorder', *Br. Med. J.*, 3, 689.

GRAY, DENNIS (1964) *On My Own Feet* London: Max Parrish.

ILLINGWORTH, R. S. and HOLT, K. S. (1955) 'Children in hospital. Some observations on their reactions with special reference to daily visiting', *Lancet*, 2, 1257.

INGRAM, T. T. S., JAMESON, STELLA, ERRINGTON, JANE and MITCHELL, R. G. (1964) 'Living with Cerebral Palsy', *Clinics in Developmental Medicine*, *xiv* London: Spastics Society and Heinemann Medical Books Ltd.

OLIVER, D. W. (1970) 'A novel way to read of handicaps', *Special Education*, 59, *iii*, 26.

REYNELL, JOAN K. (1963) 'Factors affecting response to treatment in cerebral palsy', Ph.D. thesis, University of Sheffield.

REYNELL, JOAN K. and MARTIN, M. C. (1965a) 'The response of children to physiotherapy', *Physiotherapy*, 51, 186.

REYNELL, JOAN K. (1965b) 'Post-operative disturbances in children with cerebral palsy', *Develop. Med. Child Neurol.* 7, *iv*, 360–76.

ROBERTSON, J. (1958) *Young Children in Hospitals* London: Tavistock Publications.

STEPHEN, ELSPETH (1961) 'An introductory review. Assessment, training and employment of adolescents and young adults with cerebral palsy', *Cerebral Palsy Bulletin*, 3, *ii*, 127–32.

THOMASSEN, ROLF (1957) *Beyond Today* London: Robert Hale Ltd.

WAINER, GERARDO GUIDO (1965) 'Psychotherapy in a girl with severe cerebral palsy', *Develop. Med. Child Neurol.*, 7, 175–77.

YOUNGHUSBAND, EILEEN, BIRCHALL, DOROTHY, DAVIE, RONALD and KELLMER PRINGLE, M. L. (eds) (1970) *Living with Handicap* London: The National Bureau for Cooperation in Child Care.